SALVADOR
ALLENDE
READER

SALVADOR ALLENDE READER

Chile's Voice of Democracy

Edited with an introduction by
James D. Cockcroft

Assisted by Jane Carolina Canning

*With translations by Moisés Espinoza
and Nancy Nuñez*

OCEAN PRESS
Melbourne • New York

Cover design by David Spratt

ISBN 1-876175-24-9

First printed 2000

Printed in Australia

Published by Ocean Press
Australia: GPO Box 3279, Melbourne, Victoria 3001, Australia
  • Fax: (61-3) 9372 1765 • E-mail: edit@oceanpress.com.au
USA: PO Box 834, Hoboken, NJ 07030 • Fax: 201-617 0203

www.oceanpress.com.au

Library of Congress Card No: 00-100395

OCEAN PRESS DISTRIBUTORS
United States: LPC/InBook,
    1436 West Randolph St, Chicago, IL 60607, USA
Canada: Login Brothers,
    324 Salteaux Cres, Winnipeg, Manitoba R3J 3T2, Canada
Britain and Europe: Global Book Marketing,
    38 King Street, London, WC2E 8JT, UK
Australia and New Zealand: Astam Books,
    57-61 John Street, Leichhardt, NSW 2040, Australia
Cuba and Latin America: Ocean Press,
    Calle 21 #406, Vedado, Havana, Cuba
Southern Africa: Phambili Agencies,
    PO Box 28680, Kensington 2101, Johannesburg, South Africa

Table of contents

About the editors

Dr. James D. Cockcroft is the author of 25 books on Latin America, human rights, international affairs, and multiculturalism. His most recent books are: *Latin America: History, Politics, and U.S. Policy* (2nd ed., Belmont, CA: Wadsworth Publishing/Thomson Learning, 1997); *Mexico's Hope: An Encounter with Politics and History* (NY: Monthly Review Press, 1998, Mexico City: Siglo XXI, 2000); and the forthcoming *Outlaws in the Promised Land: The Politics of Immigration* (Albuquerque: University of New Mexico Press, 2001).

Dr. Jane Carolina Canning is a sociologist and free-lance journalist who has written extensively on issues of human rights and social policy in Latin America.

To Doyle Canning, Eli Smith,
and the next generation in their struggle for peace and justice

Acknowledgments

Locating the essential materials for this book proved to be a daunting task. Although the holdings of many elite U.S. university libraries contain copies of Allende's speeches in English through the CIA's FBIS (Foreign Broadcast Information Service), they are not accessible to the public. Nor are they available through public agencies. For example, incredibly, the U.S. State Department Library does not count in its holdings the FBIS. The agency in charge of distributing FBIS documents has no records on where or how they obtained any of those documents and informed us that they "only distribute but cannot obtain" said documents (a well known form of "spookspeak").

Therefore, we wish to extend our profound gratitude to the willing, if understandably alienated, workers at the Microform Reading Room of the "Peoples Library," the U.S. Library of Congress, Washington, D.C. Their patient assistance in handling fragile materials with dilapidated and defective equipment is remarkable. It is outrageous that the use and preservation of historical archival collections constitutes such a low priority in a nation that spends billions of dollars on weapons of mass destruction.

We also wish to thank the following people whose assistance at key moments proved pivotal:

- José Del Pozo, Managing Editor of the Canadian Journal of Latin American and Caribbean Studies and professor of history at Université du Québec à Montréal, for providing essential materials and information
- Marjorie Agosín, poet and recipient of United Nations Human Rights Award (1998), for encouragement and helpful suggestions and information
- Judith Place, Bibliographer for Inter-American Studies, Head of Reference Services, State University of New York-Albany Library, for her usual prompt and efficient cooperation
- Patrick Barnard and Susan Caldwell in Canada for their cooperation in obtaining heretofore unpublished audio materials
- Steve Kahl of Librarie Abya-Yala in Montréal, Québec, for his prompt book acquisition assistance

- Rebecca Crumlish in Washington, D.C., and Manoek Ilos in Amsterdam, The Netherlands, for their timely additional research
- Ross Gandy in Mexico for his self-sacrificing efforts during a 1999 national student strike to unearth buried Allende-related manuscripts
- Amy B. Syrell, Interlibrary Loan Supervisor, Skidmore College; and Documents Librarian Alan Carter of the New York State Library in Albany for their many efforts, however often they were in vain.

The Editors

Note on Translations

The sources for translations into English appear with each chapter. I have edited the translations where appropriate to bring them into stricter convergence with the original Spanish. Necessary explanations of names or events appear either in chapter introductory paragraphs or in chapter footnotes.

Editor

SOURCES

1. **Chile's Medical-Social Reality,1939:** *Obras escogidas 1933-48*
2. **Election Day CBC Radio interview, September 4, 1970:** Tape recording from live broadcast obtained by James. D. Cockcroft
3. **Victory Speech, September 5, 1970:** Foreign Broadcasting Information Service (FBIS) Daily Report, *Prensa Latina,* September 5, 1970; *Salvador Allende: Su pensamiento político; Selección de discursos de Salvador Allende; La revolución chilena*
4. **Inaugural Address in the National Stadium, November 5, 1970** *The Chilean Road to Socialism; La revolución chilena; Salvador Allende: Su pensamiento político; Selección de discursos de Salvador Allende*
5. **Letter About Pablo Neruda, 1970:** Internet: "La página de Salvador Allende," <http://members.tripod.com/~Mictlantecuhtli/Allende/aneruda.html>
6. **Tasks of Youth and Agrarian Reform, December 21, 1970:** FBIS Daily Report, Prensa Latina, December 22, 1970; *La revolución chilena*
7. **Address to International Workers' Day Rally, May 1, 1971:** *Salvador Allende: Su pensamiento político; La revolución chilena; Selección de discursos de Salvador Allende*
8. **The Role of the Armed Forces, press conference, May 5, 1971:** *Chile: historia de una ilusión; Chile's Road to Socialism: Salvador Allende*
9. **First Annual Message to the National Congress, May 21, 1971:** *The Chilean Revolution: Conversations with Allende; Salvador Allende: Su pensamiento político; Selección de discursos de Salvador Allende*
10. **My View of Marxism, press conference, May 25, 1971:** *Chile: historia de una ilusión*
11. **First Anniversary of the Popular Government, November 4, 1971:** FBIS Daily Report, November 8, 1971; *Salvador Allende: Su pensamiento político; La revolución chilena; Selección de discursos de Salvador Allende*
12. **Interview with Salvador Allende and Fidel Castro, November 1971:** *Chile: historia de una ilusión*
13. **Farewell Address to Fidel Castro, December 4, 1971:** FBIS Daily Report, December 4, 1971; *Salvador Allende: Su pensamiento político; Selección de discursos de Salvador Allende*
14. **Speech to citizens' rally, Santiago, March 18, 1972:** *Salvador Allende: Su pensamiento político*
15. **Address to UNCTAD, April 13, 1972:** *Salvador Allende: Su pensamiento político; Selección de discursos de Salvador Allende; Chile's Road to Socialism: Salvador Allende*
16. **Interview on "The Great Inquiry," September 10, 1972:** FBIS Daily Report, September 11, 1972; *Selección de discursos de Salvador Allende*
17. **Address to the UN General Assembly December 4, 1972:** United Nations 27th Session Official Records; *Selección de discursos de Salvador Allende*
18. **Third Annual Message to the National Congress, May 21, 1973:** *La revolución chilena*
19. **Report to the Nation on the Military Uprising of June 29, 1973:** FBIS Daily Report, June 29, 1973; *La revolución chilena*
20. **Last Words Transmitted by Radio Magallanes, September 11, 1973:** "Allende's Last Speech," <http://www.derechoschile.com/english/resour.html>; "La página de Salvador Allende," <http://members.tripod.com/~Mictlantecuhtli/Allende/ultdis.html>

INTRODUCTION

Allende's Words Then and Now

by James D. Cockcroft

Radio Magallanes will surely soon be silenced, and the calm metal of my voice will no longer reach you. It does not matter. You shall continue to hear it. I shall always be at your side, and you will remember me at least as a dignified man who was loyal to his country.

President Salvador Allende's last words
to the Chilean people, September 11, 1973

On the morning of September 11, 1973, as the jet fighters completed their bombing runs, a column of thick black smoke rose from "La Moneda," Chile's presidential palace. Tanks and infantry closed in on the rubble-strewn building in preparation for the final assault.

The attackers were Chilean military personnel led by right-wing officers bent on destroying Chilean democracy in the name of "saving the country from economic chaos and communism." Their aim was to capture or kill the nation's 65-year-old president, Salvador Allende, Chile's greatest voice of democracy in history. Allende was a socialist, not a communist, and the world's first Marxist ever elected to govern a country in a free, open and democratic election.

Inside the palace ruins, on the second floor in a large room known as Independence Hall, President Allende waited, holding a submachine gun. After troops secured the first floor, they dispatched a captured defender to tell the president again that he must surrender. Once more,

Allende refused. He then told his friends and bodyguards, "There is no point in useless deaths. I order you to leave." These were his last reported words.

Most of those present obeyed their president, but five refused. As the invading soldiers climbed the stairs, they were met by a hail of machine-gun fire. The firefight raged on. Finally, at 2:20 p.m., the soldiers reached La Moneda's Independence Hall. Gunshots echoed in the great hall.

After some time, Allende's bullet-riddled body was carried out on a stretcher by firefighters and later dumped in an unmarked grave. He presumably died from bullet wounds to the head. Military officials claimed he had committed suicide.

For most Chileans and the Allende family, however, it was clear who was responsible for Salvador Allende's death and the thousands of others who died in the military takeover of September 11, 1973. As far as they were concerned, General Augusto Pinochet and his allies had murdered countless Chilean citizens — and, with them, the Chilean political system long considered one of the world's most vibrant democracies.

Today, when visitors to Chile ask for directions to Allende's gravesite, some officials claim not to know its location. But when the visitors approach workers at graveyards, they are readily told where they can find the burial site of *"el compañero presidente"* ("the Comrade President").[1]

In his final words to Chile's people, Allende was right. He *is* remembered. The calm resolve of his voice *is* still alive. So are the words he spoke that fateful day, September 11, 1973, a day he predicted would bring "infamy" down upon the heads of the coup makers — words of his "faith in Chile and its destiny" and how "much sooner than later the great avenues through which free men walk to build a better society will open."

Today, Chile's avenues are by no means fully open, but at least they are no longer closed and sealed as during the 1973-90 Pinochet dictatorship. As I write these words, General Pinochet himself is a figure of infamy. He is a prisoner, not in Chile, where he still has many fol-lowers and disciples in the upper and upper-middle classes and the military, but in England, where he awaits extradition to Spain, although a last-minute backroom deal may yet prevent that (see below). In Spain, he is charged with genocide, routine use of torture and other crimes against humanity. His arrest has galvanized hope for finally bringing to justice former dictators all over the world. As *New York Times* reporter Barbara Crossette has observed: "A new malady is stalking the presi-dential palaces and bunkers of the world. Call it the Pinochet Syndrome.... former dictators will have almost nowhere to go, in sickness or in health."[2]

In Chile, the legal proceedings against Pinochet have reawakened an entire nation from its slumber of amnesia and stimulated a dialogue about the horrors and crimes Pinochet once brought down on Chilean citizens, thousands of whom were "disappeared" after experiencing the most unspeakable forms of torture. Television shows now refer to Pinochet more often as "the former dictator" than as "senator for life," and some victims of human rights abuses have dared to go before the television cameras and express their opinions. Little wonder that Pinochet is on record as saying he does not recognize the existence of the concept "human rights." Yet, as Salvador Allende's niece and famed novelist Isabel Allende has noted, "the old dictator still holds the democratic government hostage.... fear still reigns in Chile.... the heritage of this doleful patriarch: a nation in fear. Although we still have a long way to go, it is refreshing to see the beginning of the end of the reign of fear."[3]

The Pinochet case has brought back from the shadows of obscurity the most prominent victim of his campaign of terror: Salvador Allende. Not only Chileans seeking to expand their present limited democracy but people all over the world can learn from the words of Allende, truly Chile's — and indeed Latin America's — "voice of democracy." This book, in both its English- and Spanish-language editions, means that for years to come people will continue hearing the voice of Salvador Allende and his vision of a better, more democratic, peaceful and just world.

In Chile, during the Pinochet dictatorship and even since the incomplete transition to democracy,[4] school children rarely, if ever, have had the chance to hear about Salvador Allende or his ideas. School curricula were rewritten after the 1973 coup to glorify Pinochet and the free-market economy and to vilify Allende and socialism. Today, as yesterday, insofar as Allende's name publicly comes up at all in Chile, it is usually in a negative context of someone who once caused "economic chaos" or was "a communist" — as if "a communist" were *evil* and *not a human being!* Even though a few books discussing the Allende years open-mindedly are finally beginning to appear in Chile, the country largely remains under the shadow of years of repressive rule. In more than one case, books critical of Chile's justice system have been silenced.[5] The Cold War, institutionalized by Pinochet's Chile, continues to be fought, pitting the forces of "civilization" against "evil communism." During the height of his power, Pinochet's proudest boast was that he was the only leader in the world who "got rid of the communists." Truly, the blood is on his hands for generations of citizens who lost their loved ones in the vicious campaign against opponents of his military dictatorship.

Countless older citizens of Chile, including those who contribute to the nation's large Socialist Party vote and the smaller (3.2 percent) Communist Party vote, still remember Salvador Allende with affection. He was their *"compañero presidente."* However, recognizing that the 83-year-old ex-dictator Pinochet still holds substantial power in the country, they are hesitant to speak out. Younger Chileans, kept in the dark for so many years, would like to know more about Salvador Allende, especially given the international attention surrounding efforts to bring Pinochet to trial for his crimes. True, some younger people know from family stories, or from their own experiences in the 1980s during the street battles for democracy, that Pinochet and his goons committed terrible atrocities. But their schooling painted a far different picture — of Pinochet as a national savior who "rescued" Chile from "godless Communism."[6]

In this book, Allende's voice rings out with a message of hope to all Chileans — as it did when he was president — and to those of us in other lands who, like the Chilean people, wrestle with the issue of peaceful democratic change for social and economic justice.

Just who was Salvador Allende? What did he have to say about "democracy"? How did he expand it? And, above all, why are Allende's life and words still important today?

Early Years, 1908-32:
Family Influences, Student Activism

Salvador Allende Gossens was born in 1908 in the port city of Valparaíso, Chile, where he was raised by a prosperous middle-class family. His mother, Laura Gossens Uribe, was a devout Catholic, the daughter of French immigrant professionals. His father, Salvador Allende Castro, was a lawyer serving as a government-funded public defender for those who could not afford lawyers. His father educated him about the need to introduce social reforms and to keep church and state separate (a step later inscribed in Chile's 1925 to 1973 constitution). From his mother, young Salvador, known as "Chicho," learned the positive values associated with Christianity. Chicho had a famous paternal grandfather — a medical doctor who had founded Chile's first public school and Santiago's first maternity clinic.

In 1916, at age eight, Chicho visited Santiago, Chile's capital, where his uncle, Ramón Allende Castro, was mayor. Allende later recalled his uncle's outrage at government-ordered massacres of workers: "With bullets and bayonets," his uncle had told him, "the workers aren't fed, nor are social problems resolved. Our stupid government can't comprehend this simple truth."[7]

After graduating from high school with excellent grades and winning the decathlon and swimming events at Chile's Youth Games, Chicho completed his required military service, becoming a skilled marksman. While in the service, he made friends with progressive, socially conscious soldiers and officers, including Colonel Marmaduke Grove Vallejos, whose brother had married his sister Inés. The friendship with Grove and young Chicho's military experience, along with Chile's 160 consecutive years of governance with a parliament, may have influenced Allende's later faith in the institution of Chile's military, a military that ultimately destroyed him and parliament.

In 1926, Allende entered the medical school of the University of Chile in Santiago. His studies were often slowed by his economic need for part-time jobs and by the political turmoil of the times. All of Latin America's university students were caught up in the new university autonomy movement, which passed down a tradition of student political activism in each nation's political and economic life.[8]

Allende, like so many other activist students in Chile, was arrested during peaceful demonstrations that eventually helped topple the constitutional but dictatorial regime of Colonel Carlos Ibáñez del Campo (1927-31). Having read the works of Vladimir Lenin, Karl Marx and Leon Trotsky, the young medical student soon found himself in the leadership of both the university's student federation and a more extreme leftist group he helped organize, Grupo Avance. It was the height of the Great Depression of the early 1930s and Chile's poor and disenfranchised workers and peasants, known as "*los rotos*" or "broken ones," were desperate. At a night school for workers, Allende gave classes on preventative health care. He also found some time to write poetry, a common and highly valued practice in Latin America. (Fellow Chilean Pablo Neruda, later a close friend of Allende, became known as "Latin America's poet" and in 1970 won the Nobel Prize in Literature — see Chapter 5, "Letter About Neruda.")

On June 4, 1932, the old family friend Marmaduke Grove, backed by sections of the army and air force, overthrew a right-wing caretaker government and proclaimed "the Socialist Republic of Chile." Grove's program was almost indistinguishable from the Popular Unity program of 1969 that helped get Allende elected president (for the text of the Popular Unity program, see Appendix). Grove's government lasted only 12 days. It was toppled by a military coup led by some of the Grove government's own dissident right-wing members backed by Chile's upper classes and U.S. and British industrialists. Grove remained popular and later was elected to the Senate.

Allende had the courage and honesty to speak out against the 1932 coup. For this he was arrested and imprisoned. His father was dying at the time, and later, at the funeral, Allende made "the promise that I would dedicate my life to the social struggle and the freedom of Chile."[9]

Middle Years, 1932-51:
Defending Chile's Workers and Democracy

After going through five trials, Allende was finally absolved of all charges and released from jail during a general amnesty preceding the 1932 presidential election campaign. He promptly completed his medical studies. But when he applied for jobs at Santiago hospitals, Dr. Salvador Allende learned that no one would hire a self-avowed Marxist socialist. He had to take a job performing autopsies in a morgue. Allende continued researching and writing on health problems in Chile, becoming more certain with each passing day that revolutionary democratic socialism within Chilean constitutional traditions was the only realistic and practical solution to the nation's problems.

But what did Allende mean by "revolutionary democratic socialism"? Judging from all his speeches, interviews and writings, Allende viewed revolution and socialism as a highly democratic and participatory process for all people. Upon the first anniversary of his presidency Allende would tell a mass rally at Santiago's National Stadium (Chapter 11) that his government would maintain its running "dialogue with the people" because the people "are the fundamental factor in the Chilean revolutionary process." In other words, democracy was actually the key to revolution and socialism.

For Allende, democracy meant not just political participation but also economic justice — which was why revolution and socialism were necessary in the first place. "Democracy and freedom," Allende would point out on the first anniversary of his presidency, "are incompatible with unemployment and lack of housing, the lack of culture, illiteracy and sickness. How is democracy strengthened? By creating more jobs, giving better wages, building more homes, providing the people with more culture, education and better health." As he told the United Nations General Assembly in his famous speech of December 4, 1972 (Chapter 17):

> The Chilean people... [are] engaged in the task of establishing economic democracy so that the country's productive activities will meet its social requirements and expectations and not be exploited for private gain.... [They are] laying the foundations for a pattern of growth which spells genuine development, which involves all the inhabitants of the country and which does not relegate vast sections of the people to poverty and social banishment.... while

strengthening civic freedoms, both collective and individual, and respecting cultural and ideological pluralism. Ours is a continuing struggle for the institution of social freedoms and economic democracy through the full exercise of political freedom.

Socialism meant for Allende a broad-based, well-organized people's movement to elect officials who would introduce state regulation of principle sectors of the economy and workers' control of major industries, banks, mines and farms, along with related measures to favor small and medium-sized businesses and improve the living conditions and quality of life for all. As is clear in the writings, speeches and interviews reproduced here, including one on health Allende presented at age 31 in 1939 (Chapter 1) and another he presented at age 63 as his First Annual Message to the National Congress, May 21, 1971 (Chapter 9), Allende believed socialism should use both the market and state planning as "regulators of the economic process." This is an important point that, as we shall see, is gaining favor around the world today as the "free market" celebration by the defenders of modern capitalism runs up against capitalism's predictable limits of ever greater poverty, financial market turbulence and economic collapses.

Committed to the ideas of a democratic and participatory socialism, in April 1933 Allende helped found Chile's Socialist Party. His comrades appointed him to lead its organization in his birthplace, Valparaíso. In 1935, Chile's government cracked down on striking workers, labor leaders and leftists. Allende himself was arrested in July and exiled to Caldera, a small fishing village in northern Chile, where he attended to the sick and became exceedingly popular.

At workers' meetings throughout the country, Marmaduke Grove, now a senator, called for Allende's freedom. Soon, Allende's name was known everywhere. Therefore, in late 1935, he was permitted to return to Valparaíso.

But Chile's fascist groups, like those in Hitler's Germany and Mussolini's Italy at the time, were on the rise, attacking workers' meetings everywhere. Only in unity could people opposed to fascism and in favor of social and economic democracy triumph. So Allende promptly set about bringing leftists and centrists together — unskilled workers, professionals, small and medium business people; Communists and Socialists with their historical record in leading major worker struggles; members of the pro-separation of church and state, largely middle-class Radical Party — and other centrist groups too.[10]

By 1937, a "Popular Front" of Communists, Socialists and Radicals was able to elect its best organizer, Allende, to the lower house of Congress. People liked the 29-year-old doctor's sincerity and honesty. The following year Chileans elected to the presidency the Popular

Front's candidate, Radical Party member Pedro Aguirre Cerda, a wealthy winegrower.

Allende joined President Aguirre Cerda's staff and in September 1939 became Minister of Health, a position he held for two-and-a-half years. He spearheaded many reforms, including — true to his grandfather's example — the creation of maternity care programs. He introduced larger pensions for widows, free lunch programs for children, and safety laws to protect workers in the factories. Finally, he drafted the legislation that eventually, in 1952, became Chile's National Health Service, which brought medical attention to nearly three million Chileans.

During the earthquake of January 25, 1939, Allende was in a Santiago street with others fleeing the shaking buildings, when he met Hortensia Bussi Soto, a school teacher of history who also advocated socialism. The couple soon married and went on to have a family of three daughters, Carmen, Beatriz and Isabel.

In November 1941, President Aguirre Cerda died of a heart attack. Another Radical Party member won the special presidential election but moved to the right, causing Allende to resign from the Cabinet. When some people in the Popular Front called for eliminating the Communists from the coalition, Allende opposed them. He was elected secretary general of the Socialist Party in 1943. Anticommunist Socialists quit in disgust.

After the defeat of the fascists in World War II, Allende was elected to the Senate. The anticommunist campaign in Chile heated up again, now fueled by a worldwide U.S.-orchestrated Cold War propaganda campaign and by U.S. copper companies anxious to end strikes at the mines. In 1947, Chile's government passed the "Law of Permanent Defense of Democracy," a witch-hunting "Red-baiting" device. In the Senate, Allende voted against what became known as "the Cursed Law" (*"Ley Maldita"*).

Communist leaders were rounded up and sent to detention camps in the northern desert regions. One of the world's greatest poets, Pablo Neruda, a communist, was deprived of the seat he won in the Senate. The names of 50,000 people were removed from Chile's voter registration books. U.S. copper executives were delighted by Chile's "Red scare." It helped defang the labor movement.

Allende, a true democrat and friend of Chile's workers, objected to this Chilean brand of McCarthyism, saying that Socialists would suffer the same fate as communists if they allowed such undemocratic measures to go unchallenged. When the Socialist Party fell apart on the issue, Allende and his supporters launched the Popular Socialist Party.

Final Years, 1951-73:
"A Dignified Man Loyal to His Country"

In 1951-52, Allende was still trying to cobble together a grand political coalition. However, most members of the Popular Socialist Party began to back the former dictator Ibáñez in the 1952 presidential race, since Ibáñez was running on a populist platform of social reforms and appeared likely to win. Allende returned to the Socialist Party, whose members now shared his conviction that Chile's Communist Party must be included in any progressive alliance. The party chose him to be its candidate in the 1952 presidential contest. Those Communists not in prison campaigned for Allende semi-clandestinely (the Communist Party was still illegal).

Ibáñez swept the 1952 presidential election but moved to the right, as Allende had warned he would. After a stint in the Chilean Senate, Allende ran again for president in 1958 — and almost won! He lost by only 30,000 votes to the right-wing coalition candidate, banker-industrialist Jorge Alessandri, nephew of an earlier popular president. The Communist Party had been legalized earlier in 1958 and had enthusiastically backed Allende's candidacy. It was growing rapidly and by 1970 was the world's third largest Communist Party after those of France and Italy.

Allende's near winning of the presidency in 1958 reflected the fact that much of Latin America was moving toward the left in the late 1950s. Pro-democracy forces were toppling or challenging military dictators, even though in 1954 the United States had intervened violently in Guatemala to crush a democratically elected government and restore a dictatorship in order to protect the banana interests of the United Fruit Company.

The Cuban Revolution of 1959 inspired many Latin Americans. Again the United States intervened. It set up an economic blockade against Cuba (still largely in effect 40 years later, though crumbling because of worldwide refusal to comply). In 1961, CIA-trained Cuban mercenaries loyal to the prior dictatorship and backed by U.S. ships and planes, invaded Cuba at the Bay of Pigs (*Playa Girón*). They were quickly defeated by Cuban patriots led by Fidel Castro. In Chile's local elections that year, Allende's Popular Action Front (FRAP) received more votes than any other party or coalition. The U.S. State Department was stunned.

From that point forward, as this book's "Chronology: Chile 1962-1975" spells out, the U.S. government and the CIA, acting on behalf of large U.S. copper corporations, powerful U.S. banking interests, and ITT,[11] all of which held huge chunks of Chile's economy, sought ways to "buy" Chilean elections and prevent Allende from winning the presidency. U.S. foreign policy succeeded in 1964 by financing more than half the costs of the victorious presidential campaign of Eduardo Frei, candidate of Chile's reformist PDC (Christian Democratic Party).[12] Frei promised a "revolution in liberty." First National City Bank's John M. Hennessy helped funnel the CIA moneys. Later, Hennessy joined the Nixon administration to assist it in destabilizing Allende's government of the early 1970s.

During Frei's presidency (1964-70), Allende's Senate colleagues elected him to preside over the upper house as its president. Allende was a highly respected parliamentary socialist and confirmed believer and practitioner of playing within the constitutional rules of the game. He, like poet Neruda, was widely respected throughout Chile — except among the wealthiest elite families, although even they, in public, showed him respect (as he comments in his interview with Chilean journalists on the radio show "The Great Inquiry," September 10, 1972, Chapter 16). Allende's surprising trip to northern Chile to greet fleeing guerrilla comrades of the assassinated international revolutionist Ernesto "Che" Guevara, killed in Bolivia in late 1967, earned him additional respect among those Chileans and Latin Americans who admired the principled revolutionary conduct of Che. Allende helped obtain safe passage for the few guerrillas who escaped the encirclement of the U.S.-trained and supervised unit of the Bolivian Army that captured Che.

U.S. "Alliance for Progress" aid poured into President Frei's Chile. So did U.S. corporate investments, which multiplied many-fold.[13] The AIFLD (American Institute for Free Labor Development), partly funded by the CIA and U.S. organized labor's AFL-CIO, trained 10,000 Chileans to subvert Chile's powerful left-wing labor movement and create alternative labor unions. AIFLD executive board veteran William Thayer became Frei's labor minister (and later became a mouthpiece for the Pinochet dictatorship). U.S. military aid helped to double the ranks of Chile's armed forces to 90,000 men and to train them in "domestic counterinsurgency," including more sophisticated ways to break strikes. Pinochet and other leaders of the violent military coup of September 11, 1973, had all gone to the United States at least once. The bountiful U.S. "aid" (actually, loans) saddled Chile with one of the world's highest per-capita foreign debts — a debt that Allende had to manage after he was elected to Chile's presidency in 1970.

Despite receiving so much U.S. support, the Christian Democrats failed to deliver on many of their revolutionary promises, even as Allende had predicted would happen. Unemployment rates jumped to 20 and 25 percent. Frei's program of purchasing a 51 percent share in foreign copper enterprises ("Chileanization") backfired among the electorate, so much so that in the presidential campaign of 1970 the

PDC's own candidate, Radomiro Tomic, agreed with Allende that the foreign copper companies should be nationalized as soon as possible. By 1971 not a single member of Chile's Congress dared vote against Allende's nationalization law.[14]

In brief, when Chileans elected Allende to the presidency on September 4, 1970, they were looking for a true revolution and not the fraudulent kind introduced by the PDC's Frei. Voter turnout was high — 83 percent of the electorate. Allende garnered more than a million votes (36.3 percent), a plurality in a three-way race against the runners-up, the right-wing National Party's Jorge Alessandri (34.9 percent) and Tomic (27.8 percent) of the increasingly discredited PDC.

Chile's electorate knew Allende to be a principled and honest person. Therefore, it fully expected his government to start transforming Chile in the direction of a socialist society, based on Allende's promises and the 40-point program of the multi-party leftist/centrist coalition running him, the UP (Unidad Popular or Popular Unity). The UP was spearheaded by Communists, Socialists, Radicals, and disenchanted former Christian Democrats organized into the MAPU (United Popular Action Movement) bent on practicing the revolutionary tenets of the "theology of liberation" then spreading like a prairie fire throughout Latin America.

At last, Allende had succeeded in bringing together the grand majority coalition he had so long encouraged! As he proudly told a press conference the day after his election:

> A humanistic, secular and rational way of thinking — such as that of the Radical Party — was merged into Popular Unity, even the Marxist thoughts of Communists and Socialists and the clear Christian thoughts of the friends of MAPU. No other country in the capitalist world, developed or being developed, has been able to build such a broad and profound movement.

Allende elaborated further in his victory speech of September 5 (Chapter 3):

> upon arriving at La Moneda, with the people being the government, we will fulfill the historic commitment we have made, to convert into reality the UP Program.... in no way will we... trade away the UP Program that was the [electoral] banner of the first authentically democratic, popular, national and revolutionary government in Chilean history.

According to Chilean law, however, when no candidate won a majority, Congress had to decide the winner. In the past, Congress had always

ratified the leading vote-getter. For many months prior to the election
this tradition had been disturbing powerful U.S. corporate executives
and their representatives in Washington, D.C. As later reported by the
U.S. Senate Select Committee to Study Governmental Operations in
Respect to Intelligence Activities (the so-called "Church Committee,"
named after its chairman Senator Frank Church),[15] President Richard
Nixon "instructed the CIA to play a direct role in organizing a military
coup d'état in Chile to prevent Allende's accession to the presidency."
As early as the previous March, the White House "Committee of 40,"
headed by NSC (National Security Council) chief Henry Kissinger, had
begun drawing up plans to prevent Allende's election or, failing that, to
destabilize his regime until a military coup could overthrow him —
secretly providing $125,000 for a "spoiling operation" against Allende's
UP coalition. In June 1970, Kissinger told the "Committee of 40" that
should Allende win Chile's elections, "I don't see why we need to stand
by and watch a country go communist due to the irresponsibility of its
own people." Among CIA Director Richard Helm's scribbled notes
about a September 15 meeting with Nixon and Kissinger (now also
Secretary of State) were the steps subsequently enacted to destabilize
Chile's economy during the Allende presidency, summed up in the
phrase "make the economy scream." [16]

One important individual stood in the way, however, of a military
coup prior to the Chilean Congress's vote on who should be president.
He was the Army Chief of Staff, René Schneider, a man loyal to the
constitution. The CIA decided to remove Schneider. After two muffed
CIA attempts at kidnapping him, right-wing extremists associated with
the National Party succeeded. They assassinated Schneider on October
22, 1970, and blamed it on the far left. When the true plotters were
uncovered, Chileans reacted with outrage. On October 24, 1970, Chile's
Congress confirmed Salvador Allende Gossens as president by a vote of
153 to 35.

In an unprecedented move, however, Allende's opponents had
legislated conditions on his ratification. They had passed a constitutional
reform guaranteeing noninterference by the new government in freedom
of expression, education and worship. More importantly, they barred
Allende from tampering with the country's security forces and placed
limits on the traditional presidential authority to appoint commanding
officers. Moreover, Allende was obligated to preserve the jobs of the
previous administration's state functionaries, making it difficult for him
to overcome wasteful bureaucratism. Finally, when Allende assumed
office on November 3, 1970, he controlled only the executive branch of
government — and even that power had these unprecedented limits set
upon it. For the next thousand days, then, Allende was somewhat
hamstrung in his efforts to "take the path toward socialism through

democracy, pluralism and freedom" (Inaugural Address, November 5, 1970, Chapter 4). He had to carry out his promised "revolution" in the face of not having a majority in Congress; the Supreme Court disallowing many of his reforms; and the military increasingly intervening in state affairs.

Despite the obstacles, Allende managed to introduce an expanded democracy and new economic opportunities for Chile's working people. The way he conducted the presidency set the tone. Believing that La Moneda should be a public building, Allende invited an almost constant flow of worker and peasant delegations, as well as intellectuals, to visit the presidential palace. He refused to live in the second-floor residence provided for the President and his family. Telling his friends that the place felt like "a giant mousetrap," he lived instead in a house on nearby Tomás Moro Street, where he could relax with his family, surrounded by his paintings, books and poetry.

In his first year as president, Allende began implementing the Popular Unity's "anti-imperialist" platform of building socialism within a democratic framework — the so-called "Chilean revolution," also known as the "Chilean road [or path] to socialism." He nationalized (with compensation) public utilities, non-foreign banks, and several basic industries, starting with the U.S. copper firms. He raised workers' wages, froze prices and rents, provided free milk for children, ordered hospitals to stop turning away those who could not pay for medical care, and provided tax and credit breaks for small and medium-sized businesses. In his speeches, Allende asked workers to support the revolution by producing more. They responded by increasing industrial output 14 percent in 12 months. Allende asked workers and employers to join "the People's Government" in its programs to help those without work — and unemployment plummeted to less than 4 percent. Allende's agrarian reform greatly accelerated the rate at which *fundos* (huge estates) were broken up and land was distributed to the landless. Food production and consumption rose. Unfortunately, prices also rose, as a U.S. economic blockade of Chile took hold and a CIA-funded right-wing offensive against Allende moved into high gear. Threats on Allende's life became a regular occurrence, and his bodyguard had to be beefed up.

Internationally, Allende's government inspired people everywhere. Messages of solidarity poured in from every major European country, where parliamentary socialists like him had a long tradition of governing. Other Third World countries in Asia, Africa, the Middle East and Latin America which, like Chile, were struggling with choices about economic development to overcome the legacy of centuries of political and economic submission to colonialism and neocolonialism, looked at the Chilean experiment with hope and encouragement. Those nations undergoing their own revolutions and the attempts of U.S. imperialism to crush them by means of overwhelming military force, such as Vietnam, welcomed the solidarity Allende expressed for them. A new generation of political activists in the United States, committed to ending the Vietnam War and "bringing the troops home," as well as to various liberating causes in the fields of minority rights, viewed Chile with total fascination and hope — democracy *could* work, it seemed to them, to improve people's lives and thereby avoid the need for outright revolution.

Throughout the world, there was a growing disillusionment with capitalism because of its imbalances and injustices. When some concluded that only a revolution could replace capitalism with a more humane system — called by various names, ranging from socialism, to economic democracy, to humanism, to democratic socialism — others sought to avoid the violence associated with revolution. Allende was one of these. He sought a peaceful road to social change.

On April 4, 1971, in a four-way field for elections in 280 municipalities, Allende's UP coalition garnered half the vote. For the first time in Chilean history, people 18-21 years old could vote. Young people's support contributed to the UP's huge margin of victory. It appeared that the UP was on its way to forging an absolute electoral majority for the 1973 congressional elections, which would enable it to institute a full-scale socialist program without needing the support of the other parties. Consequently, the Christian Democrats' PDC moved closer to the right-wing parties to block Allende's new legislation, although the nationalization of copper, iron ore, steel, and nitrate industries went ahead unopposed on July 11, known as the Day of National Dignity.

On November 10, 1971, Cuba's Premier Fidel Castro arrived for a whirlwind tour of Chile. The right-wing offensive accelerated. Businessmen held back basic foods, clothing and other necessities, creating artificial shortages. A black market sprang up, where the supposedly scarce items appeared in great numbers and at much higher prices. Thousands of upper-middle-class and wealthy women from Santiago's plush suburban residential area conducted a "march of empty pots and pans" in downtown Santiago. The march was organized and given its catchy name by the major CIA-funded newspaper *El Mercurio*, among others.

Alarmed, Fidel Castro quietly let Allende know that the Chilean president's trust in democracy could be his undoing, a sentiment shared by members of the small but vigorous Chilean MIR (Movement of the Revolutionary Left, some of whose members belonged to Allende's bodyguard). The MIR had repeatedly asked Allende, in vain, to arm the peasants and workers for what they felt was an inevitable clash with the right, or, failing that, to form a "worker-soldier alliance" to defend the constitution. Apparently, Allende never wavered from his faith in the armed forces' staying within the bounds of the constitution, the way he himself was doing. He felt he could pull the working-class soldiery into the social processes of the revolution (see Chapter 8).

Allende gave Castro a ringing sendoff, in which he denounced the forces of "sedition" in Chile and once more explained the peaceful and democratic "Chilean road to socialism" (see his December 4, 1971, "Farewell Address to Fidel Castro," Chapter 13).

By the end of 1971, an "invisible" U.S. economic blockade, a CIA-funded campaign of sabotage against industrial plants, and CIA financial support for Allende's opponents, especially the fascist *Patria y Libertad* (Fatherland and Liberty), were blocking the Chilean revolution's advance. A "coup team" was already operating out of the U.S. embassy in Santiago.[17]

In March 1972, syndicated columnist Jack Anderson reported in the U.S. press that secret ITT documents (soon made public) proved that ITT had dealt regularly with the CIA in efforts to bring Allende down (for details, see "Chronology: Chile 1962-1975"). Therefore, few Chileans objected to Allende's nationalizing ITT. The wealth that poured back into the Chilean treasury from ITT's lucrative subsidiaries in communications, electricity and hotels gave a modest boost to the sagging economy. But the right kept up its counterattack.

During the October 1972 CIA-funded truck owners' strike, Allende suffered a heart attack — kept secret lest the right seize the opportunity to stage a coup. Yet even as he was bedridden Allende directed negotiations on the strike. He recovered quickly and was back at his desk within six weeks to resume his 16-hour workdays.

On December 4, Allende went to New York to address the General Assembly of the United Nations (Chapter 17). Delegates from around the world listened intently as the man frequently referred to in the U.S. press as "the world's only freely elected Marxist leader" calmly informed them about the transnational corporations' mode of operation against a democratic government's introduction of profound social reforms:

> We find ourselves faced with forces that operate in shadows, without a flag, with powerful weapons, posted in various places of influence.... From the very day of our electoral triumph on the fourth of September 1970, we have felt the effects of a large-scale external pressure against us which tried to prevent the inauguration of a government freely elected by the people, and has attempted to bring it down ever since, an action that has tried to cut us off from the world, to strangle our economy and paralyze trade in our principal

export, copper, and to deprive us of access to sources of international financing.

At the end of his speech, the UN delegates gave Allende a prolonged standing ovation.

As can be readily appreciated from Allende's speeches and interviews reproduced here, Chile's masses responded to the Popular Unity government's progressive steps with great hope. A "revolution of rising expectations" had already begun during Frei's "revolution in liberty" and now, with Allende as president, it looked as if it had a chance at last to win. Citizens, including hundreds of thousands of Christian Democrats and independents, poured into the streets to back "the People's Government." In addition, in 1972 and 1973, workers began responding militantly to the right-wing counterattack by seizing hundreds of factories, sometimes at gunpoint, and operating them with workers' councils. Peasants seized farms, some of them owned by middle-class Chileans.

Amid the rising tensions of left-right conflict, 93 percent of the electorate voted in the March 1973 congressional elections. They gave Allende and the UP a strong vote of confidence, increasing an incumbent political power's vote for the first time in history in a mid-term election — by a substantial 7 percent! The opposition parties' congressional majority still stood, but it seemed more likely than ever that the UP might gain an outright congressional majority in the 1976 elections.

Therefore, military conspirators and the right sped up their target date for a coup. On June 29, 1973, an armored regiment seized the plaza in front of La Moneda and tanks began rolling toward the palace entrance. Troops loyal to constitutionalist army Chief of Staff General Carlos Prats overpowered them, but few other officers actively helped. Some, like General Pinochet, claimed they were not involved in the coup — but they carefully noted which officers and soldiers refused to join the *golpistas* (coup makers).

The MIR and other leftists once more urged Allende to form a worker-soldier alliance, or at least purge the military of right-wing generals. Allende refused, more than likely believing that the entire military would unite to overthrow his government if he antagonized the officer corps by forming a worker-soldier alliance or by removing any military officers (which the 1970 Constitutional Reform forbade him from doing in any case). Knowing that many rank-and-file soldiers held Socialist or Communist Party membership cards, Allende apparently feared a bloody civil war might erupt if he encouraged a worker-soldier alliance or challenged the caste-like officer corps.

Military purges did occur, but they were directed by right-wing officers against constitutionalists. Several navy units were purged of "leftist" elements. Some navy recruits said they were tortured until they named "pro-Allende" officers. On July 27, an Allende naval aide, Captain Arturo Araya, was found murdered. Then an event occurred that many Chileans thought ominous. On August 23, General Prats resigned, stating that he was forced to do so by a "sector of army officers." General Pinochet became the new commander-in-chief of the army. A rash of other resignations followed.

Also in August, efforts at further dialogue with the Christian Democrats' PDC failed. The PDC newspaper ran an article claiming that the Allende government had been taken over by a "Jewish-communist cell." In his Third Annual Message to the National Congress three months earlier (Chapter 18), Allende had insisted on genuine dialogue "because the alternative to dialogue is violence which, with the exception of those who are stubborn, no one in Chile wants.... the vast majority of Chileans are against political and economic chaos."

In the aftermath of the June 29 coup attempt, the MIR and left-wing elements in Allende's Socialist Party gained fresh support as workers and peasants loyal to the UP took control of still more factories and lands. Meanwhile, hoping to avoid more chaos and violence, Allende made major concessions to the right. He appointed the commanders of the three armed forces and the *Carabineros* (national police) to his cabinet and approved the eviction of workers from illegally occupied workplaces.

On September 4, 1973, more than 750,000 Chileans marched through downtown Santiago chanting "Allende, Allende, the people will defend you!" Three days later, Allende met with military officers he believed to be constitutionalists and informed them that on September 11, acting in line with provisions in Chile's Constitution, he would call for a plebiscite in which Chile's voters would declare whether or not they supported his presidency. General Pinochet attended the meeting. He realized that Allende would likely win such a referendum.

During the months leading up to the September 11 coup d'état, an estimated 100 U.S. military personnel were working with the Chilean officer corps. On September 10, Chilean Navy ships conducted joint naval maneuvers with U.S. warships off the coast. That night, those same Chilean naval ships returned to the Valparaíso port. Early on the morning of September 11, naval officers seized control of Valparaíso. Hearing of this revolt, Allende tried phoning Pinochet and other top military brass but could not reach them.[18]

It was too late! In the preceding days and hours, constitutionalist soldiers and sailors had been held in their barracks. Then, the night before the September 11 coup, the disloyal admirals and generals had ordered several hundred of them shot. Pinochet had said in 1971, "I hope the army won't have to come out, because if it does, it will be to kill." The killing had begun.

By daybreak, the swift, well-coordinated, bloody coup was in full swing. Allende rushed to La Moneda to take charge of what he realized would be an unwinnable resistance. Nonetheless, he was determined to remain loyal to his principles and to Chile. His final hours of life, like his last address to the Chilean people delivered that morning on one of the few radio stations still not seized or bombed by the military, proved how honest, loyal and dignified Salvador Allende remained to the end (Chapter 20).

Instantly, soldiers, sailors and *Carabineros* began rounding up UP officials and suspected "communists." Several officials of the different UP parties were shot on sight. "Suspects" killed or arrested included women in slacks and long-haired men, as well as supporters of the Popular Unity.[19] Bodies and several legs and arms floated down the capital's Mapocho River, where the waters turned reddish-brown. Cadavers piled up in morgues. Allende's wife Hortensia Allende Bussi fled her home on Tomás Moro Street just minutes before an air force jet bombed it. Wild-eyed militants of the CIA-backed fascistic, anti-Semitic *Patria y Libertad* torched piles of "subversive" books at street intersections. When Santiago's jails overflowed, detainees were herded into sports stadiums and military camps. More than 200,000 Chileans fled for their lives, going into exile — one out of every 55 Chileans.

Billows of smoke rose from Santiago's *cordones*, the name given to factory and residential areas having their own *comandos comunales*, or popularly elected councils. Also devastated were countless *campamentos*, self-governing slum settlements where one political party often had a majority. Even PDC *campamentos* were attacked. Peasant co-ops and "collectives" were likewise bombed, burned, searched, destroyed. All these grass-roots organizations had been viewed by Chile's wealthy elites as even more threatening than Allende's constitutional "parliamentary socialism."

During the next month, the dead bodies of priests, students, workers and others deemed subversive by the military dictatorship were left in the road and on high school and college campuses. Uncounted numbers of people "disappeared." In most cases, the "disappeared" individuals were tortured and murdered, often by being dumped from helicopters over the Pacific Ocean. Some were tossed into secret mass graves, which were later found as evidence of mass executions.[20]

Former President Frei congratulated the coup leaders for "saving Chile from a Marxist dictatorship." It was subsequently revealed that Frei had received money from the CIA to support the coup. Frei and other Christian Democrats later turned against the Pinochet dictatorship, as its frightening human rights record of routine torture, disappearances and murder became known outside of Chile.[21]

Chile fell under martial law. Congress was suspended indefinitely, as were all local elected councils. Elections, organized labor's CUT (Unitary Workers Central), strikes, political parties, an independent judiciary, a free press — all were outlawed. Chile's proud tradition of democracy was, far from being "saved from Marxism," snuffed out at the moment of its fullest expression. Chile's elites, faced with the failure of their own democratic institutions to guarantee their privileged positions, had opted for their destruction. It was a case of what a U.S. general in Vietnam had once called "destroying a village in order to save it" — destroying democracy in the name of saving it.

The coup leaders stated that their fundamental goal was nothing less than "to change the mentality of the people." General Pinochet stated in 1974 that, "Democracy is the best pot for growing Marxism.... [all government opponents] will be crushed and made to disappear."

While most of the world's governments refused to recognize the military dictatorship or broke off diplomatic relations in protest, the U.S. government immediately recognized General Pinochet as Chile's legitimate president and rushed in economic aid to his regime. Like the U.S. government, South America's dictatorships strongly backed the coup. At Santa Cruz, Bolivia, half a year earlier, Brazilian and Bolivian soldiers who had been trained at U.S. Army schools in the Panama Canal Zone instructed 250 Chileans in the techniques of terrorism. Recently released CIA and other U.S. government documents confirm extensive U.S. government foreknowledge of the military coup and its bloody aftermath.[22]

Allende's Words Today:
Democracy and Imperialism Again!

Since 1991, the word "democracy" has been bandied about propagandistically as an all encompassing slogan to celebrate capitalism's triumph over the Soviet Union in the Cold War and to drown any remaining communist countries attempting to swim against the current in the capitalist tidal wave of global "free trade." Similarly, anything smacking of socialism has been propagandistically smeared as "undemocratic" and counter to government deregulation, privatization of state enterprises, and the "free market" of "free trade."[23]

The concept "democracy" continues to embrace ideas that have profound emotional and everyday impact among working people all over the world. For example, the increase in economic democracy introduced by past communist governments like the Soviet Union's, or socialist ones like Allende's, looks attractive when compared with the massive poverty characterizing so many capitalist "democracies" of today. Worldwide there is developing a deepening discussion as to the meaning, practicality and necessity of introducing true popular democracy, both economically and politically. People are worried about the seemingly uncheckable ability of giant corporations and powerful capitalist nation states to impose their will outside the realms of democratic consultation or domestic and international law, as in the recent rash of free trade agreements and murderous "hi-tech bombings" against multiple civilian targets.

As already noted, Allende's vision itself was one of a full and true democracy for all people, not a narrow democracy for a wealthy few. Democracy for Allende had to be economic, social and political, where working people, instead of a handful of captains of enterprise or government, would have the main say. Economic democracy included the provisions of the Popular Unity Program (see Appendix) for ending "wage and salary discrimination between men and women or for reasons of age," as well as daycare centers in the poorest neighborhoods and other reforms favoring women, children or other neglected groups. Allende's policies benefited women, especially poor and working class women, with maternity leaves, daycare assistance, nutritional food programs for their children, free medicines for low-income people and improved life chances. Actually, as the speeches reproduced here make clear, no area of daily life was left untouched by the reforms introduced by Allende. Even the arts were favored, but on a basis again of encouraging the expansion of working people's culture — with such success that some of the art forms and styles introduced by Chileans in their wall and street murals of the early 1970s spread to other parts of the world, including the United States.[24]

In all his speeches, interviews and writings, Allende explained his vision of democracy, being careful to note the dangers in masking undemocratic behavior with the slogan "democracy." His words truly echoed or expanded upon the Popular Unity Program's detailed steps for extending democracy by "granting to social organizations real means of exercising their rights and creating the mechanisms which will allow them to participate in the different levels of the state's administrative apparatus.... the very opposite of that [notion of strong government] held by the oligarchy and imperialists who identify authority with the use of coercion against the people." Eventually, according to this democratic vision, a new political constitution would "validate the massive incorporation of the people into governmental power" by providing for a unicameral democratic parliament to be known as the "People's Assembly," with the people's representatives to be subject to recall.[25] A new concept of the judicial process would "replace the existing individualistic and bourgeois one."

In a short essay Allende wrote at the request of "the North American publishers" to introduce a postscript for a book containing the English translations of his February 1971 conversations with French journalist Régis Debray, Allende informed the North American public:

> Ever since my youth I have fought to bury prejudice and obsolete political frameworks for all time. Destiny has willed that I should head this democratic revolution in Chile, this struggle in which the word democracy has a much broader significance than when it is indiscriminately used to conceal essentially anti-democratic and reactionary political attitudes.... our government's action against the monopolies which have plundered the Chilean economy and our attempts to recover the basic natural resources of the country for the Chilean people will affect certain North American private interests. However, we are sure that these interests cannot be identified with the great historical purposes of the North American people.... whose progressive tradition I respect.[26]

Indeed, Allende was so preoccupied with the true meaning of democracy that he included along with the postscript for the same book a transcript of his First Annual Message to the National Congress, May 21, 1971, which lays out the five guiding principles of Chile's democratic revolution: legality, development of institutions, political freedom, nonviolence and the creation of an "area of social ownership" (see Chapter 9).

Allende was particularly sensitive to the abuses of workers' rights that regularly occur in too many so-called "democracies." As he told Chileans rallying in the streets of Santiago, March 18, 1972 (Chapter 14): "with this workers' government, the freedom to get rich by exploiting another has ended, the freedom to enrich oneself at the cost of alienated labor is over."

Finally, Allende understood the importance of resisting imperialism — a foreign power's expansion into other nations on behalf of economically powerful corporations and banks. As he told the Chilean people in mid-1972:

> I have promised to make the structural changes that Chile requires; to open the road to socialism in pluralism, democracy and freedom.... The dilemma of Chile clearly is not between Democracy and Totalitarianism. The dilemma of Chile is between Chilean interests and those of foreign capital; between patriots and anti-patriots; between the hegemony of the bosses or of the workers."[27]

Moreover, Allende, unlike Chile's supporters of the thoughts of Chinese Premier Mao Zedong, rejected Mao's notion that imperialism was "a paper tiger." In a speech critical of Chile's bureaucrats on September 30, 1971, he prophetically noted:

> Imperialism is not a paper tiger, comrades. It is a very vigorous and aggressive tiger, that moreover has native mountain cats that help it out and back it up perfectly well. So have no illusions. The struggle will be very hard.[28]

On the other hand, Allende had some grounds to hope he might eventually outflank the U.S. tiger and its Chilean mountain cats. Besides the mass mobilizations taking part in support of his government, he could take heart in the fact that, as he told a packed National Stadium on November 4, 1971:

> Today's world is changing. China has joined the United Nations. The American empire is showing signs of crisis: it is imposing a 10 percent tax on imports and stopping foreign aid. The dollar has become nonconvertible. Apparently, the definitive victory of the Vietnamese people is drawing near. The countries of Latin America are speaking the same language and using the same words to defend their rights. Nixon is taking a trip to Peking. Fidel Castro is coming to Chile. [Applause] [29]

Indeed, the Vietnamese people did achieve victory a few years later. However, the same could not be said for the Chilean people, defenseless in the face of Chile's U.S.-supplied armed forces and *Carabineros* called out by the oligarchic mountain cats.

Allende and the Socialist Challenge to Neoliberalism Today

As already explained, Allende's vision was one of a democratic socialism.

Since 1991, socialism has been on the defensive. In some parts of the world, socialism has even been relegated to the trash bin of history as being supposedly no longer relevant. Actually, socialism is more relevant than ever, which is one reason why Allende's vision has so much meaning today.

Indeed, by the end of the 1990s most of Europe's democratically elected governments were run by "socialists" (or "social democrats" as they are known) and their allies. Several of these leaders belonged to the same Socialist International that Allende belonged to — the one founded in the late 19th century which, however, during the Cold War was far more concerned with combating communism than with introducing a genuine economic democracy the way Allende attempted. The European social democrats' electoral campaign platforms of the 1990s, like those of their counterparts in Latin America and elsewhere, promised giving a "human face" to "neoliberalism" and its mean-spirited measures introduced as part of the "new economic world order" that the dominant capitalist power, the United States, was seeking to enforce globally.[30]

"Neoliberalism" is the word commonly used to describe the world's dominant economic ideology and practice that ever since the Reagan and Thatcher governments of the United States and Great Britain in the 1980s has maintained that the only viable road to successful development is the road of free enterprise capitalism, that is, the privatization of all state enterprises (including social security as in post-Allende Chile), reduced social spending and "free market" solutions to social problems. The 1980s' era of neoliberalism in Latin America earned the description of "lost decade of development" (widespread economic depression), although in Pinochet's Chile there did occur an economic mini-boom, based largely on workers' wages being kept low, the prohibition of strikes, and the restriction of labor union activities. Indeed, Pinochet's Chile became the "economic model" publicized worldwide by neoliberalism's advocates, who described it as "an economic miracle." Neoliberal guru University of Chicago economist Milton Friedman applauded the bloody coup against Allende because it removed any threat to big business's domination of society. A group of Friedman's disciples known as "the Chicago boys" helped funnel moneys to the anti-Allende forces behind the coup and then designed the economic programs of the Pinochet dictatorship that significantly de-industrialized Chile and left the economy at the mercy of foreign bankers and 12 domestic "financial groups." A 1994 World Bank report characterized Chile's "miracle" as one that redistributed income upward, allowed social service infrastructure to deteriorate, and left 40 percent of Chile's 15 million citizens able to consume only three-fourths of the calories they needed daily. Chile's unemployment rate nearly doubled in 1998-99.

In the 1990s, under the neoliberal policies of Eastern Europe's post-communist governments, East Europeans' living standards took a devastating nose-dive. During neoliberalism's heyday, unemployment plagued much of Western Europe as well, and today unemployment remains a major problem throughout almost all of Europe. In Latin America and less industrialized countries in general, unemployment and underemployment have grown during the era of neoliberalism to account for up to two-thirds of the working population.

Consequently, like socialism, neoliberalism today finds itself on the defensive. However, unlike socialism, which became discredited with the fall of the communist regimes of Eastern Europe, in some countries neoliberalism is still seen as "the only alternative." Despite this, neoliberalism's growing record of failures, including economic collapses in Mexico (1982, 1994-95), East Asia (1997-98), Russia and Brazil (1998-99), and the deepening recessions in most of Latin America, including Chile, have revealed neoliberalism's gross and ominous inadequacies, making it appear as if it, like the fabled emperor, "has no clothes." People increasingly recognize that there has to be an alternative to "the only alternative" of neoliberalism.[31]

This brings us back to the problems faced by Allende: how to correct the imbalances and injustices of capitalism. Allende's socialist development visions are more in tune with the needs of working people today than ever before. If in Allende's time societies seeking to emerge from poverty were constrained by "international forces" defending the "democratic system" against "communism," then how much does this differ from today's "market forces" and all the prattle about "globalization"? As development economist Dr. Robinson Rojas has astutely observed, in the speeches of Salvador Allende "there is no difference between the 'international' forces in 1972 and now, in the 1990s."[32]

Enter "free trade" and its ancillary organizations: NAFTA (North American Free Trade Agreement), APEC (Asia-Pacific Cooperation forum), GATT (General Agreement on Tariffs and Trade) and the WTO (the World Trade Organization, created to oversee burgeoning free-trade agreements worldwide). All these free-trade agreements and organizations are part and parcel of neoliberalism and corporate-finance capital's effort to restructure the world's economies to fit into the profit needs of the largest TNCs (transnational corporations, including banks, insurance companies and other financial institutions).

Ironically, Allende's Popular Unity Program called for removing "the obstacles in the way of free trade which, over time, have made it impossible to establish collective trade relations with all countries of the world." The Popular Unity Program saw as a major part of the problem the IMF (International Monetary Fund). As is well known today, the IMF traditionally props up nations' failing currencies with loans and economic bailout funds in exchange for the implementation of draconian neoliberal economic policies. The Popular Unity made Point 31 of its program's "First 40 Measures of the People's Government" an end to "links with the International Monetary Fund," a policy now being seriously considered by some hard pressed governments around the world. Not surprisingly, the IMF has found it necessary to search for a new public relations firm.

Once again, Allende's words become important for today. In his address to the third United Nations Conference on Trade and Development (UNCTAD), April 13, 1972 (Chapter 15), as well as in his better known United Nations General Assembly speech later that year

(Chapter 17), Allende dealt with trade, currency, debt and economic development issues. He singled out U.S.-based TNCs and GATT (the WTO did not yet exist) as perpetrators of an "unfair international division of labor, based on a dehumanized concept of mankind." Prophetically, he warned of the intentions of Japan, the United States and the European Economic Community to use GATT as a tool for the expansion through "free trade" of their own corporations' economic interests, wiping out "at a stroke of the pen the advantages of the general system of [tariff] preferences for the developing countries" — steps which the great powers are now trying to enforce through the WTO. Allende criticized GATT for having "always been essentially concerned with the interests of the powerful countries." GATT, he noted, "has no reliable linkage with the United Nations and is not obliged to adhere to its principles" and is "at odds with the concept of universal participation" (just like today's WTO).

Foreign debts, Allende observed, "constitute one of the chief obstacles to the progress of the Third World [and]... are largely contracted in order to offset damage done by an unfair trade system, to defray the costs of the establishment of foreign enterprises in our territory, to cope with the speculative exploitation of our reserves." These debts are now so high that even the creditors, knowing full well that the debts can never be paid and are an obstacle to economic growth, have accepted the need to "forgive" them to some degree with the only conflict being to what degree and on what kind of sliding scale for nations more able to pay than others.[33]

In his speech to the United Nations General Assembly, Allende urged a new technology development policy that would not be one for the profit of foreigners but rather would relate "to our own needs" and would be "prompted by a humanistic philosophy which sets up the human being as it major objective." Noting that moneys gained from disarmament "would be more than enough to start shaping a solidarity world economy," Allende concluded: "Progress and the liberation of the vast underdeveloped world depend on the urgently needed transformation of the world economic structure, on the conscience of countries, on choosing the path of cooperation based on solidarity, justice, and respect for human rights. Otherwise, on the contrary, people will be forced to take the road of conflict, violence, and suffering — precisely in order to impose the principles of the Charter of the United Nations."

Allende's frequent arguments for using both the market and state planning as "regulators of the economic process" for achieving human betterment are now finding favor throughout Europe and much of the rest of the world, including Latin America (in Asia, a strong state role in economic development pre-dates the rise of socialist alternatives and continues today).[34] In several major Latin American states and cities new socialist-oriented governors and mayors have been elected to office. In 1997, presidential hopeful Cuauhtémoc Cárdenas of the left-of-center Party of the Democratic Revolution (PRD) was elected mayor of Mexico City, the world's largest metropolis, while a year later in Brazil's economically pivotal state of Rio Grande do Sul, a UP-like popular front headed by the Workers Party (PT) won the governorship. In 1999, Tabare Vázquez, a leftist medical doctor in Uruguay resembling Allende in many ways, barely missed winning Uruguay's presidential electoral contest. Earlier, he had won the mayoralty of Uruguay's capital Montevideo. Echoing Allende, Vázquez has stated: "we will transform the country... quietly, gradually, calmly and within the constitution."[35] These and other elected officials of the left are also attempting, however erratically at times, to implement the participatory democracy that Allende so greatly emphasized. For example, in Brazil's southern industrial metropolis of Porto Alegre, the often reelected PT mayor oversees a remarkable grass-roots "participatory budget" where every citizens' group has direct input.[36]

Ironically, only in Chile does there exist such a powerful time warp that Allende's example and words are still difficult to invoke. Indeed, as part of the compromise made by Pinochet's Socialist and Christian Democrat opponents to introduce partial democracy, there has occurred a conscious political decision to forget the past, to erase it, and never to return to it. Chile's Foreign Minister Juan Gabriel Valdés, a Socialist, joins the current outgoing president, Christian Democrat Eduardo Frei Ruiz-Tagle, son of the 1960s' president, in calling for the return of Pinochet to Chile where there is little likelihood he will face his accusers. And Ricardo Lagos, the Socialist candidate of the Socialist-Christian Democrat alliance "Concertación" running for president in the December 1999 election, endorses this position while promising not to return to Allende's policies but to continue the current economic regimen. Meanwhile, in the face of an unfair electoral system favoring the right, Chile's voters often yawn — 40 percent of those eligible to vote in the December 1997 parliamentary elections either did not register, abstained, or defaced their ballots or left them blank.[37] In the December 1999 presidential elections nearly one million of an estimated eight million registered voters failed to cast ballots.

Fortunately, national memory can never be permanently erased. The past is history, yes, but history shapes the present... and the present shapes the future. The past, like memory itself, cannot be erased, and that is what the attempt to bring Pinochet to the courts of justice reflects. That too is what is reflected by the 1999 protest marches by Mapuche and other indigenous groups, university and high school students, doctors, port workers, miners and organized labor's CUT (Unitary

Workers Central), as Chile's people slowly awaken and once more seek control over their own destiny. And that is one reason why the Socialist, Lagos, won the Concertación coalition's May 30 primary election with an overwhelming 71.34 percent of the vote against his Christian Democrat rival who supported a policy of drawing closer to Pinochet in order to woo right-wing votes and who tried to associate Lagos negatively with Allende.[38]

In the December 1999 presidential elections, the Concertación's Lagos edged by only 0.4 percent the conservative coalition's candidate Joaquín Lavín, who ran as a populist supporting "change." The Communist Party candidate garnered 3.2 percent of the vote, forcing a runoff between Lagos and Lavín. On January 16, 2000, by a margin of under 2.7 percent, Lagos won the runoff election against Lavín, despite being outspent by more than three to one. Both candidates avoided speaking of the past, yet the past lingered in people's minds. In his concession speech, Lavín, an engineer trained in economics at the University of Chicago and a former Pinochet official, said he would place himself at Lagos's disposal "to help unify Chile." Some observers speculated that members of the Communist Party and two smaller parties may have swung their votes to Lagos in January. However, in both presidential contests a very large number of blank or null ballots were cast by leftists in protest against Lagos's and Lavín's coziness with Wall Street and therefore the likelihood that neither would deliver on their promises to provide more jobs. Also, many voters were critical of the softness displayed by both Lagos and Lavín on the issue of bringing Pinochet to justice should the dictator be returned to Chile.

A few days before the runoff election, in what was widely viewed as a political deal involving the governments of Chile, Britain, Spain and the United States, Britain announced it would likely release Pinochet on the basis of still private medical tests allegedly showing that the tyrant's health had degenerated to a point where he was supposedly unfit to stand trial. It is possible that Lagos's final margin of victory derived from Chileans' fear of a Lavín presidency leading to Pinochet's resurgence in the nation's politics, even though Lavín desperately tried to distance himself from Pinochet. At Lagos's victory rally on the evening of January 16, tens of thousands chanted "Trial for Pinochet!" Answered President-elect Lagos: "In my government, the courts will decide what cases to try." Many of Chile's courts remained under the control of pro-Pinochet judges. The shrewd, even if "ill," Senator-for-Life still had immunity. Most of Chile's military, some of whose officers had recently been detained to face possible trials in Chile for human rights violations, still supported Pinochet.

Human rights activists in Chile and around the world continued to contest the flaunting of international law that a release of Pinochet augured. In calling for a second medical opinion, Spanish judge Baltasar Garzón criticized Britain's "negative precedent" of skirting a criminal proceeding "for unknown medical reasons." Other physically impaired old men, such as Klaus Barbie, the Nazis' Gestapo chief in occupied France who had fled to Bolivia after World War II, had been extradited to face trials and convictions for their crimes against humanity — so why not Pinochet?"

Salvador Allende has been omitted from the basic school books of Chile's younger generations for 27 years. Yet the rest of the world remembers his visions, his example, his martyrdom. His words still echo even 27 years later, because, rightly or wrongly, they at least focus on the burning issues of social justice which plague the capitalist system today more than ever.

A specter haunts Chile and the world.... Truly it is time to say: *Compañero Allende, presente! Venceremos!*[39]

James D. Cockcroft, Editor
Friends Lake, New York
January 17, 2000

ENDNOTES

1 Actually, in the 1980s, during the long, difficult course of popular uprisings known as "National Days of Protest" that eventually led to the restoration of some of Chilean democracy and a new elected president in 1990 (even if not breaking the power of Pinochet and the other generals), the remains of Salvador Allende were moved to a mausoleum in Santiago's main cemetery. There, they were given the honors worthy of a respected head of state. For an account of the popular uprisings and Chile's still incomplete transition to democracy, see my chapter on Chile in James D. Cockcroft, *Latin America: History, Politics, and U.S. Policy*, 2nd ed. (Belmont, CA: Wadsworth Publishing/Thomson Learning, 1997), 531-66, and Cathy Lisa Schneider, *Shantytown Protest in Pinochet's Chile* (Philadelphia: Temple University Press, 1995). Salvador Allende's niece, the now famous novelist Isabel Allende, expressed one family member's view of Allende's death by saying that Allende had taken his own life but that had he accepted the generals' offer to fly him into exile: "Pinochet would have killed him during the flight. 'Kill the bitch and you eliminate the litter,' he [Pinochet] said." See Isabel Allende, "Pinochet Without Hatred," *The New York Times Magazine*, January 17, 1999.

2 Barbara Crossette, "Dictators Face the Pinochet Syndrome," *New York Times*, August 22, 1999, citing the opinion of Human Rights Watch's Reed Brody. As Brody points out in "The Pinochet Precedent," *NACLA Report on the Americas*, May-June 1999, 18-20, the House of Lords final decision to give the go-ahead to Pinochet's extradition ruled that "he could not be extradited to Spain for acts committed before Britain enacted the Torture Convention in late 1988.... The ruling means that most of Pinochet's worst crimes are excluded from the case, although the retention of a key conspiracy charge could allow a full investigation into Pinochet's role in creating a secret police apparatus and implementing plans to torture and murder political opponents in Chile and abroad." It remains to be seen if other parties involved in Pinochet's crimes, including those governments that encouraged or supported them, are ever brought to a public accounting. The remainder of this Introduction and the "Chronology: Chile 1962-1975" specify some of the governments and individuals involved. Recently released State Department documents further illustrate the U.S. Government's foreknowledge of the September 11, 1973, coup and aid to the Pinochet forces afterwards (see Lucy Komisar, "Documented Complicity," www.progressive.org/kom999. html). The sudden international publicity given Pinochet's crimes has triggered a series of renewed calls for justice from the relatives of victims of torture, disappearances and murders at the hands of not only Pinochet but of other dictators around the world, including those who ruled most of Latin America during what I have called "Latin America's long dark night of state-sponsored terror" (see Cockcroft, *op.cit.*). Unfortunately, during the "transition to democracy" out of Latin America's long dark night in the 1980s, politicians agreed to grant the departing generals, police, and goons a "general amnesty." An exception occurred briefly in Argentina after the Malvinas War but was later effectively reversed. Several organizations in different countries, including Argentina's famed Mothers and Grandmothers of the Plaza de Mayo, continue to demonstrate year after year for the bringing to justice of these criminals.

3 Allende, *op. cit.*

4 See sources cited in footnote 1.

5 In April 1999, Chilean police confiscated one day after its publication a book by investigative reporter Alejandra Matus, *The Black Book of the Chilean Justice System*. The author fled to Argentina and then Miami. Later, police arrested the general manager

and the editor of the book's publisher, the Planeta publishing company. An example of a book discussing Allende open-mindedly is Tomás Moulian, *Conversación interrumpida con Allende* (Santiago: Editorial LOM, 1998).

6 For interviews with some typical Chilean youth, see Patricio Guzmán's powerful 1997 film *Chile, Obstinate Memory (Chile, la memoria obstinada)*.

7 Quoted in Hedda Garza, *Salvador Allende* (New York and Philadelphia: Chelsea House Publishers, 1989), 32. Garza's is the only biography of Allende in English.

8 Latin America's pro-working class university autonomy movement dated back to the 1918 Córdoba University Reform in Chile's neighbor nation of Argentina. Students there won easier university entrance requirements and significant input into university governance, known as "*co-gobierno*" (joint government).

9 Quoted in Garza, 43; and "Allende: la biografía de un político ejemplar," <http://members.xoom.com/chilerebelde/compa2.htm>.

10 Chile's oldest political party, the Radical Party was founded in 1861. It was often led by members of Chile's bourgeoisie who were fairly nationalistic and favored less dependence on foreign capital. Chile's presidents from 1938 to 1952 came from the Radical Party.

11 The diversified holdings of ITT made it second to Anaconda Copper in dollar total of U.S. firms' investments in Chile.

12 The PDC espoused a populism that rejected both socialism and capitalism. Its corporatist approach sought to reorganize Chile's economy and politics by channeling social unrest through "interest groups," preserving powerful economic interests and yet modernizing Chile. The PDC brought together old-timers from the 1930s' split-off factions of the Conservative Party and younger recruits championing agrarian and other reforms in the name of "Christian humanism" and the then Vatican-approved "theology of liberation."

13 According to Rutgers University's Chile Research Group, by 1970 all but two of Chile's 18 largest nonbanking corporations heavily involved foreign capital. Twenty-four of the top 30 U.S.-based transnational corporations (TNCs) operated in Chile. An example was the Rockefellers' IBEC (International Basic Economy Corporation), which penetrated 13 of Chile's largest 25 corporations. IBEC relied on business associates like banker Agustín Edwards, whose family owned the prestigious conservative newspaper *El Mercurio* (circulation 300,000). The Edwards, together with other denationalized elites and the top echelons of the middle classes, subscribed to the ideology of anticommunism and in general voted for the conservative National Party (a 1966 merger of Liberals and Conservatives) or the PDC. They later became the main civilian supporters of the 1973 anti-Allende military coup d'état. During the Allende presidency, Edwards' *El Mercurio* was subsidized by the CIA to the tune of $1.5 billion and played the same kind of counterrevolutionary role as the CIA-subsidized *La Prensa* did against the democratically elected government of the Sandinistas in Nicaragua a decade later. For more of this background, see the research published in Dale L. Johnson (ed.), *The Chilean Road to Socialism* (New York: Anchor, 1973), *e.g.*, James Cockcroft, Henry Frundt, and Dale Johnson, "Multinational Corporations and Chile," 3-24, and various chapters in Cockcroft, *op. cit.*

14 Chile has a quarter of the world's known reserves of copper. Traditionally, copper accounted for a substantial part of government revenues and between 75 and 80 percent of Chile's export earnings (today 40 percent because of increased fruit exports by the large rural estates). Anticipating nationalization, the U.S. copper companies left Chile's mines in general disrepair and their debts unpaid, thereby handicapping the Allende government. In addition, Anaconda and Kennecott later were found to have

pocketed $774 million in excess profits during the 1955-70 period. Allende clearly explained all this in his address to the United Nations General Assembly, December 4, 1972 (Chapter 17). See also Chile Research Group, Rutgers University, "Chile's Nationalization of Copper," in Johnson, 25-41.

[15] After the investigation ended, Senator Church concluded: "Covert action is a semantic disguise for murder, coercion, blackmail, bribery, the spreading of lies, whatever is deemed useful in Washington in manipulating the internal politics of other countries."

[16] On the day after Helms took these notes, September 16, 1970, Kissinger told a group of editors that Allende's Chile could become a "contagious example" that "would infect" NATO allies in southern Europe. Allende commented on a press report about this in an address he gave to a Socialist Party convention in La Serena, Chile, on January 28, 1971, when he said that the Popular Unity would not be exported but that each nation would choose its own path to revolution — a constant theme in all Allende's speeches. An ex-aide of Kissinger's later observed: "Henry thought Allende might lead an anti-U.S. movement in Latin America more effectively than Castro, just because it was the democratic path to power." For more on the Nixon-Kissinger-Helms strategizing, see Cockcroft, *op. cit.*; *New York Times*, September 12, 1998; National Security Archive website <www.seas.gwu. edu/nsarchive>; and Robinson Rojas Databank <http://www.rrojasdatabank. free-online.co.uk/chile0.htm#Crimes> On CIA's action for a military coup to prevent Allende's assumption of the presidency, see: United States Central Intelligence Agency. Report on CIA Chilean Task Force Activities, September 15 to November 3, 1970. November 18, 1970, 1-17. IP00633 National Security Archive, Washington, DC.

[17] The "invisible blockade" consisted of U.S.-sponsored attempts to limit loans and credits to Allende's Chile; to block Chile's efforts to renegotiate its burdensome foreign debt; and to curtail all of Chile's foreign trade, especially in copper. For examples, see this work's "Chronology: Chile 1962-1975."

[18] Foreign observers, including a young American journalist named Charles Horman, said they were puzzled by the heightened presence of U.S. military and civilian personnel. Chile's military seized Horman about a week after the coup, not long after he had visited the U.S. Embassy in Santiago to ask for protection. The embassy had refused to assist him and, through its contacts in Chile's military, had found out in just a few days that Horman's body lay in the city morgue. The embassy tried to cover up Horman's death and that of his friend, Frank Teruggi, Jr., of Chicago. The 1982 Costa Gravas film *Missing* provides an account of the Horman and Teruggi family tragedies and the U.S. Embassy's unsavory role. A U.S. State Department document released in October 1999 suggests that the CIA "may have played an unfortunate part in Horman's death." A now public "SitRep" (situation report) from the U.S. military group in Valparaíso characterized Chile's September 11 coup as "close to perfect," Chile's "day of destiny," and "Our D-Day" (*NACLA Report on the Americas*, May-June 1999, 40).

[19] The Church Committee later reported that the CIA had prepared arrest lists of Allende supporters in the event of a military takeover.

[20] An October 12, 1973 CIA report released June 30, 1999, in connection with the ongoing Pinochet investigations, noted, "The line between people killed during attacks on security forces and those captured and executed immediately has become increasingly blurred." In fact, from the very start of the coup there were few attacks against security forces, since it was obvious armed resistance was futile.

21 The Catholic Church's Cardinal Silva Henríquez, one of those who initially supported the coup, was also one of the first to speak out against Pinochet. "The military tricked us all," he later explained, "because we believed that [the coup].... was for freedom and democracy... and that turned out to be false" (quoted in Patricio Guzmán's award-winning 1997 film *Chile, Obstinate Memory*).

22 Pinochet (or officials under him) even ordered the murders of his opponents in foreign lands. General Carlos Prats, the constitutionalist Commander-in-Chief of the Army whom Pinochet replaced in August of 1973, and his wife were assassinated in Buenos Aires, Argentina, in 1974. The following year, in Rome, Italy, PDC leader Bernardo Leighton and his wife were wounded in a failed assassination attempt. Then, in 1976, Allende's former Ambassador to the United States and Foreign Minister Orlando Letelier, a socialist, and his 25-year-old assistant Ronni Moffitt were blown up in Letelier's car in Washington, D.C. (Moffitt's husband Michael survived the explosion). The CIA, as well as U.S. NSC director and Secretary of State Henry Kissinger, had advance knowledge of these types of murder operations, including "Operation Condor," a notorious international state-terrorist network of planned and executed assassinations of other countries' nationals undertaken in 1975 by the dictatorships of Argentina, Bolivia, Brazil, Chile, Paraguay and Uruguay with the assistance of U.S. military aid and the cooperation of the CIA and the FBI. The targets were the opponents of these tyrannical and terrorist regimes, since overthrown or modified by their own citizens. For further information and documentation, including parts of several thousands of pages of documents released by the U.S. government in connection with Spanish Judge Baltazar Garzón's requests for additional information about Pinochet's crimes against humanity, consult: Cockcroft, *op. cit.*; *NACLA Report on the Americas*, May-June 1999; *New York Times*, June 30 and August 11, 1999; and National Security Archive website <www.seas.gwu.edu/nsarchive>.

23 Allende understood well why "privatization" of state enterprises might find favor. He explained in his First Annual Message to the National Congress (Chapter 9) the background necessary for understanding the issue today: "The state apparatus has been used by monopolies for the purpose of relieving their financial difficulties, for obtaining economic help and for strengthening the system. Up to now the public sector has been characterized by its subsidiary role in relation to the private sector. For this reason some public enterprises show large total deficits, while others are unable to produce profits comparable in size to those of some private enterprises." How convenient that the same private enterprises that have benefited for so many years from the indirect and direct subsidies of state enterprises are now able to justify their takeover in the name of "efficiency."

24 See Eva Cockcroft, John Pitman Weber, and James Cockcroft, *Toward a People's Art The Contemporary Mural Movement* (Albuquerque: University of New Mexico Press, 1998, 2nd ed., originally published in 1977 by Dutton).

25 All quotations in this paragraph are from the Popular Unity Program in this book's Appendix. The "recall" approach is a way of guaranteeing an end to corruption and has been adopted in Cuba.

26 Salvador Allende, "Postscript," in Régis Debray, *The Chilean Revolution: Conversations with Allende* (New York: Pantheon, 1971), 165-167.

27 Salvador Allende, radio and TV speech of July 10, 1972, "Capitalism Wants to End Chile's Democratic Regime," in *Salvador Allende: Su pensamiento político*. (Santiago: Empresa Editora Nacional Quimantú Limitada, 1972), 416. The original Spanish is: "Me he comprometido a hacer los cambios estructurales que Chile exige; a abrir el camino al socialismo en libertad, democracia y pluralismo.... El dilema de Chile está

ya claro que no es entre Democracia y Totalitarismo. El dilema de Chile es entre los intereses chilenos y los del capital extranjero; es entre patriotas y antipatriotas; entre hegemonía de los patrones o de los trabajadores."

28 Salvador Allende, "Crítica a la Administración Pública," in *Salvador Allende: Su pensamiento político.* (Santiago: Empresa Editora Nacional Quimantu Limitada, 1972), 220-1. The original Spanish is: "El imperialismo no es un tigre de papel. Es un tigre muy vigoroso y muy agresivo, que además tiene gatos montañeses nativos, que lo ayudan y secundan perfectamente bien. Así es que nadie de ilusiones. La lucha será muy dura."

29 Salvador Allende, "Discurso en el Estadio Nacional en la celebración del primer aniversario del Gobierno Popular," in Salvador Allende, *Selección de discursos de Salvador Allende* (La Habana: Ed. de Ciencias Sociales, Instituto Cubano del Libro, 1975), 223-4. Translation by Foreign Broadcast Information Service (FBIS) in its *Daily Report* (November 8, 1971).

30 In Latin America, there is a long tradition of populism that gives rise to presidential candidates and demagogic leaders who champion the poor while serving the rich. This further undermines the credibility of neoliberalism and helps explain why so many candidates, even the most conservative ones, typically lambaste neoliberalism. For Mexico's presidential elections in 2000, for example, more than a year before election day the most conservative candidates started criticizing neoliberalism with a vengeance. Vicente Fox of the conservative National Action Party (PAN) called for "economic growth with a human face," while the ruling Institutional Revolutionary Party (PRI) candidate, Francisco Labastida, incredibly claimed "I have never been considered neoliberal" (quoted in *La Jornada* <http://serpiente.dgsca.unam.mx/jornada/primera.html>, June 24, August 17, 1999).

31 For more analysis of neoliberalism and its failures, see articles in *Monthly Review* (New York), June 1999, 38-61. For a recent case study, see James D. Cockcroft, *Mexico's Hope: An Encounter with Politics and History* (New York: Monthly Review Press, 1998; Spanish-language edition, Mexico City: Siglo XXI, 2000).

32 Róbinson Rojas Research Unit Consultancy <http://www.soft.net.uk/rrojasdatabank/index.htm>

33 By 1999, the foreign debt of Latin America stood at $706 billion, requiring $123 billion in interest and related service payments. Between 1982 and 1996, just these payments alone came to $739 billion, that is, a sum greater than the region's total accumulated debt. For more on this, see *Desde los cuatro puntos* (Mexico City), No. 15, 1999.

34 Ironically, in the late 1960s and early 1970s, several members of Allende's Socialist Party did not share his views on the market. They were more enamored of the Cuban Revolution's approach to a planned economy, an approach that in recent years has been modified as Cuba increasingly attempts to utilize market forces.

35 Quoted in *New York Times*, July 18, 1999.

36 This experiment in popular democracy, which operates independently of the PT or organized labor, has drawn world attention. See, for example, Bernard Cassen, "Démocratie participative à Porto Alegre," *Le Monde Diplomatique*, August 1998, 3, and Mark Johnson, "Democratic and Popular Government," *International Viewpoint*, June 1999, 18-24.

37 In his article "Voting for Nobody in Chile's New Democracy," *NACLA Report on the Americas*, May-June 1999, 31-33, Alfredo Riquelme, a teacher of history at Chile's Catholic University, observes about Chile's partial democracy, "The network of authoritarian enclaves includes a non-elected set of institutional or designated

senators; a binomial-majority electoral system which guarantees the over-representation of the largest minority — the right — and the underrepresentation of the second largest minority, the non-Concertación, i.e. Communist, left; the arbitrary structure of electoral districts; and the need to find overwhelming majorities for constitutional reforms."

38 Unfortunately, it is also why the anti-Concertación right-wing coalition decided to run its candidate the extreme rightist Joaquín Lavín, who none too subtly denounces Lagos by saying, "We already had a socialist president. We don't want another." Chile's right once again waves its fake banner of nationalism, claiming that Pinochet is being detained by "foreigners" (true) and that this is an affront to Chile (false, since the affront is Pinochet himself!). Two reliable sources in English for political news from Chile and the rest of Latin America are *NACLA Report on the Americas* <http://www.nacla.org> and *Weekly News Update on the Americas* <home.earthlink.net/~dbwilson.wnuhome.html>.

39 This untranslatable idiomatic Spanish of contemporary Latin America means roughly "Comrade Allende, you are present! We shall win!"

1

Chile's Medical-Social Reality

1939

This is the opening section of a book-length government report on health written by Allende in 1939 in his capacity as Minister of Health in the Popular Front government of President Pedro Aguirre Cerda. Its passionate tone and social content reflect Allende's medical background as a doctor and his concern for people's health in Chile, as witnessed by his introduction of the legislation that eventually became Chile's National Health Service (1952).

"To govern is to educate and provide health to the people."

Pedro Aguirre Cerda

Our country is going through a moment in its history in which it struggles to unshackle itself from the old economic methods, autocratic and based on free competition, channeling its social life into a course of cooperation and well-being covering all social strata. To His Excellency the President of the Republic, the Socialist Party and its ministers, this is the fundamental significance of the Popular Front government, established by the people only a year ago; to reclaim the social wealth and the economic potential of the nation, control it, direct it, foster it in the service of all the inhabitants of the republic, without privileges nor exclusions. Also, and as a consequence, restore for the people, for the working man, his physical vitality, his virility and health, which were once his outstanding qualities; to reacquire the physiological capacity of a strong people, recover its immunity against epidemics; all of which will allow a better performance in national production while also providing a better disposition and spirit to live and appreciate life.

And finally, to conquer the right to develop our culture at all levels, regardless of social classes. A revitalized, healthy and educated people, this must be the slogan for all Chileans who have a fervent desire to serve the homeland, and who struggle without rest so that our people can overcome exploitation and ignorance.

Chile, like the majority of South American countries, has lived at the mercy of economic and cultural colonialism which has impeded its social progress and the development of its natural resources. Moreover, these factors have prevented its people from reaching living standards compatible with a civilized and relatively educated country. Some 120 years of independent political life have not been sufficient to incorporate the proletarian classes into civic life, within the standard concept of progress; they have barely been sufficient to enable a small percentage of the poor to enjoy minimal benefits of the economic, technical and cultural advances of humanity.

The formidable boom of industrialism, scientific progress, advances in hygiene and medicine, the benefits of cultural heritage, have all bypassed the great majority of Chileans, who, after all, are the ones who create public wealth. Until a few years ago, our national economy was dependent exclusively on two or three products for export, principally nitrates and copper, which became the primary sources of income for the state. The mining industries have not been exploited by Chilean capital and have always been in the hands of foreign companies and at the mercy of the interests of international economic imperialism. The agricultural and textile industries have suffered from the lack of foresight of past regimes, most of them of conservative background, with the result that technical advances have not been incorporated into farming or industry to any large degree. Our farmers continued growing the more easily marketable crops, as did the first colonizers, wasting a large quantity of land, exploiting man more than the soil, lacking an organic and methodic system of irrigation and communication, and using antiquated instruments and machinery. The light industries concentrated on those products with a secure and ready-made market, forcing us to become consumers of goods manufactured and produced by the large industrial countries. This is the reason why almost 35 percent of national income was from nitrate mining and, in lesser proportions, from copper mining, both of which had negotiated favorable tax rates.

The world economic crisis of 1929 brought a sudden decrease in the performance of our two main export industries, and the two pillars that sustained the Chilean economy were broken. The measures taken were barely able to ease the effects produced by the repercussion of the international crisis. The Chilean economy, a slave to the events, tried to find alternatives, and in the next 10 years has managed to develop some other aspects of our agriculture: new external markets have been found and, driven by small-scale national capital, the manufacturing industry has increased production which has in turn decreased imports. Despite the progress achieved, in historical terms we still remain a colonial and dependent country.

The progress obtained in national production levels has not meant a significant improvement in living standards for the poor because international capitalism — economic and financial owner of the large centers of production — is only interested in production to satisfy the market demand, and no more. The capitalist enterprises are not concerned that the working population lives in deplorable conditions, exposed to disease or condemned to obscurantism.

The motivation for production is profit, unlimited gain, with no concern that, as a result, people are perishing or suffering, not even discounting war in its obsession to conquer world markets. This has been the despicable destiny of semicolonial countries, of our South-American countries, which have been an inexhaustible emporium of riches and raw materials servicing the splendor of the great nations of the world.

This is why the action of our governments must not only be the preparatory task of guiding the people towards the future, but also to defend it from the alienation and exploitation of the economic imperialism that roams the world. This task is, without doubt, the first obligation of a popular government wishing to recover the nation's wealth and its fruits for the greater well-being.

We know that the development of our national economy is subject to the possibilities offered by world markets. The solution to our economic problems is not, as some believe, an automatic change in the ownership rights of certain export products, but rather in finding for them a secure and advantageous market. The nationalization of the production sources to satisfy nationalist sentiment resolves nothing nor does it add economic benefit. It is necessary to focus on the market and world competition. Naturally, the development of national production, by creating new jobs and incorporating great numbers of workers into remunerative activities, will increase the purchasing power of the nation as a whole. However, regardless of the modifications to our internal economic structure, its true expansion is linked, without a doubt, to the international economy. The current war, which has closed some of our habitual European markets, is irrefutable proof of this and proves that the goodwill of statesmen has its limits in the relations that the laws of world economy have imposed on secondary and dependent countries.

The above considerations have led the Socialist Party and its ministers to adopt a new criteria when faced with the responsibilities of government. Our first task is to uncover and clearly show the authentic reality of the nation, its possibilities and the resources at hand. This way we can proceed objectively and we can measure the magnitude of the problems. We know that our desire to alleviate the anguish of the Chilean people is limited by an insurmountable barrier, but this barrier also indicates an area within which there is a lot of work to be done and many conquests to achieve.

Through these considerations, it is easy to realize the state of misery that the people have lived under, the lack of hygienic habits, the predisposition to epidemics and diseases of high social impact, the degree of cultural backwardness, all of which have prevented the recognition of its own interests as the working class. But the people grow and reach a maturity and it is then that they become restless and resolve to conquer the right to well-being, health and culture. The Chilean working classes acknowledged their destiny and the deplorable reality of life and that is why they resolved to break the trend of history to install a government able to deliver the fruits of economic, social, technical and cultural progress which has always been the patrimony of a minority. That is why October 25 is such a momentous date.

We know that the task facing the government of the Popular Front is enormous. His Excellency, the President of the Republic, has understood this from the first instant and has dedicated his initial efforts to learn and revise the urgent and acute problems which need to be tackled. His trips through the country enable him to prepare to lead the recovery of the nation and it is necessary for him to view in person and in contact with reality, what immediate needs must be satisfied in order to organize the adequate measures which will accelerate the pace of economic and social evolution of the country in an efficient and vigorous manner within a fair plan.

Consistent with this objective spirit, and conscious of the responsibility on his shoulders, the Minister of Health has begun his work with a serene, documented and realistic study on the conditions of health and hygiene in the country. A succinct and cold examination of our socio-medical reality is the best way to diagnose, and therefore, to apply the adequate remedies to reestablish health and vigor in our people. This is what has moved him to tell the nation about the true hygienic and sanitary conditions of the country; to examine what has been done, good or bad; note the deficiencies and errors and put forward solutions towards finding ways to rehabilitate our race.

We must loyally declare that all those medical measures taken will only produce benefits if they are accompanied by economic and financial resolutions that permit a rise in the standard of living of our citizens. It can be said that the fundamental bases that determine the welfare and progress of nations are precisely a good standard of living, adequate sanitary conditions and a widespread dissemination of culture. It's worth noting that the volume and consistency of these latter factors depend directly on economic growth without which it is not possible to build anything serious from the point of view of hygiene and medicine, nor with respect to culture, because it is not possible to provide health and knowledge to a malnourished people, dressed in rags and working under merciless exploitation.

PERSPECTIVES AND PLAN FOR IMMEDIATE ACTION
1. Consideration on human capital

The distressing demographic and sanitary outlook of the country requires a deep reflection from all Chileans, rich and poor, left and right, governors and governed. National health is one of those problems which has consequences for everyone. No social class, however prepared biologically, can feel immune from epidemics or safe from contagious diseases. The environmental conditions affect every being. It is true that those people with a well-developed immune system can better resist the pathological risks of an unhealthy environment but it is also true that bacillus, the infectious contact, the transmitting agent, waits and attacks all citizens without distinction.

It is possible that this concise picture of our sanitary reality may shock many of our compatriots; I doubt that anyone would be indifferent. It is possible that others may react and try to find scapegoats for this invisible tragedy of the people. Not a few will resign themselves with the consolation that other countries suffer similar ills.

We cannot lie back and lament the sad reality of our present. It is essential that we test the vitality of the national organizations and the capacity of the popular masses, and aim at regaining the qualities of our race and the right to live as a cultured people. It is necessary that the whole nation mobilizes towards a reparation of all these errors, ills and lack of foresight, so that all the economic, moral and spiritual forces and reserves of our people can join in a common goal to cleanse our country, to establish conditions which will allow Chilean men to function within a favorable environment, to begin a tenacious struggle against the calamities and vices, to take to the most remote corners the advances in sanitary engineering and social medicine.

The crudeness with which we have analyzed national reality is meant to uncover the problems in all their magnitude, weighing the legacy we have received, measure the projections and study the most convenient solutions.

I know that we are distant from those days when it was not considered politic and was even seen as unpatriotic for a minister to show his citizens the bare facts. This is the reason why we inform the public, as there is no other way of learning and examining the biological realities of a people.

In matters like these there can be no subterfuges nor simulations. Social hygiene, public health, medicine do not allow compromises.

Sickness, malnutrition, alcoholism, endemic diseases, epidemics and ignorance act and erode from within and behind appearances and are inexorable in their effects. Our country has been a victim of this and that is the cause of the current alarming socio-medical reality.

Human capital, which is the fundamental base of economic prosperity of a country, has been underestimated and has been abandoned to its own fate. There lies the cause for the limited increase in our population, which must be improved and increased on the basis of numbers and in the quality of its native inhabitants. Its progressive growth is the primary condition for prosperity of a country and is a result of the state of health and culture of its components.

In historical terms, a country is valued by the quality of its inhabitants and by the size of its population rather than for its material resources. Any governmental plan requires a dense and healthy population, capable of working towards a thriving industrial and economic development. This is the mission of human capital.

All other forms of wealth: raw materials, instruments of work and the rest, lose their significance for the country that owns them, if it doesn't have at its disposal men who value and defend them, or, in summary, a robust and strong people to guide its destiny.

Our human capital has been seriously affected by abandonment and lack of social prevision. We have, of course, almost the highest mortality rate for children and adults, comparable only to the more backward countries. National health statistics are atrocious, with the state unable to significantly reduce the ravages of tuberculosis, syphilis and other contagious diseases. The population increase is below the norm which means that in 60 years, Chile's population has only increased from 2,075,871 habitants in 1876 to 4,200,000 in 1936. The average span of life of Chileans, according to statistics, is at most 24 years, while in Switzerland, Germany, Denmark and England it is above 50.

The enormous number of deaths and the high level of disease registered in our demographic records, apart from indicating the stagnation of the population, also influence the volumes of production and greatly affect the general economic possibilities, because the lost working hours and the decrease in consumption that follows, signify a considerable decline in national wealth.

Our social pathology shows that 20 percent of the active population is unable to work, reducing by a similar figure the value of national production. This is the same as if a fifth of the workers were on strike and, despite this, neither the employers, nor society are moved, nor are they interested in looking for causes and remedies. Add to this the temporary interruption to work of those who are sick or those whose organic inadequacies have not yet been expressed through an accident.

Let's add, finally, the enormous percentage of malnourished people who are easy prey for epidemics and other calamities; the lack of shelter and housing; the reduced level of urbanization existing in the country; the increasing occurrence of inbreeding among the population; the high number of illiterates and we have the true projections of the social reality of Chile.

Past governments considered the necessities of national salubriousness as deferrable and of secondary importance. They never moved to prevent, or stop to think that human capital, the basis of all wealth, constitutes the maximum responsibility of a modern state.

All progressive spirits will agree with the Minister of Health that we cannot waste any more time and that we must plan, organize and put into action a massive project aimed at restoring our nationality in its three fundamental aspects: effective economic improvement of the working classes; intensifying and extending the measures of prevention in national health programs; and an intense literacy campaign in the lower layers of the country. In order to carry out this immense task, the Popular Front was born.

The Medical Convention of Chile, held in 1936 in Valparaíso, had declared that "our socio-economic structure must undergo fundamental modifications to guarantee citizens optimal conditions of welfare through an equitable distribution of the fruits of work." It also declared that the state must regulate "production, distribution and price of articles of food and clothing." It affirmed that "housing, as property, is by essence a social function and the state must intervene in establishing norms and quality of housing." Finally, it also affirmed "that the problems related to work must constitute a medical concern due to the disastrous working conditions, the high number of accidents registered among the working class, and the deficient regulations covering the relations between capital and labor." With this, the convention stressed that the solution to the socio-medical problem of the country required precisely a solution to the economic problems affecting the proletarian classes.

With the honesty that has characterized his political action and perfectly committed to his present responsibility, the Minister of Health warns that the country must be considered to be in a state of emergency and points to the imperative necessity to use all means to deal with the dangers that threaten the existence of the country. It is necessary that the well-off contribute without haggling, for their own security. It is necessary that each and every one of our citizens support the gigantic task of lifting our country economically, health-wise and culturally, and thus bring the most dignified and effective benefit for the republic.

Let's help His Excellency the President with loyalty, in the task of rehabilitating our race, in his desire to return its creative capacity to the people.

Let's remember that Chile is, at present, a tense country, in pursuit of its rights; a country trying to mark its own destiny.

2

Election Day Interview with Canada's CBC Radio

September 4, 1970

In live election day coverage of the presidential contest by Canada's CBC (Canadian Broadcasting Corporation) on Toronto's "Radio Free Friday," spontaneous street celebrations can be heard as word spreads of Allende's impending triumph — 30 percent of the vote is in and Allende is ahead. People in the background are singing and cheering "Venceremos! Venceremos!" ("We shall win!"). It is history in the making as the CBC voice-over announces: "Very shortly the world will learn whether or not the South American country of Chile is about to get the first freely elected communist government in Latin America. If Dr. Salvador Allende, the Communist-supported Socialist Party candidate for the presidency of Chile, wins... it promises to transform radically the face of that troubled South American continent." Allende grants a hastily arranged mid-afternoon interview at his modest home in a Santiago suburb for CBC's "Radio Free Friday." How the interview was arranged reveals much about Allende the man. Earlier that day at the crowded National Headquarters of the Socialist Party of Chile in downtown Santiago, freelance journalist Patrick Barnard, working for the CBC, was introduced to Allende and asked for a 3:00 p.m. interview. Allende informed Barnard he would be lunching with his family at home at that time. "Come to my house," Barnard later recalled Allende telling him, as the president-to-be opened his wallet to show "a small piece of cardboard inside with his private Santiago telephone number scrawled in handwritten letters." After getting past the lone Chilean Army guard at the front door (Allende's life had been frequently threatened), Barnard was "ushered into Allende's small, book-lined library where I was to wait while the Allende family had lunch in an adjoining room." Soon Allende "came into the library with his nephew who could speak French. Toronto called. The Canadian host of Radio Free Friday, Peter Gzowski, asked questions in English which were translated into French in Toronto, then translated into Spanish for Allende by his nephew. Allende's Spanish answers were instantly translated into French by the nephew, and subsequently converted into an English voice-over in Toronto." In a letter dated July 29, 1999, to the editor of this volume, Barnard went on to recall: "On arguably the most important day of his life, Salvador Allende took a good half hour to talk to people in Canada, to reach out and explain to North Americans his hopes for reviving his country. During that short portion of an afternoon, Dr. Allende's grace and vivacity illuminated his sense of a fuller politics for all of the Americas." Speaking to the Canadian audience, Allende expressed the hopes which the impending victory had aroused for Chile and the other countries of Latin America. He answered questions about the U.S. reaction, the effect of the election outcome on other revolutionary movements, the role of the armed forces, and the foreign policy stance of a Popular Unity government. Finally, Allende offered an ironic and ultimately prophetic forecast of what would happen should any subversion of the election results occur.

Question: Given the fact that a large part of this capital [to be nationalized] is foreign, and particularly American, what do you expect the reaction of American private interests to be toward your program of nationalization?

Salvador Allende: The United States needs to understand that countries have an obligation through their governments to provide for the needs of their people: food, shelter, jobs, education, recreation, culture and health. It needs to understand that the people of Latin America can not live indefinitely in their current state of misery and poverty while at the same time financing the richest and most powerful country in the world. The United States needs to realize that there is a clear direct causal relationship between underdevelopment and imperialism. There is underdevelopment because of imperialism and imperialism because of underdevelopment. As far as the reaction of the United States is concerned, it seems to us that the US government is becoming aware of a growing moral attitude around the world, one that seeks social justice and the rights of people who have traditionally been exploited. The interventions of the United States and the reactions to the war in Vietnam have had a great effect on this growing spirit of international solidarity.

Question: What effect will the victory of the Popular Unity have on other revolutionary movements in Latin America?

Allende: I believe that the victory of the Chilean people in the election will certainly open a road for many countries in the same situation as ours. However, there are also countries which have very different conditions and where present guerrilla activity is the only path available for the forces of change. The Chilean situation is unique. For the first time in history, a revolutionary party can take political control by means of the electoral process. At least, we feel that the electoral process provides the best way for the people to achieve the type of government control that will lead ultimately to the building of a socialist society.

Question: Will the Chilean armed forces remain loyal to a revolutionary government?

Allende: As far as the armed forces are concerned, they are complete professionals. They have always been respectful of our citizens and the Chilean Constitution. In this case, I am sure that they will continue this great tradition.

Question: In the event of victory [in today's elections], what are the outlines of your government's foreign policy?

Allende: We want to have political, economic and cultural relations with every country. We only ask that the rights of the Chilean people and those of Chile itself be respected with regard to our liberty and our right to choose our form of government. We are firmly committed to the rights of all countries to control their own destinies. We are also committed to the principal of nonintervention in the affairs of other nations. We understand that each country will choose the form of government it prefers, although corruption and foreign interests can undermine the ability to choose. All that we ask is that we in Chile be allowed to decide our own future and that our independence be respected.

Question: If you lose... [VOICE-OVER of radio announcer: "Well, we'll put this on anyway."] ...lose tonight, what will this mean for Chile, for Latin America, and for the ballot box as an effective weapon for left-wing parties throughout Latin America?

Allende: There is the possibility of an eventual defeat for Chile and Latin America and for electoral tactics as a whole. It seems incontestable that a defeat in the election would cause a loss of confidence by the people. It is very significant for any revolutionary movement to win power through free elections. But if threats and corruption forestall this victory by a powerful and popular political movement in Chile, we can very well foresee an acceleration of armed struggle everywhere in Latin America. The corollary of our defeat is a triumph by the oligarchy and the suppression of the real desires of the people.

[VOICE-OVER of radio announcer: "It may be too soon to call the results of the election, but certainly, at this moment as we heard direct from Santiago, Salvador Allende may become the first elected radical socialist communist left-wing leader in Latin America."]

3

Victory Speech
to the People of Santiago

September 5, 1970

In this victory speech to a happy throng of hundreds of thousands in Santiago the day after his election to the presidency, Allende says that the election was won cleanly and that the transition should be kept clean, peaceful and joyous. "This is your government," he says, and "I am your compañero presidente." Together all will make a "revolutionary government." Revolution "does not mean to destroy but to build." Describing the occasion as "the second triumph of the Chilean Revolution" (the first was independence from Spain, won in 1817), Allende calls for a serene attitude of peace in implementing the full program of the UP (Unidad Popular, or Popular Unity).

People of Santiago, people of Chile: I speak to you with deep emotion from this improvised speaker's platform and from these deficient amplifiers. More significant than my words here is the presence of the people of Santiago, representing the people of Chile, who are gathered here to reaffirm the victory which we honestly achieved today and which opens a new path for the country and whose most important actor is the Chilean people.

It is especially significant that I am able to address the people of Chile and Santiago from the Federation of Students building [on Alameda Bernardo O'Higgins not far from La Moneda]. This is meaningful and of deep significance. Never before has a candidate victorious as a result of the will and sacrifice of the people, used a speaker's platform with greater significance, for the youth of this country was the vanguard of this struggle. This was not the struggle of one man but the struggle of the people and it is Chile's victory that is honestly achieved this afternoon.

I beg you to understand that I am only a man with all of man's weaknesses, and I was able today to endure the failures of the past because I was fulfilling a task. I accept this victory without arrogance or a spirit of vengeance. It is not a personal victory, I owe it to the Popular Unity, to the social forces with us. I owe it to the Radicals, Socialists, Communists, Social Democrats, people from the Unitary Popular Action Movement and from the Independent Popular Alliance, and to thousands of independents. I owe it to the country's anonymous and sacrificed men. I owe it to the humble women of our country. I owe it to the Chilean people who will be with me when I enter La Moneda National Palace on November 4.

The victory you have achieved has great national significance. From here I solemnly state that I will respect the rights of all Chileans, but I also state, and I want you definitely to know this, that when I enter La Moneda — since the people are the government — I will carry out the historic commitment to make a reality of the Popular Unity program.

I have said that we do not have nor could we have any vengeful purpose; it would belittle our victory. But if we do not have any purpose of vengeance, we are not under any circumstances going to back down in our dealing with the Popular Unity program that was the people's combat flag. I will not be just another president; I will be the first president of the first truly democratic, popular and revolutionary government in Chilean history.

I have said it and I must say it again: If victory was not easy, it will be more difficult to consolidate our victory and to build a new society, the new social life together, the new morality, and the new homeland. But I know that all of you who made it possible for the people to become the government tomorrow will have the historic responsibility of doing what Chile is hoping for — to make the country a beacon in progress, in social justice, in the rights of each man, each woman, and each young person in our land.

We have won in order to overthrow once and for all imperialist exploitation, to put an end to monopolies, to carry out a serious and profound agrarian reform, to control the import and export trade, and to nationalize credit. These things will make Chile's progress possible and will create the social capital which will promote our development. That is why I would like tonight to express my deep appreciation to the men and women, to the militants of the popular parties and members of the social forces who made this victory possible — this victory which has repercussions that reach beyond the borders of our country.

For those in the plains and in the mountains, for those who are listening to me in the coastal areas, for those working in the sierras, for the simple housewife or for the university professor, for the young student, for the small businessman or for the industrialist, for Chile's men and women, for our youth, for all of them I am committed with my conscience and with the people to be completely loyal to the great common and collective task. I say this: My only wish is to be your president.

Chile's anonymous men and forgotten women are the ones who made possible this important social event. Thousands and thousands of Chileans staked their sorrow and their hopes on this hour which belongs to the people. The victory is viewed with satisfaction from other borders, from other countries.

Chile opens a way that other American countries and the world may follow. The vital force of unity will break the dikes of dictatorship and will open the floodgates so that people may be free and build their own destiny.

We are sufficiently aware that each country and each nation has its particular problems, its own history, and its particular reality, and that in the face of this reality it is up to the political leaders of each country to decide what tactics to follow. We can only maintain the best political, cultural and economic relations with all the countries of the world. We only ask that they respect — and they will have to respect — Chile's right to a Popular Unity government.

We are and we will continue to be respectful of the thesis of nonintervention and of self-determination, but this does not mean that we will be silent about our support for those peoples who struggle for their economic independence and to dignify mankind in all continents.

I do not want to receive credit in history for what you have achieved — defeating the arrogance of money, pressure, threat, twisted information, the campaign of terror, of plotting and of evil. People who are capable of this will also be capable of understanding that only by working more and producing more will we be able to make Chile progress and make it possible for the men and women of our land, the human couple, to have an authentic right to work, housing, health, education, rest, culture and recreation.

We will put all the country's creative force to work to make possible the fulfillment of all the human goals included in the Popular Unity platform. Together with the efforts of all of you we are going to have a revolutionary government. Revolution does not mean to destroy but to build, not to raze but to construct. And the people of Chile are ready for this great task in this important hour of our history.

Comrades, friends: How I wish communications were such that I could speak longer and be heard by every one of you, that each person could hear my words, full of emotion yet firm in the conviction of the great responsibility that we now have and which I fully assume. I ask that this unprecedented demonstration be converted into a manifestation of the awareness of a people.

You will all retire to your homes without provoking anyone and without being provoked. The people know that their duty is not to break windows or to stone automobiles, and those who have said that disturbances would characterize our victory will encounter your awareness and sense of responsibility. You will all go to work Monday happy and singing of the legitimate victory won, singing to the future that with the callous hands of the people, the tender hands of the women, and the smiles of the children we shall make possible in a struggle that only aware, disciplined people can accomplish.

Latin America and countries beyond the borders of our country, beyond our continent, are looking to our future. And I am fully confident that we shall be sufficiently strong, sufficiently calm, to open the fortunate road to a different and better way of life and to begin the march along the hopeful avenues of socialism that the people of Chile are about to construct with their own hands.

I repeat my expressed gratefulness to the militants of the Popular Unity and to those of the Radical, Communist, Socialist, Social Democratic, Unitary Popular Action Movement, and the Independent Popular Action Parties, and to the thousands of independent voters of the left who have supported us. I also express my affection and public gratitude to the leaders of those parties who went beyond the limits of their own parties to strengthen this unity, which the people made their own. The victory has been possible because of the people's unity. This is the people's victory.

The fact that we are happy and content does not mean that we will become careless in our vigilance. This weekend the people will take over the country, from Arica to Magallanes, from the mountains to the sea. We will dance a grand *cueca* [Chilean national dance] to show the joy of our victory. But at the same time our Popular Action committees will be on the alert, ready to answer the call of Popular Unity if necessary so that the committees in commerce, factories, hospitals, the Neighbors Councils, the neighborhoods and the working class districts may begin to study the problems and their solutions, because we will have to put the country on the move immediately.

I have faith, deep faith, in the honesty and the heroic attitude of every man and woman who made this victory possible. We are going to work more and produce more, but we will work more for the Chilean family, for the people, and for Chile with the pride of Chileans and with the conviction that we are undertaking a great and wonderful historic task.

I can feel within me as a man, deep down within me as a human being, as a struggler, that which you have given to me. This effort ends a long struggle. I simply took in my hands the torch that was lighted by others who struggled with the people and for the people. This victory should be a monument to those who fell in this social struggle, who sprinkled with their blood the fertile seed of the Chilean revolution that we are going to bring about.

Before closing — and it is only honest to do this — I want to acknowledge that the government has published the correct figures on the results of the election. I want to make it known that General Valenzuela, the military commander, authorized this mass rally. He was convinced that I was telling the truth when I said that the people would behave themselves responsibly, knowing that they have achieved the right to be respected, to be respected in their victory. These people know that they will enter La Moneda Palace with me on the fourth of November.

I want to emphasize that our Christian Democratic adversaries have issued a statement acknowledging our victory. We are not going to ask the right to do likewise. We do not need to do this. We hold no grudge against the right, but they will never be able to recognize the greatness of the people in their struggles, the greatness that is the fruit of their pain and hopes.

Never before have I felt so much human warmth and never before has the national anthem had so deep a meaning to you and to me as now. In our speech we said that we are the legitimate heirs of our country's fathers and that together we will bring about the second independence: the economic independence of Chile. Citizens of Santiago, workers of the homeland, you and only you are the victors. The popular parties and the social forces have provided a great lesson which projects, I repeat, beyond our borders.

I urge you to return home with the joy of a clean victory achieved. And tonight when you caress your children and prepare for bed think of the difficult days ahead when we will have to have more passion and more affection to make Chile even greater and life in our homeland even more just.

Thank you comrades. I have said once before that the best that I have was given to me by my party, the unity of the workers and Popular Unity. Your loyalty will be equaled by my loyalty. I shall show the loyalty of the ruler of the people; the loyalty of your *compañero presidente*.

4

Inaugural Address in the National Stadium

Santiago, November 5, 1970

Allende calls the October 22 assassination of Army Commander-in-Chief René Schneider an unsuccessful attempt to start a civil war. He denounces "the criminal insanity of those who know that their cause is lost," saying that, "We Chileans reject fratricidal struggle." Allende quotes the motto on Chile's national coat of arms, "By Reason or Force" — and reminds his audience that Reason is placed first. He emphasizes that "Respect for others, tolerance for others, is one of the most important sources of our cultural wealth" and that Chileans must always maintain "the operation of and respect for democratic values, the recognition of the will of the majority." Allende attributes Chile's difficulties to the inherited problems of underdevelopment, unemployment, inflation, and social inequalities caused by "this dependent capitalist system." The great task of the new "People's Government" is "to build a new society." He speaks of putting an end to corruption; of implementing a "true land reform"; and of "reclaiming our natural resources." He concludes on a note of international solidarity, asking foreign dignitaries present to tell the world that Chile's people are "taking the helm of their destiny to embark on a democratic course toward socialism."

The people said: "We will win," and we have won, so, comrades, here we are today to celebrate the start of our victory...

This victory belongs to the workers, to those who suffered and endured for more than a century and a half, under the name of independence, the exploitation of a ruling class which was unable to provide progress and wasn't even concerned about it.

We all know the truth, that the backwardness, ignorance and hunger of our people and of all the peoples of the Third World exist and persist because a few privileged people profit from them.

But the day has finally come to say enough — enough of economic exploitation, enough of social inequality, enough of political oppression.

Today, inspired by the heroes of our country, we gather here to celebrate our victory — Chile's victory — and to mark the start of the liberation of the people, who are at last in power and are taking over control of their national destiny.

But what kind of Chile are we inheriting?

Excuse me, comrades, that, on this happy day and before the delegations from so many countries that are honoring us with their presence, I should have to discuss such an unfortunate subject. It is our right and duty to denounce age-old sufferings, as Peruvian President Velasco Alvarado has said: "One of the great tasks facing the revolution is that of breaking out of the encirclement of deceit which has made all of us live with our faces turned away from reality."

We must say that we, the underdeveloped peoples, have failed in history.

We were colonies in the agrarian-mercantile civilization. We are barely neocolonial nations in the urban-industrial civilization, and, in the new civilization which threatens to continue our dependency, we have been the exploited peoples — those who existed not for themselves, but rather to contribute to the prosperity of others.

And what is the reason for our backwardness? Who is responsible for our underdevelopment?

After many deformations and deceptions, the people have understood. We know from our own experience that the real reasons for our backwardness are to be found in the system, in this dependent capitalist system which counterposes the rich minority to the needy majority internally and the powerful nations to the poor nations externally, a system in which the many make possible the prosperity of the few.

We have received a society torn by social inequality; a society divided into antagonistic classes of the exploited and exploiting; a society in which violence is part of the institutions themselves, which condemn man to a never-satisfied greed, the most inhuman form of cruelty and indifference in the face of the suffering of others.

We have inherited a society wracked by unemployment, which throws growing numbers of the citizenry into a situation of forced idleness and poverty. These masses are not, as some say, the result of overpopulation; rather, with their tragic destiny, they are living witnesses to the inability of the regime to guarantee everyone the elementary right to work.

We have received an economy plagued by inflation — which, month after month, eats up the miserable wages of the workers, leaving them with next to nothing to live on in the last years of their lives, when they reach the end of an existence of privation.

The working people of Chile are bleeding through this wound, and it will be difficult to heal. But we are confident we will be able to heal it, because the economic policy of the government will, from now on, be aimed at serving the interests of the people.

We have received a dependent society, one whose basic sources of income were alienated by the internal allies of the great international firms. We are dependent in the economic, cultural, technological and political fields.

We have inherited a society which has seen its most deeply felt desire of independent development frustrated, a divided society in which the majority of families are denied the right to work, education, health care, recreation and even the hope of a better future.

The people of Chile have risen up against all these forms of existence. Our victory was the result of their crystallized conviction that only a genuine revolutionary government could stand up to the power of the ruling classes and at the same time mobilize all Chileans to build a republic of the working people.

This is the great task which history has given us. To carry it out, I call on you, workers of Chile, today. The only way we who love this country and believe in it can overcome underdevelopment and build a new society is by putting all our shoulders to the wheel.

We are living at a historic time, that of a great transformation of the political institutions of Chile, a time in which the parties and movements which represent the most neglected social sectors are assuming power by a majority will.

Let us stop and think a moment and cast a glance back over our history. The people of Chile are proud of having made the political road prevail over the violent one. This is a noble tradition, a lasting achievement. Throughout our permanent battle for liberation, the slow and hard struggle for justice and equality, we have always preferred solving social conflicts by means of persuasion and political action.

From the bottom of our hearts, we Chileans reject fratricidal struggle — but without ever giving up the defense of the rights of the people. Our coat of arms says "By Reason or Force," but it puts Reason first.

This civic peace, this continuation of the political process, is no accident. It is the result of our socioeconomic structure, of a particular relationship of social forces which our country has been building in keeping with the reality of our development.

In our first steps as a sovereign country, the determination of the men of Chile and the ability of its leaders helped us to avoid civil war.

In 1845, Francisco Antonio Pinto wrote to General San Martín, "I think we will solve the problem of knowing how to be republicans while continuing to speak Spanish."

From that moment on, the continuity and institutional stability of this country was one of the greatest in Europe and America.

This republican and democratic tradition thus became a part of our identity and the collective conscience of all Chileans.

Respect for others, tolerance for others, is one of the most important sources of our cultural wealth.

And when, amidst this institutional continuity and within the basic political norms, the class antagonisms and contradictions come forth, they do so in a political way. Our people have never broken this historical pattern; the few breaks with institutionalism were always caused by the ruling classes. The powerful were always the ones who unleashed the violence, shed the blood of Chileans and blocked the normal progress of the country.

This was what happened when Balmaceda, aware of his duties and a defender of national interests, acted with a dignity and patriotism that posterity has since recognized. [1]

The persecution of trade unions, students, intellectuals and workers' parties is the violent reply of those who are defending their privileges. However, the ceaseless struggle of the organized popular classes has, little by little, succeeded in its demands for recognition for civil, social, public and individual liberties.

This particular evolution of institutions in the context of our structures has made possible this historic moment, in which the people are taking political control of the country.

The masses, in their struggle to overcome the capitalist system, which exploits them, are arriving at the presidency of the republic, united in People's Unity and in what constitutes the most extraordinary demonstration in our history: the operation of and respect for democratic values, the recognition of the will of the majority.

---

[1] José Manuel Balmaceda was a wealthy Liberal who became president in 1886 and instituted many reforms designed to help the impoverished of Chile. One of his proposed programs involved the purchase of the nitrate fields by the government from private owners, with the government to then use the nitrate income to pay for industrialization, public works, health services, schools and land reform — an early version of a socialist-type program. The British nitrate magnates, the Chilean land-owners and other capitalists who would be hurt by Balmaceda's nationalization plan opposed it. In 1891, a civil war between pro- and anti-Balmaceda forces broke out; 10,000 Chileans died in the conflict and Balmaceda was unseated. He took refuge in the Argentine embassy, where he committed suicide.

Without renouncing the revolutionary goals, the popular forces have adjusted their tactics to the concrete reality of Chilean structures, viewing victories and setbacks not as definitive victories or defeats but rather as stepping stones on the long, hard road to emancipation.

Chile has just provided an indication of its political development, which is completely unprecedented anywhere in the world, making it possible for an anticapitalist movement to take power by virtue of the free exercise of the rights of all citizens. It takes power to guide the country toward a new, more humane society, one whose final goals are the rationalization of economic activity, the progressive socialization of the means of production and the end of class divisions.

As socialists, from the theoretical and doctrinal points of view we are well aware of what the forces and agents of historical change are. And I know very well, to quote Engels, that "We can conceive of peaceful evolution from the old society to the new in countries where the popular forces hold all power; where, in keeping with the constitution, it is possible to do everything one wants from the moment there is majority support."

And that is the case of Chile. Here, what Engels wrote is at last a reality.

However, we must point out that, in the 60 days that have followed the elections of September 4, the democratic vitality of our country has been put to the strongest test it has ever had to face. After a dramatic series of events, our dominant trait has once again prevailed: confrontation of differences through political channels. The Christian Democratic Party has recognized this historical moment and its duty toward the nation, and it is but right that we declare this here today.

Chile is beginning its march toward socialism without having had to undergo the tragic experience of a fratricidal war. And this fact, in all its grandeur, has an influence on the way in which this government will undertake the task of transformation.

The will of the people gives us legitimacy in our tasks. My administration will respond to this confidence, making the democratic traditions of our country real and concrete. But, in these 60 decisive days through which we have just passed, Chile and the rest of the world have witnessed admitted attempts to fraudulently alter the spirit of our constitution; mock the will of the people; attack the economy of the country; and, above all, effect cowardly acts of desperation designed to provoke a bloody clash between our citizens.

Personally, I am convinced that the heroic sacrifice of a soldier, General René Schneider,[2] the commander-in-chief of the army, was an

---

[2] General Schneider, commander of the armed forces, was assassinated in a right-wing conspiracy to prevent Allende from taking office.

unforeseen event that saved our homeland from civil war. Permit me, on this solemn occasion, by honoring him, to voice our people's thanks to the armed forces and to the *Carabinero* corps, which abide by the constitution and the rule of law. This amazing episode, which lasted barely a day and will go down in history as a civil war in the embryonic stage, has once more demonstrated the criminal insanity of those who know that their cause is lost.

They are the representatives, the mercenaries of the minorities who, ever since the time of Spanish rule, have borne the unenviable responsibility for having exploited our people for the sake of their own selfish benefit and for having handed our wealth over to foreign interests. These are the minorities who, in their wanton desire to perpetuate their own privileges, did not hesitate in 1891 and have not hesitated in 1970 to create a tragic situation for the nation.

But the law will be implacable with them and provide just punishment for them. They failed in their unpatriotic designs. They failed when they came up against the strength of the democratic institutions and the firmness of the will of the people, who were determined to confront and disarm them in order to secure tranquility, the nation's confidence and peace from now on, under the responsibility of people's power.

What is people's power?

People's power means that we will do away with the pillars on which the minorities have found support — those minorities that always condemned our nation to underdevelopment. We will do away with the monopolies, through which a handful of families control the economy. We will put an end to a fiscal system that serves those who seek lucre, a system which has always borne down hard on the people and touched but lightly on the rich, a system which has concentrated the nation's savings in the hands of the bankers in their greed for amassing greater riches. We will nationalize money lending and place it at the service of the prosperity of Chile and the people.

We will put an end to the *latifundia*, which condemn thousands of peasants to subjugation and poverty and keep the nation from getting from the land all the foodstuffs we need. A true agrarian reform will make it possible to do just what we are saying — feed the people. We will call a halt to the ever more massive process of denationalization of our industries and sources of work, a process which subjects us to foreign exploitation. We will reclaim Chile's basic wealth. We are going to reclaim the large copper, coal, iron and nitrate mines for the people.

It is in our power — the power of those who earn their living by their work and who hold power today — to do these things. The rest of the world may sit back and observe the changes that are wrought in our country, but we Chileans cannot be satisfied with such a role for ourselves; we must play the leading role in the transformation of our society. Everyone must be fully aware of our common responsibility. It is the essential task of the People's Government — that is, of every one of us — to create a new, just state, one that can offer a maximum of opportunities to all of us who live in this land.

I know that the connotation of the word "state" causes a certain apprehension. The word has been much abused, and it is often used to discredit a just social system.

Don't fear the word "state," because you, all of us, form part of the state, of the People's Government. Working together, we should improve it and make it efficient, modern and revolutionary. But I wish to be understood correctly when I say "just," and this is precisely what I want to emphasize.

Much has been said about the people's participation, and this is the time to put it into practice. All Chileans, of any age, have a task to fulfill. In that task personal interest will merge with the generous conduct of collective work. No state in the world is rich enough to satisfy all the aspirations of all its citizens if these do not first wake up to the realization that rights go hand in hand with duties and that success has more merit when it stems from one's efforts and sacrifice.

The full development of the people's awareness will result in spontaneous voluntary work, which has already been proposed by the young people.

Those who wrote on the walls of Paris [1968] that the revolution had to be made first in the people and later in things were right.

Precisely on this solemn occasion I wish to speak to the young people, to those standing on the lawn, who have sung their songs for us.

A rebellious student in the past, I will not criticize their impatience, but it is my duty to ask them to think calmly.

Young people, yours is that beautiful age during which physical and mental vigor enable you to undertake practically any endeavor. For that reason you are duty-bound to help us advance. Turn your eagerness into more work, your hopes into more effort and your impulsiveness into concrete accomplishments. Use your drive and energy to be better — the best — students and workers.

Thousands upon thousands of young people have demanded a place in the social struggle. Now they have that place. The time has come for all young people to participate in the action.

To those who have not yet taken part in this process, I say, "Come on, there's a place for everyone in the construction of our new society."

Escapism, decadence, superficiality and the use of drugs are the last resort of young people who live in countries which are notoriously opulent but are devoid of any moral strength. That cannot be the case of the young people of Chile.

Follow the best examples, the examples set by those who leave everything behind to build a better future. That is why I've been deeply moved by the sight of portraits of the immortal Che Guevara.

What will be our path, our Chilean way of action, to defeat underdevelopment?

Our path will be that built on the basis of our experience; the path legitimized by the people in the elections; the path contained in the program of Popular Unity; the path toward socialism through democracy, pluralism and freedom.

The basic conditions which, used with prudence and flexibility, will enable us to build a new society, based on a new economy, are now to be found in Chile.

Popular Unity adopts this watchword, not as a simple slogan but as its natural way.

Chile has the unique virtue of having the social and political institutions necessary for carrying out the transition from backwardness and dependence to development and autonomy along the socialist path.

Popular Unity is, constitutionally, the exponent of such a reality. Let no one be deceived; the theoreticians of Marxism have never pretended, nor has history shown, that a single party is a prerequisite in the process of transition toward socialism.

Social circumstances and political vicissitudes — both internal and international — may lead to this situation. Civil war, when imposed upon the people as the only way toward emancipation, leads to political rigidity; foreign intervention, in its frenzy for maintaining domination at all costs, makes the exercise of power authoritarian; and poverty and generalized backwardness make it difficult for political institutions to act dynamically and the people's organizations to grow stronger.

To the extent that such situations do or do not arise in Chile, so will our country, on the basis of its traditions, organize and create the mechanism that, within the pluralism supported by the great majorities, will make possible the radical transformation of our political system.

This is the great legacy of our history. It is also a most generous promise for our future. It is up to us to see to it that it does, someday, become a reality.

This decisive fact is a challenge to all Chileans, regardless of their ideological orientation, to contribute to the autonomous development of our country. As president of the republic, I can affirm, recalling all those who have preceded us in the struggle, face to face with the future that will be our judge, that every one of my actions will constitute another effort at fulfilling the aspirations of the people in keeping with our traditions.

The people's victory marked the maturity of the awareness of a vast sector of our population. It is necessary that that awareness develop even more. It must flourish among thousands upon thousands of Chileans who, even though they were not with us in a part of the process, are now determined to join the great task of building a new life with a new morality.

Together with this new morality, patriotism and revolutionary feeling, will be present the behavior of the government officials. From the outset, I must point out that our administration will be characterized by absolute responsibility — to such an extent that, far from being prisoners of controlling institutions, we will demand that they operate as a permanent conscience, in order to correct mistakes and denounce all those who carry on abuses either within or outside the government. To each one of my countrymen who shares a part of the task to be carried out, I say that I am adopting Fidel Castro's statement that, "In this government anybody may make mistakes, but nobody will ever be allowed to be on the take."

As president of Chile, I shall be unflagging in my watchfulness over the morality of the regime.

Our program of government, endorsed by the people, is founded on the fact that the best guarantee of our democracy is the people's participation in our activities. Our democracy will contribute to increasingly strengthen all human liberties, in accord with the greater participation of the people.

The people are taking over the executive power in a presidential regime in order to start the progressive construction of socialism, through conscientious, organized struggle in free parties, in free labor unions.

Our road, our path, is that of liberty — liberty for the expansion of our productive forces, breaking the chains that have smothered our development thus far; liberty for each citizen, according to their conscience and beliefs, to collaborate in the collective task ahead; and liberty for all Chileans who work for a living to gain social control over and ownership of their work centers.

Simón Bolívar forecast for our country, "If there is one republic that will stand for a long time in America, I am inclined to believe that it is Chile. The spirit of liberty has never been extinguished there."

Let us remember the Liberator at this hour of our homeland.

Our road, our Chilean way, will also be that of equality — equality to overcome, progressively, the division existing between Chilean exploiters and Chileans who are exploited; equality so that everyone shares a part of the collective wealth, according to their work and at a level to meet their personal requirements; and equality for reducing the enormous wage differences that exist between similar jobs.

Equality is a *sine qua non* for investing all individuals with the dignity and respect they are due.

Within these directives, true to these principles, we will march onward toward the construction of a new system.

The new economy which we will build will seek to have the resources of Chile produce for the benefit of the people of Chile. The monopolies will be nationalized, because the interests of the nation require it, and, for the same reason, we will give full guarantees to the small and medium-sized firms, which will receive all possible assistance from the state to carry out their activities.

The People's Government has already worked out laws which will make it possible for it to fulfill its program.

The workers, employees, technicians, professionals and intellectuals will have economic and political control of the country.

For the first time in our history, four workers are a part of the government as ministers of state.

Only by advancing along this path of basic transformations in the political and economic fields will we be able to draw ever nearer to the ideals which are our objective:

To create a new society in which men can fulfill their material and spiritual needs without having to resort to the exploitation of other men.

To create a society which guarantees each family — every man, woman and child — rights, securities, freedom, hope and other basic guarantees. We aim to have all the people filled with a sense of their being called upon to build a new nation which will also mean the construction of more beautiful, more prosperous, more dignified and freer lives for all.

To create a new society capable of making continuous progress in the material, technical and scientific fields; capable of guaranteeing its artists and intellectuals the necessary conditions for reflecting a true cultural rebirth in their works.

To create a new society capable of getting along with all the other peoples, including those of the advanced nations, whose experience can help us greatly in our efforts toward self-improvement.

A society capable of living together with all the other independent nations everywhere, to whom we wish to extend our fraternal solidarity.

Our international policy today is based, as it was yesterday, on respect for international commitments freely assumed, self-determination and nonintervention.

We will collaborate resolutely in the strengthening of peace and coexistence among nations. Every nation has the right to develop freely, marching along the path it has chosen.

However, we are well aware of the fact that, unfortunately — as Indira Gandhi stated in the UN, "The right of the peoples to choose their own form of government is accepted only on paper. In reality," Indira Gandhi affirmed, "there is considerable interference in the internal affairs of many countries. The powerful make their influence felt in a thousand different ways."

Chile, a country which respects self-determination and practices nonintervention, has the legitimate right to demand that all countries treat her the same way. The people of Chile recognize only themselves as the controllers of their destiny.

And your government, comrades, the government of Popular Unity, will firmly see to it that this right is respected.

I wish to extend a special greeting to all the official delegations which are honoring us with their presence.

I also wish to greet the nonofficial delegations from those countries with which we still do not have diplomatic relations. Chile will do them justice by recognizing their governments.

Gentlemen, representatives of governments, peoples and institutions, this mass rally is a fraternal and deeply felt tribute to you.

As a Latin American, I consider the common problems, aspirations and interests of all the people in the continent to be my own. That is why, at this moment, I send my greeting, as a head of state, to our brothers in Latin America, hoping that one day the mandate of our process will be fulfilled and we will all have but one, great, single continental voice.

We also have here with us the representatives of workers' organizations from all over the world and intellectuals and artists of universal renown who wish to demonstrate their solidarity with the people of Chile and celebrate, together with us, a victory which, while ours, is considered as their own by all those who struggle for freedom and dignity.

To all those gathered here — ambassadors, artists, workers, intellectuals and soldiers — Chile extends the hand of friendship.

Distinguished guests, permit me to say that you are witnesses to the political maturity attained by Chile.

To you, who have seen with your own eyes the poverty in which many of our compatriots live; to you, who have visited our marginal towns, the *callampas,* and have seen to what depths of subhuman existence men can be sunk in a fertile land brimming with potential resources and who must have recalled Lincoln's words when he said of his country, as I say of mine, "This nation cannot endure permanently half slave and half free": to you, who have been informed of the way Popular Unity will carry through the program supported by our people — to you I wish to make a petition:

Take back to your respective countries this image of the Chile that is and of the Chile that will be.

Tell your people that here history will take a new course, that here the people have succeeded in taking the helm of their destiny to embark on a democratic course toward socialism.

This Chile in the process of renovation, this Chile in the springtime and an atmosphere of festivity wants, as one of its greatest aspirations, every man in the world to know that we are his brothers.

5

Letter About Pablo Neruda

on the occasion of his
Nobel Literature Prize, 1970

World-renowned poet and Communist Party member Pablo Neruda was serving as Chile's ambassador to France in 1970 when it was announced that he had just won the Nobel Prize in Literature. The arts flourished under Allende's Popular Unity government, affecting trends in music, literature and art all over the world. "Sometimes we poets wait for miracles," Neruda told reporters, "and here it seems one has happened." Shortly after Chile's September 11, 1973 military coup d'état, popular folksinger Víctor Jara, under arrest with 10,000 others in Santiago's National Stadium, had his hands broken by officials so that he could not play his guitar; they then beat him to death. A few days later, Neruda, afflicted with cancer, passed away — some say "of a broken heart."

D ear Compatriots: the Nobel Prize of Literature has been awarded to a Chilean — Pablo Neruda. This award, that grants immortality to one of ours, is the victory of Chile and its people, as well as of Latin America.

This extraordinary and significant distinction could have and should have been achieved by Neruda years ago, without belittling the work and literary merit of those who did receive it.

However, at this moment, it is for us also an obligation, as well as highlighting that Chile is a land of poets, to bring forth the memory of that woman that once also obtained the Nobel Prize of Literature,

Gabriela Mistral, and point to the profound human and social content that is a background for the work of both.

Certainly, while this is not the time to point out or outline, even superficially, the work of Pablo Neruda, whose prodigious imagination reaches all aspects of life, I wish to emphasize that nothing has escaped the imagination of this poet of ours. His books and poetry have been translated into many languages. However, it is useful to say that this is the award for a poet who is committed to his people, who have journeyed along his verses for significant periods of his work; so it is natural that at this time it is the people who happily celebrate their compatriot, their brother.

Neruda, a distinguished humanist who has beautifully narrated the existential concerns of men; Neruda's poetry reflects all of Chile, with its rivers, its mountains, its eternal snow and torrid deserts, but, above all, its men and women and this is why love and social struggle are ever present.

I reiterate that the distinction given to Neruda is a distinction that reaches Chile and all Chileans. It is undeniably a national and patriotic feeling of satisfaction that I express here.

However, I must mention that Pablo Neruda, ambassador of the government of the people in France, has been during all of his existence a combatant with a firm ideological position, a militant of one of the parties that make up the Popular Unity and an active member of it.

Personally, I have very special motives for being moved by the distinction awarded to Pablo, with whom for so many years I participated in popular struggles. He was a comrade in many tours of the North, the Center and the South of Chile. I will always remember with emotion how the people who listened to our political speeches would listen with emotion and expectant silence to Pablo's readings of his own verses. How good it was for me to see the sensitivity of the people, and to see how the verses of the poet fell into the hearts and conscience of the Chilean masses.

That is why I send him a fraternal embrace on behalf of the Chilean people. The quality of Neruda the poet, our country with its popular government and the Communist Party of Chile are being recognized.

It is an event that ennobles a man who is the ambassador of Chile in France, representing the word of the popular government.

We are enthused because, I repeat, the poet's quality, as well as other facets, are being recognized. I believe that this joy is unanimous.

6

Missions and Tasks of Youth and Agrarian Reform

Speech in Santiago Plaza, December 21, 1970

Here Allende speaks to the nation's youth, peasantry and Mapuche people and other indigenous groups. Allende was the first president in Chilean history to take the needs of these groups seriously enough to initiate major reforms on their behalf. Allende uses this occasion to announce the nationalization of copper, the creation of peasant councils, and the start of a voluntary work campaign to be sparked by young people. He also explains the violence occurring in the countryside, urging peasants not to seize lands or "run for fences" (a method used by indigenous peoples to recover their stolen lands) but to wait for the implementation of the agrarian reform. He denounces those large estate owners who are behind the countryside's armed violence, saying that "steel should not be turned into weapons for Chileans to confront Chileans" but "into hoes, picks, hammers, into work tools."

Comrade members of Popular Unity, comrades and friends, national leaders of the peoples' parties, ministers, under secretaries, and officials of the popular government. Accompanying me on this speakers platform, as a symbol of those gathered in this plaza, are three comrades who represent the youth, the peasants and the copper comrades.

As we repeatedly told you, the popular government will always keep the people informed of its actions and its significance in the life of Chile and each individual Chilean. We have called you here this afternoon so that you may understand the tremendous importance of this forthcoming action in which youth, peasants and copper workers play an important part. Youth could not be a spectator of this great economic and social transformation of Chile, youth had to be and is a most important part of this era in the national life. We need, we demand and ask for the creative energy of youth. Its revolutionary loyalty will be placed fully at the service of Chile and its people. That is why today we begin an act of profound solidarity and of great human significance. Chilean youth will go through the valleys, the countryside, the villages, the towns, carrying the message of redemption — the will, the popular government's creative and revolutionary decision, carrying this shining faith to tell the old man from whom he gets his experience that his centenary weariness will be replaced with the energy of youth to make Chile a different country, a community of all Chileans, independent economically and sovereign politically.

Youth must be the essential factor in the changes demanded by this uneven society in giving way to a new society, and youth's presence is equally or more necessary when in our country — we can proudly say that we are a young country — more than 60 percent of the population is younger than 30 years; that is, more than 4.6 million Chileans are younger than 30. In addition, it is also right to recognize that among those over 50 years old who belong to the popular parties, there is a consciousness of youth and also a youthful will, because the struggle of the people of Chile is not a struggle of generations. The presence of youth in voluntary work — in the democratic work of Popular Unity — pointing out that it understands the historic work in which we are engaged and youth, with its creative spirit, its moral force, will erect a dam against juvenile corruption, against those who waste time, against those who use drugs to escape a society that does not satisfy them and in which they feel alienated. Popular Unity youth should set an example in work, in studies, in loyalty to the people and in the heroic vocation to serve Chile above all.

As a governmental need, I will sign before you, on this fine afternoon, the decree that creates the General Secretariat of Youth. The decree reads as follows: Whereas the Executive has special interest in increasing the political participation of youth and its capability of action in the leadership of a new homeland, giving its most determined and efficient cooperation to the popular government plans, with this in mind: It is necessary to create a youth organization to cooperate with the government in the preparation of policies relative to the problems which concern the young and their participation in said plans, I hereby decree:

First Article: That there is now created the General Secretariat of Youth, dependent on the presidency of the republic, whose objective will be to cooperate in the preparation and execution of plans in policy relative to the young.

Second Article: The job of the Secretariat is to propose to the Executive concrete plans on organized youth participation in the initiation of voluntary work, teaching literacy, reforestation, housing construction, for example; dissemination and execution of government measures, dissemination of the Popular Unity program, and the increasing of political participation by the Chilean masses. The Secretariat will be especially concerned about specific youth problems, in areas regarding education, labor, health, nutrition, recreation or sports; coordination with state organizations, especially with the education under-secretariat, the state's sports administration, planning office, the culture department of the Education Ministry, tourism administration, Labor Ministry, National Scholarships and Educational Aid Board, and in general, with the ministers, under-secretariats and general directorates.

Along this line, there will be close coordination with the Family Ministry, for which a proposal will be sent to the National Congress prior to December 31. In addition, the Secretariat of Youth must suggest to the government the legal and administrative measures it deems adequate for the accomplishment of its respective program and plans; consult, coordinate and plan with the Chilean youth mass organizations, such as student federations, the trade union confederation, peasant youth organizations, municipal, slum, sports and cultural organizations.

Third Article: The General Secretariat of Youth will be composed of six representatives appointed by the president of the republic, on the basis of suggestions from the national leaders of the Popular Unity Youth Command. The members of the General Secretariat will not be paid. The General Secretariat of Youth can request of the public agencies all the background information, reports or services it considers appropriate for the best performance of its mission. These agencies must provide such information and services as quickly as possible.

Transitory Article: The General Secretariat of Youth will be attached to the presidency of the republic. In this way I wish to emphasize the importance I attach to this Secretariat and the presence of youth in the popular government and in our people's struggle.

I am going to sign the respective decree.

I have said, people of Santiago, that this afternoon I want to inform you of all the important initiatives which the government has resolved to make a reality, thus fulfilling the Popular Unity program and satisfying our consciences. I wish to emphasize, that on this occasion there is no thought of giving a recapitulation of the work done in the months and days we have been in government. I shall speak to the nation before the end of the year, over the state radio and television, and on a voluntary, non-compulsory network to tell what has been done in this period.

I wish now, in the same way, to point out the importance that the creation of the National Peasant Council holds for us.

We seek, as we have repeatedly stated, an economic development which will give wealth, which will promote the progress of the nation.

But we also seek an economic development which will bring a more just social system, which will give man greater freedom by guaranteeing him against life's risks, which will end his alienation — in other words, safeguard him against disease, unemployment, ignorance, lack of housing, ill-health, and provide recreation and rest.

To be able to achieve this imperative necessity, the people must understand that this task cannot be carried out by one man or a government alone: This is a task which can be carried out only on the basis of a great spirit of awareness on the part of the popular masses, of the irrevocable determination of a people to produce more, to try harder, and to sacrifice more, if necessary, for Chile and to improve the living conditions of people. But the people must also remember what I have said so many times: We are going to produce more, we are going to work more, we are going to try harder, but this will not be for the benefit of a minority, but rather for the benefit of the majority of Chileans, for the benefit of Chile and of the people.

And in regards to the agrarian reform, I want to clearly say to the people who are listening, that yesterday I was in the province of Cautín, where there is a very tense climate, artificially created in part.

There, I publicly said that it was not my intention to unearth the war axe, symbol of the Mapuches, and nor did I hypocritically exhibit a white and warm dove of peace either. I was taking the responsible word of a governor of the people, to tell the workers of the land, to tell the Mapuches that, while recognising the justice of their hopes and yearning for land, I demanded that they no longer participate in the seizing of land or "run for fences." With that, I added, they encouraged exploitation and the ill-conceived campaign to accuse this government of going too far, that the law is not respected and that there is anarchy in this country. I pointed out that in this government there is one who is responsible, that the President of the Republic supports their determination through his moral strength and through the influence he has among the popular masses.

I said at the same time that, while we were going to organize the National Peasant Council, while we were also going to deal with the Mapuche situation with decisiveness, speed and responsibility, I also pointed out that there were two types of landowners: those who have abided by the law, who have worked the land, who have respected those who have collaborated with them and who have respected the dignity of the peasant; while on the other hand, unfortunately, there is the other sector of landowners — I'm not referring to the labor union entities — who were linked to reactionary activities, to conspiracies, who acted in a sinister manner, even smuggling arms.

In relation to this matter, I want to be very precise with my words, since a newspaper asserts that arms have arrived from Argentina, without specifying facts. That type of landowner has smuggled arms. In the south of Chile, especially in the provinces of Cautín, Bío-Bío and Malleco, there are landowners who are armed, who have long range weapons and machine guns, which they have already used and have announced that they will keep using. I have said, categorically, that we don't want violence, that we are opposed to violence, that we don't want Chilean steel to be turned into weapons for Chileans against Chileans, that we want steel to be turned into hoes, picks, hammers, work tools. But I have maintained that if these landowners do not understand, it will be the government itself that will impose respect for the law and for the lives of the workers of the land. I have had talks with the unions, or rather, with the representatives of the managers' union of the National Society of Agriculture, and have told them that the memorandum they gave to the Minister of Agriculture will be replied to shortly. Out of the 20 questions that they have raised, we will not avoid answering any of them. I want all landowners to know what our attitude will be and what path we will take. Indisputably, the small and medium landowners, those that work the land well, will know that the Popular Government will go to their aid. But we will irrevocably carry out the agrarian reform as a social and economic necessity; we will even modify the current law, but certainly via legal channels. If we demand from the Mapuche, the indigenous, the worker of the land, respect for the law, we will relentlessly demand it of those who have a higher obligation to respect the law because of their cultural and educational level.

Meanwhile, I must point out that this government has not infringed the law. I bring this up because the Santiago newspapers have already made public a document emanating from the Christian Democrat parliamentarians from the province of Cautín. They should not forget that the expropriations in this province started in June of this year, and that there were more estates seized in the months of June and August than there were after the elections. Similarly, there was moving of fences in the same magnitude as there is now. I have wanted to remind these parliamentarians that this government has not transgressed the legal regulations. I want to remind the whole of Chile that it was a group of estate owners who were disrespectful towards President Frei's ministers in an act of the National Society of Agriculture. I want to remind you that it was the landowners who blocked the roads with their cars and wagons, to express their protest at the previous government's proposal to fix the price of wheat. I want to remind you that staff members of INDAP were run down, shot at and wounded in the province of Linares. I want to remind you that journalists were beaten and, last but not least, I want to remind you of the assassination of a government employee who had gone to carry out the law, who was even under police protection: I'm referring to engineer Mery.

It is not us who have impinged on the law, and in the cases where the seizing of estates has taken place, we have made the workers see reason. We know that some sections of land have been seized because their owners do not work them, they have abandoned them. In other cases, where the conflicts have been extraordinarily lengthy, it is undeniable that it was desperation which drove the agricultural workers to act in the way that is now well known. In these cases we have provided administrators. We have given them very clear instructions because we need those farms to keep producing in order to ensure that the people of Chile are better nourished and this is a responsible attitude on our part.

I want to tell the people of Chile what I learned yesterday in Cautín, while the Second Mapuche Congress took place: it should be known that in Chile there are 3,048 indigenous reservations, between Bío-Bío and Llanquihue, with 392,616 Mapuches, and the highest concentration being in Cautín with 189,000; in Malleco there are 89,000; in Valdivia 3,000; 5,000 in Arauco, etc. The basic activities of the Mapuches are agriculture and cattle breeding. However, many of them only feed on pine kernels, especially in the agricultural sectors of the coast of the Bío-Bío province.

I want to tell you that the race that heroically defended the initial stages of our history, have gradually lost their land and have been increasingly neglected. I want to point out that the law granting them certain privileges has a paternalistic tone and, therefore, the Mapuches cannot dictate their own conduct. They cannot alienate themselves from their land or lease it out. Their affairs have to be processed by the Indigenous Courts, which are few in numbers and, furthermore, function for a limited number of hours in the day. I want to point out that each Mapuche is entitled to about one-and-a-half or one-and-a-quarter hectares, and only 60 percent of this land is cultivable. And I want to say that the living conditions of these people are dramatically deplorable. I want to stress that there are 77,800 school-aged children and that there is a shortage of schools and teachers; above all, teachers who understand and comprehend Mapuche anthropology. I want to tell you that there are over 37,000 pre-school children in absolute abandonment and 27,000 children in breastfeeding ages without medical attention; many of whom have never drunk a glass of milk. I want to say that it is a national obligation, it is an imperative of our conscience, to not forget Chile's debt to the people of the Araucanian race, who are our ancestors. Therefore, the Popular Government will confront this situation with responsibility.

It will raise the material and spiritual levels of the Araucanian, of our Mapuches; it will legislate with a different sense; it will give them lands and dignify their existence, as an urgent necessity of their human presence in the life of the people of Chile.

That's why, yesterday I said to the Mapuches that the youth were meeting today, here in Santiago, to initiate their voluntary work. I ask more than that, I urge the young students in their fifth and sixth year of medicine, the students in their last year of dentistry, I ask young doctors and dentists to go with haste, with affection, with humane tenderness to work for one or two months there in the communities; so that they can relate to the dramatic reality of the Mapuche people; that they take with them, along with technology, an encouraging word in their remedies and diagnosis. Let the teachers and student-teachers also go. On our part, we will mobilize INDAP, CORA and all the organizations necessary to change the life and the work of the Mapuche. This is a commitment of honor and I know that the youth that are listening to me will consider my request and my mandate, a mandate that emanates from the pain and the hope of the Araucanians in the south of Chile.

7

Address to
International Workers Day Rally

Santiago's Bulnes Plaza, May 1, 1971

Speaking out on the issues of nationalization of industries and land reform, Allende explains that "Copper is the wage (sueldo) of Chile" and "Land is the nourishment (alimento)." He acknowledges the right to dissent but cautions that criticism must take place within legally acceptable avenues. Recognizing that the whole world is watching how "for the first time in history, a people have chosen the path to revolution at a small social cost" (meaning without violence and bloodshed), Allende defines "people's power" ("poder popular") as going beyond the consolidation of a People's Government to include the daily social mobilization of the people "because class conflict occurs every day." To the workers he says: "We are depending on you to win the great battle of production" — which will determine if Chile's political future is a happy one or one of disillusionment. "The workers," whom he defines broadly to include peasants, technicians, white collar employees, intellectuals, professionals and small and medium-sized business people, "have the responsibility" over Chile's future.

Workers of Chile: This is not a day for festivities, this is a day for remembrance. A day for looking back, within and beyond our borders and paying tribute to all those who fell fighting in different countries in the pursuit of a better life for humanity and the conquest of true liberty.

Today brings to an end a week in which the government of the people, through me as a medium, has held talks with the most diverse national sectors. We have spoken with the youth of the Popular Unity, with recently graduated doctors in order to stress the responsibility involved in practicing their profession; we have attended meetings with the important United Nations organization CEPAL where we presented our thinking and highlighted the reality of smaller developing countries in the face of industrial countries, pointing out, once again, the harsh exploitation to which we are and continue to be subjected, and to demand the right to self-determination and to non-intervention.

And once again, not as a politician, but as their general-in-chief, a title that is bestowed on me by the constitution, I have spoken with the representatives of the armed forces, in this case with the Santiago garrison. As well as reaffirming our respect for the professional performance of our armed forces and the Police Force and their adherence to the constitution and the law, we also stressed that they cannot be an independent entity, separate from the great process of transformations that Chile faces on the economic, social and cultural fronts, in order to make the lives of the people in our land more just and dignified. Furthermore, I spoke with the university community of the State Technical University; with trade union delegates of Yarur [textile plant] and with the workers that came from Panguipulli to tell me of the plight of the wood and sawmill workers. This act today marks an end to this week; with this May Day so different from other May Days of the past.

We are here today on this day that has such profound and deep significance; it is significant because you, the workers of Chile, are here together with us, because the government and the people are here, because the people are the government, and therefore they voice the yearnings and wishes of the majority.

We have achieved government and we advance towards the conquest of power. The difference with the past is noticeable, not only because of the massive numbers here present, which triples the numbers of rallies from previous years but also because I see thousands and thousands of women. I pay tribute to them, symbolized by the two elderly women that I have been observing for more than an hour, and who have come despite their tiredness to show us, with their example, their support and deep feelings for the Popular Government.

I salute those who have come from other countries as representatives of trade unions, bringing to us their words of solidarity. I salute the representatives of friendly countries, diplomats or heads of business delegations; and I highlight a very significant thing which fills me with pride: the presence on this platform of the head of the Chilean Church, Cardinal Raúl Silva Henríquez. His presence is extremely significant, because he is aware that under the government of the people, all beliefs are and will be respected. With the Catholic Church being the largest in Chile, it receives popular affection because its word is closer to the thought of Christ.

And I salute all the Chilean trade union officials, my comrades from the CUT (Unitary Workers Central). I pay homage to those who, even though having already fulfilled their duties, never left their place alongside the workers, like the first president of the CUT, my dear friend Clotario Blest.

We have come to speak to the people; to speak to them about their rights and their fundamental duties and responsibilities. I would like you to meditate on the implications and the content of my words. Something big and transcendental has occurred in the country with the victory on September 4. It hasn't happened by chance; it has been the effort and sacrifice of thousands and thousands of anonymous Chileans who had faith in themselves, who joined the popular parties and understood the great historical task we must accomplish. This has been the fervor of generations and generations who have known of imprisonment, exile and death, giving us the opportunity to reach government and achieve power. But the victory obtained at the polls entails a great responsibility and I want that to be clearly understood. Of course, let's make it known, let it be appreciated, let us ponder on what it means for a people who, for the first time in history and within the legal parameters of bourgeois democracy, attain government to transform society and to begin the road to deep structural transformations that will lead to socialism. I reiterate: this is the first time that this has occurred. We want the political liberties we have achieved to turn into social liberties. We want every worker to understand that revolutionary theory teaches that one does not destroy one regime completely, in order to build another. One takes all the positive aspects of the previous regime to improve them, to use them and expand them. It is important that this is understood and that it gets into the consciousness of each and every one of you.

We will maintain the political gains because the people obtained them through their struggle and they have been consecrated by Chilean law and the Chilean Constitution. And the positive achievements in the economic area, derived from the Popular Government of Pedro Aguirre Cerda and reflected in the industries of steel, transport, energy, fuel and electricity, will be focal points in our endeavors to extend and organize the social capital that we have spoken so much about.

On another point, it is important to never forget that we have a commitment and that we will carry it out: to respect the right to opinion, the right to be critical. And from here I respond to the youth of the Catholic University — so restless — that the government of the people will respect those who disagree with it. Criticism does not worry us, all we ask is that it is expressed within the legal context that we abide by.

I want to reiterate that for the first time in history, a people has consciously chosen the path to revolution with the least social cost. And it is essential that this fact is understood: with respect for all ideas and with unrestricted respect for all beliefs.

I want to remind you that we have a program that will be implemented no matter what difficulties we may have to overcome. In order for Chile to break with its backwardness, its unemployment, its inflation, its physiological and moral wretchedness; so that our children can have a future and our old folks peace, we must make good use of the surplus produced, investing it in a planned way into the economic and social development of our country. This is why nationalizations are essential in order to strengthen the social economy that our program refers to. That is why we have begun to nationalize our essential resources currently in foreign hands, as well as the monopolies held by foreign capitalists and national capital.

We want to do it in accordance with the needs of Chile and its people, taking into account our technical capacity to maintain the strategic industries, and aiming to surpass current levels of production. It is essential to understand this and to also realize that it is up to the government to accelerate or slow down this process according to the current reality. I appeal to the conscience of the workers so that they understand that it is their government that determines the technique and the methods on how to proceed and they must place their trust in the government if we are to reach the goals we have set.

We are opening a new horizon for you in Chile. In the social and mixed sectors of the economy the workers will no longer just be simple wage earners. Hear me well, they will stop being simple wage earners because they will join with the representatives of the state — who are yourselves — in assuming the management of these companies, respecting the trade union organizations who have a different role. While we propose this in relation to the public and mixed sectors, it must be understood that it is essential for production monitoring committees to function in private companies. There are more than 35,000 companies, and we, at this point, are only going to nationalize less than 1 percent — hear me well — and in Chile there are 35,000. Therefore it must be understood that the role of the companies that are not nationalized, the small and medium-sized companies, is indispensable to the process of economic development. We want them to have production committees, because the worker is not a machine but a human being that thinks, suffers, has hopes and can contribute to the improvement of production, even in those organizations.

Comrade Víctor Díaz, whose documented speech was necessary so the workers could become aware of the reality that confronts us, has pointed out that the government, through me, has agreed to give Balmaceda Radio to the CUT (Unitary Workers Central). In regards to this I tell you: Did the workers, the journalists, the commentators, those that work there, know the truth about this company? I will tell you. In the first place, its broadcasting license expired more than two years ago. The Christian Democrat government did not grant it a new license and Balmaceda Radio, with a capital of 300 million, today owes 3.8 billion pesos. It has obtained 2.8 billion from the Bank of Credit and Investments without any collateral, and obtained another 700 million on other loans to deal with this enormous liability. I will be clear, I don't think that the acquisition of this radio by the Christian Democrat Party would be a good thing as this signifies, if not a conflict of interest — a strange act for a political party. That radio station has lost 10 times its capital; that radio must belong to the workers, because I have not given it to the socialist workers nor the radicals or the communists; I have given it to the trade union confederation (CUT) where, luckily, there are also Christian workers, there are Christian Democrat workers.

I have said that all public and private enterprises must have production committees, because our most basic need, our first priority, is to increase production. I have said it many times and will say it many more times: the people only progress by working, producing more and studying more. But it is very different — and they understand and know this — working for a minority and working and producing for all Chileans. That's why I emphasize and insist on the importance of a bigger effort, a bigger sacrifice and a bigger patriotic determination to work and produce more, because in doing this you will be securing the future of our homeland and defeating those who conspire against it and its government. That's why I express my approval of comrade Víctor Díaz's words in highlighting the significance of the efforts of the coal workers, of Purina, the nitrate miners and nationalized textile sectors. It demonstrates an awareness that is important to highlight and an example we should imitate. It is important to know that the new meaning of work now involves new obligations. Before, when the state was at the service of capitalists, the workers of the private and public sectors inevitably adopted a demanding attitude, proposing salary and wage increases in accordance with the rise in the cost of living. That is to say, they fought for their interests. Today, you have to understand, the workers are the government; the people are the government. The public sector is not financing a minority. It's putting its economic surplus at your service, at the service of the people and Chile. That's why it's necessary to look at it from the other side of the fence, in order to assume the responsibility, the enormous and important responsibility involved in being the government.

A part of the state is in the hands of the workers, through the popular parties and of the CUT, which represents all levels of trade union organization. If I say "a part of the state," it is because there are other powers, such as judiciary or legislative, in which we do not have a majority. That's why it must be understood that together with the difficulties inherent to these circumstances, today we have to set different objectives. First of all, to consolidate the political power. Second, to broaden that political power, the people's power. And do these in the easiest and most realistic way in accordance with Chilean conditions.

When I speak of broadening political power I think that, beyond the limits of the Popular Unity, there are thousands and thousands of citizens who could join with us; there are hundreds and thousands without a political home, and there are others who have one and yet cannot ignore principles or ideas. That is why we call on them, fraternally and honestly, to work for the new Chile, for the better homeland that we want for all Chileans.

Consolidating and broadening people's power presupposes the vitalization of the popular parties, on the basis of effective unity, maintaining ideological dialogue, controversial, critical, but with loyalty and without partisan prejudices, always aware of the great common responsibility that falls on us.

To strengthen people's power and consolidate it means strengthening unions with a new awareness, the awareness that they are a fundamental pillar of the government, and that they are not dominated by it but that they consciously participate, support, assist and criticize its actions.

To consolidate power it is necessary to organize the mobilization of the people, not only for elections, but mobilise it daily because class conflict occurs every day, at all hours, every minute. And we have to be aware of this.

A disciplined, organized, and conscious people, together with the clear loyalty of the armed forces and the police force, is the best defense for the Popular Government and the future of the country.

To strengthen, broaden and consolidate people's power means *winning the battle of production.* Hear me well comrade workers: *to win the battle of production.* I have for you here, in my hands, the summary of a document published in the United States by a financial weekly. This is not reproduced in Chilean newspapers. But what does it say? What does it point out? What is meant between the lines? It affirms that the loans from the World Bank are not directly controlled by the Unites States but a large part of this capital comes from the treasury of that country, and thus, surely, Washington can influence the bank's decisions. They want to close our line of credits, they intend to go down that road. They say that every activity, and they refer to the loans, seems to be contrary to existing legislation which, to any sound mind, would indicate a ban on aid from the United States to Chile. It goes on to add, with the best possible disposition, that the United States could do little or nothing to save Chile from disaster. How pious and compassionate they are towards us! No? Because, according to them, Chilean workers now have less, and much less, to buy. And they add that there won't be any production in Chile. And they say, "The workers have little time for work." In Valparaíso, absenteeism in the docks averages 25 percent a day and they add with irony, "except on Mondays when it reaches 40 percent." This has not been published in Chile but reflects an intent that the people must watch out for: to start to create economic difficulties for us, that will impact on the political power bases that sustain the government. Our newspapers, the same newspapers that demand freedom of the press, while they publish whatever they like, reproduce articles from many capitals of Latin America and Europe where, unfortunately, they write against us, distorting what we are, what we want and where we are going. But next to this, which we knew was going to happen, we see the broad solidarity, the respectful attitude from governments that, without sharing our orientation, have similar concepts and principles in relation to self-determination and non-intervention. We have the presence of workers who have manifested their support for Chile in the industrial capitalist countries and in the industrial socialist countries; we have the support from the Latin American workers, whose solidarity we feel so close, because we know it is loyal, because the history of yesterday and today will make possible a more intimate, a more profound struggle of our people.

I want to highlight an act of great moral and significant solidarity: the word of Cuba. Not long ago in Havana, a huge rally took place, because it was the anniversary of the victory of the people at the Bay of Pigs. Chile was represented by the senator of the Popular Unity, comrade and friend Volodia Teitelboim. Fidel Castro, along with making a historical synthesis of Latin American struggles and that of Cuba, had words for Chile that reflect his broad and great spirit of solidarity, echoing the fraternal spirit of the people of Cuba towards us. What did Fidel Castro say in his speech which has only been published partially, distorted, with paragraphs extracted and analyzed out of context by the reactionary sectors? What did Fidel Castro say in relation to us? He said, "Logically, our wholehearted support is with Chile and we are prepared to show our solidarity in any field. We have now, for example, re-established commercial relations with Chile. We send them sugar, which is a very important product for Chilean popular consumption. They send us beans, garlic and onions.

"As long as the Chileans can pay for our sugar and can send us food and can send us wood, we will receive food and we will receive wood; but if as a result of counterrevolutionary ploys from imperialism and from the internal counterrevolution they manage to sabotage the production of food in Chile and tomorrow they could not send us garlic or onions or beans, it doesn't matter, we would not stop sending our sugar to the people of Chile." And he adds, "To our brothers in Chile, to the government of the Popular Unity, to President Allende we say: the people of Chile will not be left without sugar, we will do whatever is necessary, with more production, even giving from our own consumption." And he concluded: "I express to the people of Chile, selflessly, fraternally, and in the spirit of Girón [Bay of Pigs], that, should they need to, they can count on our blood; that, should they need to, they can count on our lives." This is solidarity; this is the concept of a revolution without frontiers.

Here they have tried to say that, because of the offering of lives of Cubans, Fidel thinks that Chile does not have in its armed forces or in the police force or in the people the capacity for resistance in the face of a threat. No. It should suffice to remind those who distort Fidel Castro's words that our people were born into political independence because men born in different countries raised a common flag, and Bolívar and Sucre and San Martín and Martí and O'Higgins were Latin Americans who fought with arms for its independence.

So don't come and distort history or the roots of the fraternal spirit that other people have for our government and for our struggles. But I reiterate, the great struggle, the great battle of Chile is now and will always be that of production. Production, understand it, let it stay in your minds and hearts for always, I repeat, the battle now and always is that of production. We have to produce more. And in order to increase production in the long term we also need to increase the investments and the surplus, hear it well, the surplus of companies. The companies' profits will partially serve to improve the wages and salaries of those that work there, but the greatest percentage of those profits and surplus should be invested to create new jobs and new companies; to increase the now dormant capacity of many of them. That's why comrade Víctor Díaz has done so well in pointing out that there cannot be exaggerated petitions. Do not overstep the limits because we will not accept it. We are not playing a game of hopscotch, what is at stake here is the destiny of Chile; there cannot be any privileged sectors here, there cannot be an aristocracy of workers or white collar employees or technicians, here we all have to tighten our belts.

Comrades, imagine if public companies don't have profits, imagine it! If we spent it all on wages and salaries, what would happen? How could we advance? We would take them straight into bankruptcy and ruin. And you must understand this clearly: the companies in the mixed sector, or those from the social sector do not belong to them. The CAP does not belong to the steelworkers. Chuquicamata, El Salvador and El Teniente do not belong to the copper workers. They belong to the workers of the whole country. And the workers in the copper and steel industries should be proud of working in them, but above all, they should be proud of working for the rest of their class brothers, for the whole of Chile.

I wish to cite two examples and I want you to pay attention (it's quite late and you are going to get home with quite an appetite and most of your ladies won't have any lunch for you.) I want to present two examples: copper and land. So listen comrades. Copper: *copper is the wage of Chile.* The North American government and the North American people must also understand this. When we propose to nationalize our mines we are not doing it to attack U.S. investors. If they were Soviet, Japanese, French or Spanish investors we would do the same. We need the profit that goes beyond our frontiers from those companies to boost the development of our nation, along with the iron, nitrate and all of the nationalized enterprises. Remember that in just over 50 years, more than $3 billion in profits from copper have left the country. Now with nationalization, we should have an additional $90 million annually. This means that in the next 20 years, at the price of 50 cents a pound, $1.830 billion. If the average price reaches 55 cents a pound, the figure would be $2.114 billion. This surplus, this higher income is needed to get the economic development of Chile underway, along with the surplus of other companies and industries in the hands of the state, together with the taxes that we all pay, that all Chileans pay. This is why it is essential to understand the importance of copper and to ensure that the people understand the inherent responsibility of the workers, technicians and Chilean professionals.

Some 240 U.S. technicians at the Chuquicamata mine have left or are about to leave Chile. We have not thrown them out, but they are leaving. We have to replace them with our own technicians and our own workers, we have to improvise technology no matter what the cost, and we have to produce more at Chuquicamata. *The workers there will have to sweat copper in order to defend Chile.* And they will have to do it, because we, the people, are asking and demanding it of them.

Yesterday, comrades, I endured some bitter hours. I was told that during the week three sections of Chuquicamata had stopped for no justifiable reason. And this happens now, when there are workers in the management of those companies. I was told they were demanding that all workers be paid severance, only to be re-hired when we finally take over the companies. It struck my conscience and, as a revolutionary, it hurt that this was true. This morning I had a call from Antofagasta and was told that the trade union assembly rejected the untimely proposal made by some workers and what's even worse, by some vote-chasing political leaders. This shows the conscience of the workers in Chuquicamata and, from here, I congratulate them because their stance represents an essential contribution to the homeland.

I have said that, as well as copper, there is the problem of the land. And you have to understand. You that live in Santiago, the majority of you in this great mass rally, who are not peasants. But I am sure that I am being heard by agricultural workers throughout Chile. This is a very serious problem. *If copper is the wage of Chile, land is the nourishment for hunger,* and it cannot continue producing what it has produced up until now. That's why the agrarian reform has been introduced; that's why land property laws have been modified, that's why the methods of land exploitation must be changed; that's why we have to provide credit, seeds, fertilizer and technical assistance to the peasant, the small and medium-sized farmers; that's why the smallholdings have to be eliminated long with the large estates. Take notice, comrades, who listen to me throughout Chile: 300,000 or more Chileans are born every year. And despite the high infant mortality rate, there are many new mouths to feed. If agrarian production were to remain at the current levels, which only represents an increase of 1.8 percent, whilst the population increases by 2.5 to 2.7 percent each year, we would find that by the year 2000 (a year that you and I will both reach, eh?) we would have to import, hear me carefully, $1 billion in meat, wheat, fat, butter and oil. Today we import $180 to $200 million a year. And in 2000 we would have to import $1 billion. The whole of Chilean exports reaches $1.05 billion. Consider the drama that we are facing and the huge responsibility attached to agrarian reform. That's why I say very clearly; that's why I have said to the people of Chile; I have said it to the workers of the land; I have yelled it out with passion so that Cautín, Valdivia, Llanquihue and Osorno can understand; in the agrarian provinces of the center and the north: *we will apply agrarian reform quickly and thoroughly. We are going to eradicate large estate holdings.* This year we are going to expropriate 1,000 estates that surpass the legal limit, and we will eliminate the tiny parcels too small to survive. But it is not enough to expropriate, we have to make the land produce and *we have to respect the law.* We cannot accept the violation of the legal rights of the estate owners. We cannot bring chaos to production. We cannot expropriate land and then leave it unproductive. The government has to respect the determination and the planning of the Executive.

I tell you, and I say it to the officials of INDAP and CORA: you cannot bypass the law. What would a man do, what would I do if I had been a farmer for 40 or 50 years of my life and I only had my house and bread for my children, if the law gives me a right and then officials come who don't respect the law? What does that man, who cannot find other work at his age, do? Why wouldn't we have a sense of humanity and justice? I call on the people who work the land, I call on the peasants to have trust in us, that's why we have created the Peasant Council. Not one large estate will survive in Chile, but the medium and small landowners will have our support, our help. We will provide the necessary technicians, seeds and fertilizer, in order to meet the goals of production essential to feed our people, comrades.

That is why we must have the awareness: *the revolution is not made with words, comrades, but with actions.* And it is not easy to achieve, otherwise many other peoples in other areas and other continents would have achieved it.

It is necessary to have a political awareness, and have the necessary responsibility to understand it. It is not enough to talk about the revolution. We have to carry out an internal revolution which will give us the authority to make demands on others, and that's why I speak to you like this, on May Day, with passion, in the face of the responsibility we have with Chile and with history. New goals, more organization, more discipline, detachment, unselfishness; look beyond the small horizons of each company, each industry or each fence, in order to see the problem of class as a whole, be they peasants, workers, white collar employees, technicians or professionals. That's why I must tell you that I have read, with great concern, a document published on April 29 in the newspaper *La Prensa*, in which they interviewed a peasant leader, a comrade by the name of Fuentes. This has not been refuted, that's why I'm commenting on it. What does this leader say? He said that he supports the government, but if it stops half way then he will continue on. They say that they have the autonomy to do whatever they want, they say that despite the fact that the government will expropriate all estates, they still think that it is necessary and that's why they do it and will continue to do it and they add, "because we must stop comrade Allende and comrade Baytelman in their tracks."

Comrades, Comrade Víctor Díaz said: "Keep going forward, comrade Allende." I will keep going forward, I will not step on the brakes, comrades. But know this once and for all, especially the members of the Popular Unity: we have here a government and a president and if I go forward it is because my pants are well fastened and I do not accept... (I'm sorry, Cardinal Silva Henríquez, for using this expression but I know that you understand and share my view.)

Well, I have used that example because if everybody chooses their own way then there will be chaos here, comrades, and that's what they want: they don't want the land to produce; they don't want industries to produce, they want difficulties. The purchasing power that you have today has meant that sales are at an all-time high. But we have to balance certain things. Within 15 days to two months, stocks will be gone and if the industries don't produce, Chile is not used to rationing and we don't want it. That's why we have to produce in the countryside, in the industries, comrades. And that is why I want to tell you, quite calmly, as your comrade, that I have a report by the Comptroller of the Republic, elaborated at my request. The report is based on a study of two state companies, one in particular, and here are the figures that show the percentage of absenteeism of its workers and employees. (This is what is published with such joy in that American weekly I mentioned earlier.) And the worst is that this report confirms what I said to the people at the other square a few days ago. I said that, unfortunately, there is absenteeism by workers and employees who fake illness and I added that, unfortunately, there were also medical professionals with no sense of responsibility, with no understanding of their Hippocratic oath, who issue false medical certificates. Workers and employees that earn more by not working, because the law is absurd and because doctors receive a percentage from every certificate they give out. There are some that have obtained 50, 60, 80 million pesos this way. I have informed the Medical School of this. I have been president of this school for five years; I have a moral authority to say this, because I created that law, in conjunction with the National Health Service, I also created the Statute of the Medical Servant. The medical profession in this country has never fallen to the moral standards that some people have intended. We cannot accept the collusion between workers and employees and doctors to swindle the Treasury, the people and Chile itself, comrades.

To conclude — it's just that I don't like the exploitation of men by men — you know already what the government has done and comrade Víctor Díaz has just gone through it in detail. From the half a liter of milk, to controlling 53 percent of bank shares, and to granting nationalized banks control of the dollar market. From the nationalization of monopolized companies to the recovering of the basic resources in the hands of foreign capital. We have made and will continue to make all the necessary efforts to stop inflation and to reduce unemployment. But inflation will not be stopped if we don't produce more, comrades. Because if we generate more demand and don't increase production, prices will go up and, who pays the consequences? You do. And above all, the pensioners, the retired, those who receive a dependant's pension, those on fixed incomes, salaries or wages. The government does, fulfills, acts, but it is not only up to the government. You, too, have responsibilities. Essentially, it is the workers' responsibility.

When I speak of workers I speak of peasants, employees, technicians, intellectuals and professionals. I speak of small and medium-sized industrial and commercial businessmen. *The onus is on the workers.* All that which debilitates also divides the workers, debilitates the government and this must be understood. Whatever strengthens the workers also strengthens the government and this must be understood. The future of the Chilean revolution is, today more than ever, in the hands of those who work. Whether we win the great battle of production depends on you. Day to day, the government shows what it's capable of doing. But it will not be able to do much more if we cannot count on the support, the conscientious and revolutionary will of you, comrade workers.

That's why — as I was saying — we have to revitalize movements, unions, popular parties, and, above all, the peasants and the workers must be conscious of their responsibility...

The revolution, the destiny, the future of Chile is in your hands. If we fail in the economic arena, we will fail in the political arena, and this will bring disillusionment and bitterness for millions of Chileans and for millions of brothers from other continents who are looking at us and support us. We have to realize that far beyond our frontiers, from Africa and Asia, and here in the heart of Latin America, there are men and women who are looking with passionate and fraternal interest at what we are doing. Think, comrades, that in other places people have risen to make their revolution and were crushed by the counterrevolution. Torrents of bloodshed, incarceration and death mark the struggle of many peoples, in many continents, and even in those countries where the revolution has triumphed, the social cost has been high, a social cost in lives which do not have a price, comrades. Social cost in human existence of children, men and women that cannot be measured by money. Even in those countries where the revolution triumphed they had to overcome the economic chaos created by the struggle and the drama of combat or civil war. Here we can make the revolution through the channels that Chile has sought with the least social cost, without sacrificing lives and without disorganizing production. I call on you with passion, I call on you with affection, I call on you as an older brother to understand our responsibility; I speak to you as the Comrade President to defend the future of Chile, which is in your hands, workers of my country.

8

The Role of the Armed Forces

From press conference with foreign journalists, Santiago, May 5, 1971

Allende explains why the armed forces must be incorporated into the social processes of Chile's reforms and maintain their strength and professionalism. He commends their tradition of loyalty to the constitution and notes their working-class and peasant composition.

We are proud of the professional role of our armed forces. The great characteristic of the armed forces of Chile has been their obedience to the civil authority, their unquestioned regard for the public will as expressed in the ballots, for the laws of Chile and for the Chilean Constitution. It is my firm intention, as it is of Unidad Popular, that the armed forces will maintain their professional attitude.

The armed forces of Chile are the armed forces of the country. They are not at the service of one man, nor of one government. They are of the nation, and this is one of the factors which characterizes Chile and distinguishes it from other countries.

But we believe that the armed forces should not remain on the fringes of what is now taking place and that consequently they should be integrated directly with Chile's process of development. We cannot have powerful armed forces in a country with high rates of mortality and sickness. We cannot afford to have armed forces which are technologically advanced and disproportionately well-equipped in a country whose economic development is inadequate. Either we spend the greater part of our budget on them, as happens in other countries, where up to 70 percent of the budget goes on the armed forces while the people die of hunger (and in fact these armies are basically weak), or quite simply, the armed forces participate — without detriment to their professional status and with no attempt being made to politicize them in the direction of one or another party or group of parties — in the broad policies of the nation.

We have tried to make clear what we mean in such a case, for example, by pointing out that the armed forces should be represented in those organizations where they might be interested for technical reasons.

For example, how could it not be important for the armed forces to participate in the control of the copper industry, since a percentage of the income obtained from copper is destined by law to finance the needs of the armed forces to participate in steel production? Or that they participate in the Commission for Atomic Energy? How is it not important for the armed forces to be involved in the Council for Research and Scientific Development, the nature of which is profoundly universal?

These are brief examples of what I am proposing. But I expect the professional character of the armed forces to remain unquestioned and there will be absolute respect for this character on the part of the government throughout their participation in aspects of economic developments of vital concern to Chile, and which should also concern the armed forces. How could we not be concerned for example if ASMAR, which is a small shipyard, were to become the only shipyard? That lies in the hands of the armed forces. How would it not concern us if the FAMAE munitions factory were not able to reach a level of production to supply its fixed percentage of the army's needs? But the fact is that for this to happen there must be available certain established grades of steel, and so the presence of men from the armed forces in the CAP (the Pacific Steel Company) is important, just as from the economic angle their presence will be important in the copper industry.

How could it not be important for Chile to exploit capacities — which they possess to a high degree — of officers and other leaders in the Chilean armed forces? How could it not be important to exploit them not in their military capacity but in the field of scientific knowledge? That is what we have the Polytechnic Academy for, in order to train leaders to a high standard. Why should we waste these capacities? We are not giving them a political role but adapting them to processes of which no government could disapprove. What government could say that it is a mistake to increase steel production and to produce different grades of steel? What government could say that it was not important, indeed decisive and essential, for Chile not only to produce more copper but to produce it in treated and semi-treated forms?

We fully recognize that the armed forces have by tradition a sense of professional standing and that it is their duty to maintain Chile's integrity and full sovereignty along her frontiers. But they have also at all times had an important social function, especially in the southern areas. The planes of the armed forces have been a unifying factor for the people. They have helped and cooperated on the canals, where great professional and technical skills are needed. They carry merchandise, they transport settlers, establish communications, carry supplies to lighthouses and so on. The army is on the frontiers or near them and the barracks are no doubt an element in equipping the citizen with national awareness — not a chauvinistic or mock-heroic patriotism, but a deep and sober sense of nationhood. We must realize that those who come to the barracks are sons of the land, sons of workers.

Why should we not use to the full this energy, in the fields where the armed forces, and particularly the army, can and wish to cooperate? We have discussed this subject in public because it is a need felt strongly by the country and clearly recognized by the armed forces.

9

First Annual Message to the National Congress

May 21, 1971

In this traditionally required presidential address to the new legislative session of the Congress, President Allende lays out a philosophical framework for the reforms his administration is introducing. Refusing to engage in a typical annual message's litany of statistics and self-praise, he instead explains the unique Chilean road to socialism with its five principles of legality, development of institutions, political freedom, nonviolence, and the creation of an "area of social ownership." He points out that a revolutionary government does not discard the bourgeois gains of the past but instead builds on them to construct — within democracy and pluralism — a broader people's regime with social and political liberties for all. A ringing call to "Marxist humanism" and "the socialist ideal," this speech includes special appeals to Chile's young people, farmers, professionals, small and medium-sized business enterprises, and, in the end, all of society — even the one-time capitalist monopolists! It rationally lays out the steps "our transitional regime" will take in moving Chile not into "state capitalism" but toward a socialism that uses both the market and state planning as "regulators of the economic process." Allende states his confidence in the professionalism and constitutionalism of the armed forces, along with his faith in "those who live by their work" and their ability to direct the state and build "the new social regime" to bring about the "triumph of the revolution." He concludes: "We shall overcome."

F ellow citizens of Congress:
Appearing before you in fulfillment of the constitutional
mandate,[1] I attribute a two-fold importance to this Message. It is
the first message of a government which has just taken office, and it
corresponds to unique demands in our political history.

For this reason I wish to give it special content in accord with the
present significant moment and because of its implications for the
future.

For 27 years, I have attended this House, nearly always as a member
of the parliamentary opposition.[2] Today I attend as chief of state, elected
by the will of the people as ratified by the Congress.

I am well aware that here were debated and established the laws
which set up an agrarian structure based on big estates; but here too,
obsolete institutions were abolished in order to lay the legal foundations
of the land reform which we are now carrying out. Here were
established the institutional procedures for the foreign exploitation of
Chilean national resources; but this same Congress is now revising these
in order to return to the Chilean people what belongs to them by right.

Congress makes the legal institutions which regulate the social order
in which they are rooted; for this reason, for more than a century, it has
been more responsive to the interests of the powerful than to the
suffering of the people.

At the very commencement of this legislative period, I must raise this
problem. Chile now has in its government a new political force whose
social function is to uphold, not the traditional ruling class, but the vast
majority of the people. This change in the power structure must
necessarily be accompanied by profound changes in the socio-economic
order, changes which parliament is summoned to institutionalize.

This step forward in the liberation of Chilean energies for the
rebuilding of the nation must be followed by more decisive steps. The
land reform which is now in progress,[3] the nationalization of copper

---

[1] According to Article 56 of the Constitution: "Congress shall convene its ordinary
session on May 21 of each year, and adjourn on September 18. The President of the
Republic shall report to Congress on the administrative and political state of the
country at the inauguration of each ordinary legislative session."

[2] President Salvador Allende first won election as a Deputy in 1937, a position he
resigned in 1939 to become Minister of Health in the Popular Front Government of
Pedro Aguirre Cerda. He was a Senator from 1945 until his election to the presidency
in 1970, and President of the Senate from 1966 to 1969.

[3] Law 16,640 of July 28,1967, empowered the Executive to expropriate abandoned or
poorly cultivated plots and all first-class irrigated land exceeding 192 acres, or its
equivalent, in Santiago province. The previous government had expropriated 1,410
plots; in the first six months of the present administration, 504 plots have been
expropriated.

which is only awaiting the approval of the Plenary Congress,[4] must be followed by new reforms — whether these are initiated by parliament or by government proposal, or by the combined efforts of both powers, or by plebiscite,[5] which is a legal appeal to the foundation of all power, the sovereignty of the people.

We have accepted the challenge to reexamine everything. We urgently wish to ask of every law, every existing institution and even of every person whether or not they are furthering our integral and autonomous development.

I am sure that on few occasions in history has the parliament of any nation been presented with so great a challenge.

Overcoming capitalism in Chile

The circumstances of Russia in 1917 and of Chile at the present time are very different. Nevertheless, the historic challenge is similar.

In 1917, Russia took decisions which have had the most far-reaching effects on contemporary history. There it was believed that backward Europe could face up to advanced Europe, that the first socialist revolution need not necessarily take place in the heart of industrial power. There the challenge was accepted and the dictatorship of the proletariat, which is one of the methods of building a socialist society, was established.

Today nobody doubts that by this method nations with a large population can, in a relatively short period, break out of their backwardness and attain the most advanced level of contemporary civilization. The examples of the Soviet Union and of the Chinese People's Republic speak for themselves.

Like Russia then, Chile now faces the need to initiate new methods of constructing a socialist society. Our revolutionary method, the pluralist method, was anticipated by the classic Marxist theorists but never before put into practice. Social thinkers believed that the first to do so would be the more developed nations, probably Italy or France with their powerful Marxist-oriented working-class parties.

Nevertheless, once again, history has permitted a break with the past and the construction of a new model of society, not only where it was theoretically most predictable but where the most favorable concrete conditions had been created for its achievement. Today Chile is the first

---

[4] The Plenary Session of Congress, on July 11, 1971, approved a constitutional amendment which provides the legal means for the nationalization of the five largest cooper mines currently operating in the country. The Plenary Session is the meeting of both houses of Parliament, the Chamber of Deputies (lower house) and the Senate, as one body.

[5] The constitution provides for a plebiscite on certain matters when the Executive and Legislative branches cannot reach agreement.

nation on earth to put into practice the second model of transition to a socialist society.

This challenge is awakening great interest beyond our national frontiers. Everybody knows or guesses that here and now history is beginning to take a new direction, even as we Chileans are conscious of the undertaking. Some among us, perhaps the minority, see the enormous difficulties of the task. Others, the majority, are trying to envisage the possibility of facing it successfully. For my part, I am sure that we shall have the necessary energy and ability to carry on our effort and create the first socialist society built according to a democratic, pluralistic and libertarian model.

The skeptics and the prophets of doom will say that it is not possible. They will say that a parliament that has served the ruling classes so well cannot be transformed into the parliament of the Chilean people.

Further, they have emphatically stated that the armed forces and the corps of *Carabineros*, who have up to the present supported the institutional order that we wish to overcome, would not consent to guarantee the will of the people if these should decide on the establishment of socialism in our country. They forget the patriotic conscience of the armed forces and the *Carabineros*, their tradition of professionalism and their obedience to civil authority. In the words of General Schneider, the armed forces are "an integral and representative part of the nation as well as of the state structure, that is, they belong both to the permanent and the temporary spheres, and are therefore able to organize and counterbalance the periodic changes which affect political life within a legal regime."

Since the National Congress is based on the people's vote, there is nothing in its nature which prevents it from changing itself in order to become, in fact, the parliament of the people. The Chilean armed forces and the *Carabineros*, faithful to their duty and to their tradition of nonintervention in the political process, will support a social organization which corresponds to the will of the people as expressed in the terms of the established constitution. It will be a more just, a more humane and generous organization for everybody, but above all for the workers, who have contributed so much up to the present and have received almost nothing in return.

The difficulties we face are not in this field. They reside in the extraordinary complexity of the tasks before us: to create the political institutions which will lead to socialism, and to achieve this starting from our present condition of a society oppressed by backwardness and poverty which are the result of dependence and underdevelopment; to break with the factors which cause backwardness and, at the same time, to build a new socio-economic structure capable of providing for collective prosperity.

The causes of backwardness resided and still reside in the traditional ruling classes with their combination of dependence on external forces and internal class exploitation. They have profited from their association with foreign interests, and from their appropriation of the surplus produced by the workers, to whom they have only awarded the minimum indispensable for the renewal of their laboring capacities. Our first task is to dismantle this restrictive structure, which only produces a deformed growth. At the same time, we must build up a new economy so that it succeeds the previous one without continuing it, at the same time conserving to the maximum the productive and technical capacity that we have achieved despite the vicissitudes of our under-development; and we must build it up without crises artificially provoked by those whose ancient privileges we shall abolish.

In addition to these questions, there is another which is an essential challenge of our time: How can people in general and young people in particular develop a sense of mission which will inspire them with a new joy in living and give dignity to their existence?

There is no other way than that of devoting ourselves to the realization of great impersonal tasks, such as that of attaining a new stage in the human condition, until now degraded by its division into the privileged and the dispossessed. Today nobody can imagine solutions for the distant future when all nations will have attained abundance and realized the satisfaction of material needs and at the same time have assumed the cultural heritage of humanity. But here and now in Chile and in Latin America, we have the possibility and the duty of releasing creative energies, particularly those of youth, in missions which inspire us more than any in the past. Such is the aspiration to build a world which does away with divisions into rich and poor; and for our part, to build a society in which the war of economic competition is outlawed; in which the struggle for professional privileges has no meaning; in which there is no longer that indifference to the fate of others which permits the powerful to exploit the weak.

There have been few occasions in which men have needed so much faith in themselves and in their capacity to rebuild the world and regenerate their lives.

This is an unprecedented time, which offers us the material means of realizing the most generous utopian dreams of the past. The only thing that prevents our achieving this is the heritage of greed, of fear and of obsolete institutional traditions. Between our time and that of the liberation of man on a planetary scale, this inheritance has to be overcome. Only in this way will it be possible to call upon men to reconstruct their lives, not as products of a past of slavery and exploitation, but in the most conscious realization of their noblest potentialities. This is the socialist ideal.

An ingenuous observer from some developed country which has these material resources might suppose that this observation is a new manner that backward people have found of asking for aid — yet another plea of the poor for the charity of the rich. Such is not the case, but its opposite. With the internal authority of all societies brought under the hegemony of the dispossessed, with the change in international trade relations simulated by the exploited nations, there will come about not only the abolition of poverty and backwardness but also the liberation of the great powers from their despot's fate. Thus, in the same way as the emancipation of the slave liberates the slave owner, so the achievement of socialism envisaged by the peoples of our time is as meaningful for the disinherited peoples as for the more privileged, since both will then cast away the chains which degrade their society.

I stand here, members of the National Congress, to urge you to take up the task of reconstructing the Chilean nation according to our dreams, a Chile in which all children begin life equally, with equal medical care, education and nutrition. A Chile in which the creative ability of each man and woman is allowed to develop, not in competition with others, but in order to contribute to a better life for all.

Our road to socialism
To achieve these aspirations means a long road and a great effort on the part of all Chileans. It also implies, as a basic prerequisite, that we are able to establish the institutional apparatus of a new form of pluralistic, free socialist order. The task is one of extraordinary complexity because there are no precedents for us to follow. We are treading a new path. We are advancing without guides across unknown territory, but our compass is our faith in the humanism of all ages and particularly in Marxist humanism. Our aim is the establishment of the society that we want, the society which answers the deep-rooted desires of the Chilean people.

For a long time, science and technology have made it possible to create the productive system which will assure that everybody enjoys those basic necessities which today are enjoyed only by a minority. The difficulties are not technical, and — in our case at least — they are not due to a lack of national resources. What prevents the realization of our ideals is the organization of society, the nature of the interests which have so far dominated, the obstacles which dependent nations face. We must concentrate our attention on these structures and on these institutional requirements.

Speaking frankly, our task is to define and to put into practice, as the Chilean road to socialism, a new model of the state, of the economy and of society which revolves around man's needs and aspirations. For this we need the determination of those who have dared to reconsider the world in terms of a project designed for the service of man. There are no previous experiments that we can use as models; we shall have to develop the theory and practice of new forms of social, political and economic organization, both in order to break with underdevelopment and to create socialism.

We can achieve this only on condition that we do not overshoot or depart from our objective. If we should forget that our mission is to establish a social plan for man, the whole struggle of our people for socialism will become simply one more reformist experiment. If we should forget the concrete conditions from which we start in order to try and create immediately something which surpasses our possibilities, then we shall also fail.

We are moving towards socialism, not from an academic love for a doctrinaire system, but encouraged by the strength of our people, who know that it is an inescapable demand if we are to overcome backwardness and who feel that a socialist regime is the only way available to modern nations who want to build rationally in freedom, independence and dignity. We are moving towards socialism because the people, through their vote, have freely rejected capitalism as a system which has resulted in a crudely unequal society, a society deformed by social injustice and degraded by the deterioration of the very foundations of human solidarity.

In the name of the socialist reconstruction of Chilean society, we have won the presidential elections, a victory that was confirmed by the election of municipal councilors. This is the flag behind which we are mobilizing the people politically both as the object of our plans and as the justification for our actions. Our government plans are those of the Popular Unity[6] platform on which we fought the election. In putting them into effect, we shall not sacrifice attention to the present needs of the Chilean people in favor of gigantic schemes. Our objective is none other than the progressive establishment of a new structure of power, founded on the will of the majority and designed to satisfy in the shortest possible time the most urgent needs of the present generation.

Sensitivity to the claims of the people is in fact the only way we have of contributing to the solution of the great human problems; for no universal value is worth the name if it cannot be applied on the national or regional scale and even to the local living conditions of each family.

---

[6] Unidad Popular is the name of the coalition formed by the Socialist, Communist and Radical Parties, the Movement of United Popular Action (MAPU), the Social Democratic Party and the Independent Popular Action (API). These parties form the base of the present government. The election for municipal councillors, held on April 4, 1971, saw the governing Popular Unity winning 49.7 percent of the vote in a four-way field.

Our policy might seem too simple for those who prefer big promises. But the people need decent housing for their families, with proper sanitation; they need schools for their children which are not expressly intended for the poor; they need enough to eat every day of the year; they need work; they need care during sickness and in old age; they need to be respected as people. That is what we hope to offer all Chileans in the foreseeable future. This is what has been denied the people in Latin America throughout the centuries. This is what some nations are now beginning to guarantee their entire population.

But beyond this task, and as a fundamental prerequisite for its achievement, there is another equally important one. It is to engage the will of the Chilean people to dedicate our hands, our minds and our feelings to the reassertion of our identity as a people, in order to become an integral part of contemporary civilization as masters of our fate and heirs to the patrimony of technical skills, knowledge, art and culture. Turning the nation's attention to these fundamental aspirations is the only way to satisfy the people's needs and to wipe out the differences between them and the privileged classes. Above all, it is the only way to provide the young with a mission by opening up broad perspectives of a fruitful existence as builders of the society in which they will live.

The mandate entrusted to us embraces all the nation's material and spiritual resources. We have reached a point at which retreat or a standstill would mean an irreparable national catastrophe. It is my obligation at this time, as the one primarily responsible for the fate of Chile, to indicate clearly the road which we are taking and the dangers and hopes which it offers.

The Popular Government knows that the transcendence of a historical period is determined by social and economic factors which have already been shaped by this same period. These factors embrace the agents and modes of historical change. To ignore this would be to go against the nature of things.

In the revolutionary process which we are living through, there are five essential points upon which we shall concentrate our social and political campaign: the principle of legality, the development of institutions, political freedom, the prevention of violence, and the socialization of the means of production. These are questions which affect the present and the future of every citizen.

The principle of legality
Legality is a governing principle today in Chile. It has been achieved as a result of the struggle of many generations against absolutism and arbitrary exercise of state power. It is an irreversible achievement for as long as differences exist between rulers and ruled.

It is not the principle of legality which the mass movements are protesting against. We are protesting against a legal system whose basic assumptions reflect an oppressive social order. Our legal norms and the regulating machinery of Chilean social relationships correspond at the present time to the needs of the capitalist system. In the transition to socialism, legal norms will correspond to the needs of a people engaged in building a new society. But there will be legality.

Our legal system must be modified. Hence the great responsibility of the two Houses at the present time: to help and not to hinder the changes in this system. On whether the Congress takes a realistic attitude depends to a great extent whether capitalist legality will be succeeded by socialist legality in conformity with the social and economic changes we are making and without a violent break in jurisdiction which would open the door to arbitrary acts and excesses which we, as responsible people, wish to avoid.

The development of institutions
The obligation to organize and govern society according to the rule of law is inherit in our system of institutions. The struggle of the popular movements and parties which are now in the government has contributed greatly to one of the most promising situations to obtain in this country. We have an open system which has defied even those who would seek to infringe upon the will of the people.

The flexibility of our institutions allows us to hope that they will not be a bitter bone of contention. And that, like our legal system, they will adapt to new needs in order to give rise, by constitutional means, to the new institutions required by the overthrow of capitalism.

The new institutions will conform to the principle which justifies and guides our actions, that is, the transference of political and economic power to the workers and to the people as a whole. In order to make this possible, the first priority is the socialization of the basic means of production.

At the same time, political institutions must be adjusted to this new situation. For this reason we shall, at an opportune moment, submit to the sovereign will of the people the necessity of replacing the present constitution, with its liberal foundations, by a constitution of a socialist nature and of replacing the bicameral system by a single house.

It is in accordance with this that we have committed ourselves in our government program to the realization of our revolutionary task while respecting the rule of law. It is not simply a formal commitment but an explicit recognition that the principles of legality and institutional order are inseparable from a socialist regime despite the difficulties involved in the transitional period.

To maintain these institutions while changing their class basis during this difficult period is an ambitious undertaking of decisive importance for the new social order. Nevertheless, its achievement does not depend solely on our will. It will depend fundamentally on the planning of our social and economic structure, on its short-term evolution and on the degree of realism shown by our people in their political action. At the moment we believe that it is possible, and we are acting upon that assumption.

Political freedom
It is also important to remember that for us, as representatives of the popular forces, political freedom represents the achievement of the people on the difficult road to emancipation. It is an element of real achievement in the historical period that we are now leaving behind. And for this reason, freedom must remain. That is why we respect freedom of conscience for all creeds. That is why we are happy to underline the words of the Cardinal Archbishop of Santiago, Raúl Silva Henríquez, in his message to the workers: *The Church which I represent is the Church of Jesus, the son of a carpenter. It began as such, and as such we go on loving it. Its greatest sorrow is that people believe it has forgotten its cradle, which is among the humble.*

But we would not be revolutionaries if we limited ourselves simply to preserving political freedom. The Popular Unity Government will strengthen political liberties. It is not sufficient to proclaim them verbally, because this makes them a source of frustration or mockery. We shall make them real, tangible and concrete, and practicable in the process of achieving economic freedom.

In consequence, the Popular Government bases its policy on a premise which some people artificially reject, that is, on the existence of social classes and sectors with opposing and mutually exclusive interests, and on the existence of unequal political levels within the same class or group.

In the face of this diversity, our government is concerned with the interests of all those who earn their living by their own labor: workers, members of the professions, technicians, artists, intellectuals and white collar workers. These are a group which is growing as a result of capitalist development and becoming more united because of its members' common condition as wage-earners. For the same reason, the government gives protection to both the small and the medium-sized business sectors, that is, to all sectors which, to a greater or lesser extent, are exploited by the minority who hold the centers of power.

The multi-party coalition of the Popular Government corresponds to this reality. And in the daily confrontation of its interests with those of the ruling classes, it uses the techniques of bargaining and agreement established by the legal system, recognizing at the same time the political freedom of the opposition and keeping its own actions within institutional limitations. Political freedom represents the achievement of the entire Chilean people as a nation.

As president of the republic, I have fully ratified all these principles of action, which are supported by our revolutionary political theory, conform to the present national situation, and are included in the program of the Popular Unity Government.

They form part of our plan for developing to the maximum the political potentialities of our country so that the stage of transition towards socialism will be characterized by the selective overcoming of the present system. This will be achieved by destroying or abandoning its negative and oppressive features and by strengthening and broadening its positive features.

Violence

The Chilean people are achieving political power without having to use arms. They are taking the road of social emancipation having had to fight only the limitations of a liberal democracy and not a despotic or dictatorial regime. Our people legitimately hope to go through the stage of transition to socialism without having recourse to authoritarian forms of government.

Our wishes are very clear on this point. But the responsibility for guaranteeing the political evolution towards socialism does not reside only in the government and in those movements and parties which it comprises. Our people have stood up to the institutionalized violence which the present capitalist system has held over them. And for this reason we are changing the basis of that system.

My government owes its existence to the popular will freely expressed. It answers to this alone. The movements and parties which are included in it reflect the revolutionary conscience of the masses and express the people's ambitions and interests. They are directly responsible to the people.

Nevertheless, it is my duty to warn you that a danger may threaten the straight road to emancipation and could radically alter the direction which our situation and our collective conscience have marked out for us. This danger is violence directed against the people's determination.

Should violence from within or without, should violence in any form, whether physical, economic, social or political, happen to threaten our normal development and the achievement of our workers, then the integrity of our institutions, the rule of law, political freedom and pluralism will be put in the greatest danger. The fight for social emancipation and for the free determination of our people would necessarily take a different form from that which we, with legitimate pride and historical realism, call the Chilean road to socialism. The determined attitude of the government and the revolutionary energy of the people, the democratic resolution of the armed forces and the *Carabineros*, will see that Chile advances surely along the road to emancipation.

The unity of the popular forces and the good sense of the middle sectors give us the necessary superiority to prevent the privileged minority from having recourse to violence. If violence is not released against the people, we shall be able to change the basic structures on which the capitalist system rests into a democratic, pluralistic and free society, and to do this without unnecessary physical force, without institutional disorder, without disorganizing production, and at a speed which the government will determine according to the needs of the people and the level of development of our resources.

The attainment of social freedom

Our aim is the attainment of social freedom through the exercise of political freedom, and this requires the establishment of economic equality as a basis. This is the road which the people have decided upon because they know that the revolutionary transformation of a social system must go through intermediate stages. A revolution that is simply political may consume itself in a few weeks. A social and economic revolution takes years. Time is necessary for the conscience of the masses to be penetrated, for new structures to be organized and made operable as well as to be adapted to the existing ones. It is sheer utopianism to imagine that the intermediary stages can be skipped. It is not possible to destroy a social and economic structure and existing social institutions without at least having first developed a replacement. If the natural exigencies of historical change are not recognized, then reality will remind us of them.

We are very well aware of the lesson of victorious revolutions, the revolutions of those countries which, faced with foreign pressure and civil war, had to speed up their social and economic revolution in order not to fall back into bloody despotism and counterrevolution. Only recently, decades afterwards, have they organized the necessary structures for the definitive overthrow of the previous regime.

The direction which my government has planned takes into account these facts. We know that to change the capitalist system while respecting law, institutions and political freedoms demands that we confine within certain limits our actions in the economic, political and social fields. This is perfectly well known to every Chilean. These limits are indicated in the government program which is being carried out resolutely and without concessions, and in the manner and at the speed which we have previously made known.

The Chilean people, showing their increasing maturity and organization, have entrusted the Popular Government with the defense of their interests. This obligates the government to act on the basis of its total identification and integration with the masses whose will it interprets and orients and prevents it from distancing itself from the masses and acting in a dilatory or precipitate manner. Today more than ever, the synchronization between the people, the popular parties and the government must be precise and dynamic.

Every historical change corresponds to conditions established at previous stages and creates the elements and agents which are to follow. To pass the transitional stage without restriction of their political liberties, without having a legal or institutional vacuum, is a right and a legitimate demand of our people, its full material realization in concrete terms being presumed in a socialist society. The Popular Government will fulfill its responsibility at this decisive time.

The principal constructive agent of the new regime consists in the organization and the conscience of our people, in permanent mobilization in many forms— political parties of the masses, labor unions — according to the objective needs of each moment.

We hope that this responsibility, which is not necessarily that of the government alone, is shared by the Christian Democratic Party,[7] which must demonstrate consistency in adhering to the principles and programs which it has so often laid before the country.

Socialization of the means of production

Fellow citizens: In six months of government, we have acted with decision on all fronts. Our economic work has been aimed at breaking down the barriers which impede the complete fulfillment of our material and human potentialities. In six months of government, we have advanced energetically along the path of irrevocable change. The printed statement which we have just distributed gives a full and detailed account of our activities.

Chile has begun the definitive recovery of our most fundamental source of wealth: copper. The nationalization of our copper is not an act of vengeance or hatred directed towards any group, government or nation. We are, on the contrary, positively exercising an inalienable right on behalf of a sovereign people: that of the full enjoyment of our national resources exploited by our national labor and effort. The recovery of copper is a decision by the whole of Chile, and we demand that all countries and governments respect the unanimous decision of a free people. We shall pay for the copper if it is right to pay, and we shall

---

[7] The Christian Democratic Party, headed by President Eduardo Frei, governed the country from November 4, 1964, to November 3, 1970.

not pay if it is unjust. We shall watch over our interests. But we shall be implacable if we find out that negligence or fraudulent activity on the part of any persons or entities has harmed the country.

We have nationalized another of our basic resources: iron. A short time ago, negotiations with the Bethlehem corporation were concluded,[8] and as a result, iron mining passed over completely to public ownership. We are now studying the constitution of the national steel complex which will group six companies together around the CAP.[9] The agreement with North American industry has once again shown that the government is offering a fair settlement to foreign capital without sacrificing the fundamental interests of our nation. But we are not prepared to tolerate the contempt for our laws and the lack of respect for established authority that we find in some foreign firms. We have also taken over coal as collective property.[10]

The nitrate resources are also ours.[11] According to a settlement by the previous government, we owed $24 million in debentures payable in 15 years, which with interest amounts to $38 million. The shares belonging to the North American sector were theoretically worth $25 million. All this has now been redeemed for $8 million payable in two years.

We have incorporated various firms — among them Purina,[12] Lanera Austral, and the Bellavista Tomé, Fiap and Fabrilana textile plants[13] — into the area of public ownership; we have requisitioned the cement industry and the Yarur [textile] industry when supplies were threatened. In order to prevent bankruptcy, we have acquired an important share of the assets of the Zig Zag Publishing House, which forms a big part of our graphics and publishing industry, so that it can satisfy the cultural needs of the new Chile.

---

[8] The government of Chile bought the stock of Bethlehem Steel following negotiations toward a contract signed in March of 1971.

[9] The National Steel Complex will comprise the state-owned Compañía de Aceros del Pacífico (CAP, Pacific Steel Industry), and a number of related industries dealing with iron ore, industrial or metallurgical processing and certain areas of household appliances (white line). The 60 percent of CAP's stock that was privately owned in the past was purchased by the state in March 1971.

[10] The state bought, through the Corporación de Fomento de la Producción (Development Corporation), 51 percent of the stock of the Lota Schwager Company; the remaining 49 percent is in the hands of small private stockholders.

[11] Since 1967, the exploitation of nitrates had been carried on by a mixed enterprise, in which the state owned 37.5 percent of the stock, the rest belonging to Anglo Lautaro Company. In 1970 the state's share rose to 51 percent, and on May 28, 1971, the state legally purchased the remainder of the stock.

[12] Animal-feed industry. The state entered negotiations for the purchase of its stock at the beginning of 1971.

[13] The government's actions have been directed towards the establishment of a national textile complex that would increase output and prevent unemployment in this area.

In all the firms that have been taken into public ownership, the nation can bear witness to the determined support of the workers, the immediate increase in productivity, and the active participation of workers, white-collar personnel and technicians in management and administration.

We have speeded up land reform and have already achieved a major part of this year's plan: the expropriation of 1,000 big estates. The reform is going forward in accordance with existing legislation, and is protecting the interests of the small and medium-sized farmers. We want to build up a new and more vigorous agriculture, more solid in organization and more productive. We want the men who work the land to benefit fairly from the fruits of their labor. The state ownership of banks has been a decisive step.[14] With absolute respect for the rights of the small shareholder, we have established state control over nine banks and are on the point of obtaining majority control in the others. On the basis of previous experience, we are hoping for a reasonable settlement with foreign banks. We are thus trying to gain control of the financial apparatus and to widen the social area in the sectors which produce material goods. We want to place the new banking system at the service of the socialized area and of the small and medium-sized industrialists, merchants and farmers, who until now have been discriminated against.

Our present economic policy
These have been our first acts towards the initiation of the essential and definitive change in our economy. But we have done not only this. We have also planned a short-term policy whose central objective has been to increase the availability of material goods and services for consumption, and we have directed that increase towards the less-favored sectors.

We are carrying on a fierce struggle against inflation,[15] and this is the key to our policy of redistribution. The fight against inflation has acquired a new political connotation; it will be a dynamic element in the popular struggle. To halt the rise in prices means that the people will maintain the increased spending power that has been given them, and this will be definitively consolidated with the deeper entrenchment of socialist organization. At the same time, independent businessmen can

---

[14] As of June 30, 1971, the state had obtained a majority control of the stock of 11 of the 20 national private banks existing in the country. The government was carrying on negotiations with each of the six foreign banks operating in the country. The objective of this nationalization is to democratize credit, that is, to facilitate a more even distribution by location and economic activity and to make credit available to a larger number of people.

[15] The consumer price index for the first six months of 1970 rose by 23.9 percent. The figure for the same period in 1971 was 11.1 percent.

earn fair profits, the higher volume of production compensating for the smaller profits on each item. In practice this policy has borne appreciable fruits in terms of redistribution. Nevertheless, we know that this planned reactivation faces obstacles. On the one hand, some groups of business are attempting to hinder the success of our measures by means of an open or a covert slowdown in production. On the other hand, some sectors which are imprisoned in a traditional model of low production and high profit lack audacity and are unable to understand the present juncture or to play a greater part in the productive process. To do so is, nevertheless, their social duty. To those who do not fulfill this duty, whether deliberately or not, we shall apply all the legal resources within our power to go on urging them and, if necessary, to make them produce more.

We are also carrying out a social policy to improve the diet of our children; to provide speedier medical care; to increase substantially the capacity of our educational system; to initiate the necessary housing construction program; and to plan greater absorption of the unemployed as an urgent national need. We are doing this without disorder and with justice, endeavoring always to keep the social cost as low as possible. Today the citizen of our nation has greater buying power, consumes more and feels that the fruit of the common effort is better distributed. At the same time, he has the right to feel that he owns the mines, the banks, industry and the land, that he owns the future.

We are neither measuring ourselves against nor comparing ourselves with previous governments. We are fundamentally different. But if that comparison were to be made, using even the most traditional indicators, we would come out favorably. We have achieved the lowest rate of inflation in recent years; we have begun the most effective redistribution of revenues that Chile has ever seen. We shall build more houses this year than have ever been built before in a similar period. Despite the gloomy predictions, we have maintained the normal flow in supplies of essential goods.

Limits on government action
We are fundamentally different from previous governments. This government will always speak the truth to the people. I believe it is my duty to state honestly that we have committed mistakes; that unforeseen difficulties are slowing down the execution of plans and programs. But although the copper produced was not up to the target and although nitrate production did not reach a million tons, although we did not build all the houses that we planned, in each one of these sectors we have surpassed the highest rate of copper and nitrate production and of housing construction that our country has ever recorded. We have not

managed to coordinate adequately the various institutions of the state sector, owing to inefficiency in some decisions. But we are designing more expeditious methods of rationalizing and planning.

Immediately on assuming power, we set ourselves to fulfill our promises to the country. Together with the Unitary Workers Center[16] we studied the Readjustments Law[17] and signed the CUT-government agreement. We have sent a bill to Congress in which we propose for the public sector a pay increase 100 percent equal to the rise in the cost of living, and an increase on a greater scale in the corresponding minimum wages in the private sector. But I believe it was a mistake not to come to a broad agreement with the workers in order to arrive at more precise readjustments applicable in both the public and the private sectors.

Another limitation that we have suffered lies in the administrative, legal and procedural deficiencies of some of the basic government plans. For this reason the housing project, for example, got off to a slow start; and this has prevented the reactivation of certain industries and the absorption of a greater number of unemployed. In the months of April and May, economic activity connected with building began to get under way.

There is a vast area of public activity, comprising the public service sector, where there are deep-rooted evils. Millions of Chileans are the daily victims of bureaucratic paperwork, of delays and red tape. Each step requires dozens of transactions, forms, signatures and official stamps. How many hours are lost by every Chilean in his fight against red tape, how much creative energy is lost, how much useless irritation suffered. The government authorities have still not directed sufficient effort towards eradicating this endemic evil. The most responsible sectors of white-collar workers have called attention to it.

We have also moved slowly in outlining the social machinery for the participation of the people. The bill which will give legal status to CUT is now ready; it will institutionalize the participation of the workers in the political, social and economic management both of the state and of economic enterprises. But we have barely outlined the form their participation will take in the regions, in the communities and in private organizations. We ought to guarantee not only a vertical participation of workers in their separate branches — that of industrial workers, for example, in their plants — but also a horizontal participation which allows peasants, manufacturing workers, miners, white-collar workers and members of the professions to come together and discuss the problems of a particular economic region or of the country as a whole.

[16] Central Unica de Trabajadores (CUT), national workers confederation of Chile.

[17] Ley de Reajustes. Every year Congress passes legislation specifying the scale of remuneration of government employees; remunerations in the private sector are affected by the setting of minimum levels for this sector.

These types of participation not only tend to bring about a fairer distribution of income but also help to ensure a greater yield.

This horizontal integration of the people is not easy and will doubtless require political maturity and collective consciousness, but it is well for us to start realizing now that the improvement of production on a collective farm depends also on workers in machinery and in tool and fertilizer plants, on the workers who build new roads, and on the small and medium-sized merchants who distribute the goods. Production is the responsibility of the working class as a whole.

Another criticism which we have to make of ourselves is that in these first six months we have still not managed to mobilize the intellectual, artistic and professional capacity of many Chileans. There is some way to go before all scientists, members of the professional classes, builders, artists, technicians, householders, all those who can and wish to cooperate in the transformation of society, find a place in which they can use their talents.

The immediate tasks
In the remaining months of 1971, copper will definitely come under Chilean ownership. On the efforts of the workers, white-collar personnel and technicians of the Chuquicamata, El Teniente, Exótica, El Salvador and Andina mines[18] depends to a great extent the volume of production which we shall achieve this year, and therefore our ability to obtain foreign exchange and so maintain normal supplies and realize our investment programs. Copper represents the livelihood of Chile. Those who administer this wealth and those who extract it from the earth hold in their hands not only their own destiny and their own well-being but also the destiny and well-being of all Chileans.

We must extend land reform and if necessary modify the law, for if copper is Chile's livelihood, the land is its bread.

The land must be made to produce more. This is the responsibility of the peasants and of the small and medium-sized landowners, but the government recognizes its mistakes and it is fair that others should also recognize theirs. The occupation of land by squatters, the indiscriminate occupation of agricultural terrains, is unnecessary and harmful. Belief in the government is warranted by what we have done and by our attitudes. For this reason, the plans made by the government and the time fixed for their execution must be respected. We invite political

---

18 These are the five largest copper-mining enterprises and constitute what is called the *Gran Minería* (Great Mining). They have operated in the last few years as mixed enterprises in which the state controlled between 25 and 51 percent of the shares. The companies, who owned the rest of the shares, were Anaconda Company (El Salvador, Exótica and Chuquicamata), Kennecott Copper Corporation (El Teniente) and Cerro Corporation (Andina).

groups and individuals who are not in the Popular Unity to meditate seriously upon this.

Fellow citizens: The creation of the area of social ownership is one of our great objectives. The incorporation into this area of the major part of our basic wealth, the banks, the big estates and a large proportion of our foreign trade as well as of industrial and distributive monopolies is a task that we have already begun and that must now be amplified.

On the economic plane, the establishment of socialism means replacing the capitalist mode of production by a qualitative change in the relations of ownership; it also implies a redefinition of the relations of production. In this context, the creation of the area of social ownership has a human, political, and economic significance. The incorporation of large sectors of the productive apparatus into a system of collective ownership puts an end to the exploitation of the worker, creates a deep feeling of solidarity, and permits the individual worker and his efforts to form part of the common work and the common endeavor.

In the political field, the working class knows that it is fighting for the socialization of our principal means of production. There is no socialism without an area of social ownership. To incorporate new firms day by day requires a permanent state of vigilance on the part of the working class. It also requires a high degree of responsibility. To construct socialism is not an easy task; it is not a short task. It is a long and difficult task in which the working class ought to participate in a disciplined, organized and politically responsible manner, avoiding anarchistic decisions and inconsistent voluntarism.

The importance of the public sector is traditional in our country. Approximately 40 percent of spending is public. More than 70 percent of investment is of state origin. The public sector was created by the national bourgeoisie in order to promote private accumulation and to consolidate the means of production, concentrating their technological resources and ownership.

Our government wants to make this sector quantitatively more important, but also to make it qualitatively different.

The state apparatus has been used by monopolies for the purpose of relieving their financial difficulties, for obtaining economic help and for strengthening the system. Up to now the public sector has been characterized by its subsidiary role in relation to the private sector. For this reason some public enterprises show large total deficits, while others are unable to produce profits comparable in size to those of some private enterprises.

Besides, the state machinery of Chile has lacked the necessary coordination between its different activities. As long as this is the case, it will be impossible for it to make a decisive contribution to a socialist economy. The control of some branches of production does not mean that the public sector has the machinery to direct and fulfill the objectives of socialism with respect to employment, saving, increase in productivity and the redistribution of income.

It is therefore necessary to widen the scope of public ownership and give it a new outlook. The expropriation of the most important means of production will permit the attainment of the degree of cohesion in this public machinery indispensable for the realization of the great national objectives. Hence one of the general criteria for the definition of the area of public ownership is the need to conceive this as a single, integrated whole, able to realize all its potentialities in a short or medium term.

This implies an urgent need to set up a planning system which devotes the economic surplus to the different productive assignments. This year we have begun to set up such a system, creating advisory bodies such as the National and Regional Development Councils.[19] The Annual Plan for 1971 has been laid down and for the rest of the year the planning organizations will work out the national economic plan for 1971-1976. It is our intention that no investment project shall be carried forward unless it is included in these centrally approved government plans. In this manner, we shall put an end to improvisation and begin to organize socialist planning in agreement with the Popular Unity program. The existence of socialized ownership requires, by definition, a planning method which is both capable and effective and which is endowed with sufficient institutional power.

The advantages of socialism are not spectacularly displayed in the first stages of construction. But the creation of a real morality of work and the political mobilization of the proletariat not only around the government but also around the means of production will overcome the obstacles.

The establishment of the area of public ownership does not mean the creation of a state capitalism, but the true beginning of a socialist structure. The sector of public ownership will be directed jointly by the workers and by representatives of the state, as the uniting link between each enterprise and the whole of the national economy. It will not be inefficient bureaucratic enterprises but highly productive units which will lead the country's development and confer a new dimension on labor relations.

---

[19] The National Development Council is chaired by the president of the republic and consists of several Cabinet ministers, the leadership of various economic institutions, and management and worker representatives. Its objective is to assist the president in formulating plans for development. The Regional Development Councils are formed by local authorities and include worker and management representatives; their function is to assist the President in setting guidelines for development policies for each region.

Our transitional regime does not consider the existence of the market as the only regulator of the economic process. Planning will be the main guide for the productive processes. Some will believe that there are other ways. But the formation of workers' enterprises integrated into the liberal market would mean dressing up wage-earners as so-called capitalists and pursuing a method which is a historical failure.

The supremacy of social ownership implies holding back and utilizing the surplus that has been produced. It is therefore necessary to guarantee that the financial sector and a large part of the distributive sector be included in the area of public ownership. In short, we have to control the productive, and financial processes and also, to some extent, the trade sector.

We have to strengthen the area of social ownership, pouring the power of the state, expressed in its economic policy, into this task; our credit policy, our fiscal, monetary and wage policies, our scientific and technological policies, our trade policy, must all be subordinated to the needs of socialist accumulation, that is to say, to the interests of the workers.

Simultaneously, we must help the small and medium-sized industrialists, shopkeepers and farmers, who have for many years belonged to a sector exploited by the big monopolies, to make their contribution. Our economic policy guarantees them a fair deal. There will be no more financial exploitation, and the large-scale buyer's extortion from those who sell on a small scale will end. The small and medium-sized industries will play an active part in the new economy. Within a more rationally organized machinery which is directed towards production for the great majority of the nation, they will appreciate the support of the public sector. The limits of the private, mixed and public sectors will be precisely drawn.

We are facing an option for change unique in economic history. No country has achieved an acceptable economic development without huge sacrifices. We do not pretend to have discovered the recipe for making economic progress and achieving a fairer social system without cost. We are not offering to build overnight a socialized economy with fair distribution of income, with monetary stability and full employment, with high levels of productivity. On the other hand, we are offering to build that society at the least possible social cost imaginable in our circumstances.

Socialism is not a free gift which people happen to find in their path. Neither is the liberation that accompanies it.

Attaining it means postponing some present possibilities in exchange for founding a more humane, richer and more just society for the future.

Our foreign policy

The same principles which inform our internal policy inform the foreign policy of the country. In agreement with the United Nations Charter, our country resolutely supports nonintervention in the internal affairs of nations, juridical equality between them, and respect for their sovereignty and for the exercise of their right to self-determination.

My government's foreign policy is directed both bilaterally and multilaterally towards the consolidation of peace and towards international cooperation. As a result, Chile has extended its diplomatic relations to new countries. Our first decision, in obedience to the wish of the majority of the Chilean people, was to reestablish relations with Cuba, upon which unjust sanctions had been imposed. We have also established diplomatic and economic relations with China, Nigeria and the German Democratic Republic. We have established commercial relations with the Democratic Republics of Korea and North Vietnam, and within the Latin American sphere we have supported the reduction of arms before the Organization of American States.[20]

Chile collaborated in the "Declaration of the Principles of International Law for Friendship and Cooperation Between Nations," adopted by the General Assembly of the United Nations at the end of last year. We have also supported a program of action to apply the "Declaration on the Granting of Independence to Colonial Nations and Peoples," and we have taken part in the formulation of the international strategy for the "Second Decade of the United Nations Development Program."

Our fight against underdevelopment and against dependence on foreign hegemonies gives Chile a community of interests with the peoples of Africa and Asia. For this reason the Popular Government has decided to participate actively in the group of so-called unaligned nations and to take a determined part in their deliberations and agreements. Our concept of the universal scope of the United Nations leads us to vote in favor of the legitimate rights of the Chinese People's Republic. Our respect for the independence of all countries requires us to condemn the Vietnam war and its extension into Laos and Cambodia.

Within the general lines of this policy, we are collaborating in the United Nations Commission for Trade and Development (UNCTAD), the third world conference of which will take place in Santiago in April 1972. Furthermore, I have the honor to inform you that I have received repeated invitations to visit countries of this and other continents. I have thanked these nations for their courtesy in the name of Chile.

It is the purpose of this government to maintain friendly and

---

[20] A regional organization comprising the nations of the Western Hemisphere, except for Cuba, which was excluded in January 1962, and Canada, which never joined.

cooperative relations with the United States. We have persevered in creating the conditions for making our position understood in order to avoid the outbreak of conflict and to prevent inessential questions from hindering this purpose and making it difficult to negotiate the friendly settlement of any problems that might arise. We believe that this realistic and objective course of action will be respected by the people and the government of the United States.

We have raised our voice as a sovereign people respected by all nations, and with the dignity of those who speak in the name of a worthy country. This we have done in ECLA[21] and CIAP,[22] and in all the special meetings where our representatives have expressed our thinking.

We have spoken repeatedly of the deep crisis which the inter-American system and its representative body, the Organization of American States, are passing through. The said system is based upon a supposed equality among its members when, in fact, there is absolute inequality, when the marked imbalance in favor of the United States protects the interests of the most powerful and prejudices those of the weaker nations. This takes place in a global context of dependence whose negative effects are evident at all levels. Thus the present dollar crisis, which had its origin in the internal and foreign policy of the United States, threatens to injure all the industrial capitalist countries. But it will have even more harmful repercussions upon the Latin American economies to the extent that it reduces our monetary reserves, diminishes our credit and restricts trade relations.

We also insist that the multilateral character of international financial organizations must be maintained free of all political pressures.

The member countries of these institutions cannot have their rights questioned because of the form of government they have chosen. And the international financial organizations cannot act on behalf of powerful countries against the weak. To use direct or hidden pressure in order to hinder the financing of technically suitable projects is to alter the declared aims of these organizations and represents a perverse way of interfering in the internal affairs of those countries in defiance of their needs.

Our efforts to broaden and strengthen all kinds of relations with the countries of Western Europe have been greeted with definite interest on their part, an interest which has already had real results.

---

21 The Economic Commission for Latin America, a subsidiary body of the United Nations Economic and Social Council with headquarters in Santiago. The Commission was created in 1948 to provide studies, analyses and recommendations for the development of the region.

22 The Inter-American Committee for the Alliance for Progress, created in 1963 to make an annual examination of the progress of development of the member nations and make recommendations for the assignment of funds.

In the increase in exchange and collaboration with the socialist countries my government sees a suitable method of protecting our interests and simulating the economy, technology, science and culture as a means of serving the working class of the entire world.

Latin America is in an abject state which none of its countries have been able to change by the traditional and ineffective means.

For some time Colombia, Peru, Bolivia, Ecuador and Chile proposed replacing the old formulas by new ones which, through regional integration, will permit the harmonious development of our resources in favor of our common objectives. The Andean Pact[23] is an exemplary undertaking into which the Popular Unity Government is putting all its efforts. We have demonstrated as much both in Lima and Bogotá.

My government attaches special importance to maintaining the best possible relations with the sister nations of the continent. It is our fundamental aim to strengthen all the links which will increase our continued friendship with the Argentine Republic, eliminating the obstacles which stand in the way of realizing this objective. The anomalous state of our relations with the Republic of Bolivia conflicts with the aims of both peoples, and for this reason we shall do everything in our power to restore them to normal.[24]

The workers' leading role
Everything we have discussed in the political, economic, cultural and international fields represents the task of a whole nation, not that of one man or one government.

Between the months of November and February, the number of workers who have been obliged to go on strike has decreased from 170,000 to 76,000. The Popular Government's identification with the workers who share its successes and setbacks has made disputes unnecessary which were formerly inevitable. This year there have been no strikes in the coal, nitrate, copper, iron and textiles industries, the health services, education or railroads. In other words, there have been no strikes in those sectors which are vital to the nation's progress.

I should like to emphasize that for the first time in Chile, voluntary work has been introduced on a permanent basis in some state enterprises. And also, that for the first time it is being carried on in all areas of national life and on a massive scale from Arica to the Straits of Magellan. Soldiers, priests, students, workers, members of the professions and shopkeepers, old and young, are participating freely, spontaneously and in their own time in the common tasks. It is a much

---

23 A regional agreement between Colombia, Ecuador, Bolivia, Peru and Chile, signed at Cartagena, Colombia, in May 1969, for the purpose of economic cooperation.
24 Chile and Bolivia broke off diplomatic relations in October of 1962 because of a disagreement over the use of waters of the border river Lauca.

more creative development than working for profit. And it is an eloquent reply to those who, inside and outside Chile, would like to believe things that have never happened never will. In this country there is and there will be a government which knows what methods to apply and when to apply them. As president, I assume responsibility for this.

The great achievements that lie before us will depend on the responsible and determined identification of the worker with his own real interests, which are more far reaching than the small or big problems of this day, this month or this year. In the solidarity of the workers and their political representative, the Popular Government, we have an invincible instrument.

Those who live by their work have in their hands today the political direction of the state. It is a supreme responsibility. The building of the new social regime is based on the people, who are its protagonist and its judge. It is up to the state to guide, organize and direct but never to replace the will of the workers. In the economic as well as in the political field, the workers must retain the right to decide. To attain this means the triumph of the revolution.

The people are fighting for this goal. They are fighting with the legitimacy that comes from respecting democratic values; with the assurance given by our program; with the strength of being the majority; with the passion of the revolutionary.

We shall overcome.

10

My View of Marxism

From press conference, May 25, 1971

In his response to a reporter's question about his First Annual Message to the National Congress, Allende expresses his view of Marxism as "a method for interpreting history" and not a dogma. He also distinguishes Chile's democratic path to socialism from the notion of "a dictatorship of the proletariat."

Question (EFE Agency): Mr. President, in the Message to Congress on May 21 you had the opportunity to give the most complete definition yet of the political process that the country is going through. If I am not mistaken, you stated that it is the second model for a transition toward socialism. For some Marxist theorists your words could seem, from what I understand, somewhat heterodox. For others they are really a manifestation of the richness of the doctrine, that allows for this other manifestation. Given this, I would like to ask you to elaborate in relation to these two interpretations.

Salvador Allende: Your question, without a doubt, is very important. I must make it clear that I am not a theorist of Marxism. I am a man who has read some theorists of Marxism. However I do not have the arrogance to think that I am an authority on this matter. I am, however, pleased that what I have said has at least provoked some reflection. Not wanting to make wild or pedantic statements — but as a man who is not a theorist — I will say that Marxism is not a static thing; I believe it is a method to interpret history. It is not a recipe to be applied by a government. I intentionally said that some countries have gone through the so-called transition stage, what is termed as the dictatorship of the proletariat. Within this, there are two aspects: one political and one social. The political one is the dictatorship and the social one is the proletariat. We have changed here the dimension of dictatorship for a different tactic; but the other factor, the social one, is present. I have spoken, and I believe that it is difficult to use such terms in a bourgeois parliament, about the proletariat. I have spoken about the workers and I have said that this is a government of the workers. And, if you speak of workers, the most important factor, without argument, is the proletariat. Thus, I believe that orthodox Marxists will allow me this incursion, which does not pretend to theoretically set a doctrinal position, but rather shows what we believe to be a tactical application in accordance with Chilean reality. And if we broke with the virginity of the orthodox but got things done, then I would choose the latter.

11

First Anniversary of the Popular Government

National Stadium, Santiago, November 4, 1971

Addressing an enthusiastic throng, Allende notes that each May 21, Chile's president is obligated to "render accounts" ("dar las cuentas") to Congress. He then announces he intends to break with that old framework by going directly to the people "in this stadium, or in larger places, dialoguing with the people and telling them that they are the fundamental factor in the Chilean revolutionary process." He talks about the difference between achieving the reins of government and achieving real political power. Speaking of achievements during his first year in office, he notes that it is now "our copper, our iron, our nitrates"; that unemployment is way down; and that special measures have been adopted to meet the needs of Chile's Mapuche people and other indigenous groups. He addresses the free milk program for children; agrarian reform; penal reform ("not one political prisoner"); maternity care and other social services; law and order; protection of small and medium-sized businesses; reforestation; the foreign debt; and bureaucratism. He lauds the armed forces and Carabineros (national police). Denouncing the forces of fascism and infantile leftism ("extremism," an implicit reference to "ultraleft" groups), Allende concludes with a renewed plea for unity and a ringing series of "we shall win's."

C hileans, people of Santiago. A year ago in this same big place, I said, "The people said we shall win, and we did."

Today, with authentic pride, the Comrade President also says, "We said we were going to accomplish things, and we did." I was told: "You will not be able to fill the stadium." I was told that the galleries were going to be deserted, that the people were not going to come. I wish our enemies could see this marvelous spectacle of workers, students youth, women, peasants and — thanks also to those fathers and mothers who have brought their children — the children of Chile, to them my affection and consideration.

I greet and am grateful for the presence here of diplomats and representatives of friendly countries who have willingly come to be with us. I greet the members of the Chilean trade union confederation [CUT], its President Comrade Luis Figueroa, and its secretary general who have come to this ceremony.

I greet the representatives of the parties and groups that make up the Popular Unity. I also pay homage to the thousands and thousands of workers who fill the galleries, and those who built floats with their own hands and funds. I greet and I pay homage to an exemplary worker, Comrade Barría. This anonymous worker, with a new awareness and a new spirit, built a new machine at the Andina Mine which has greatly increased production. I greet the new revolutionary awareness of the Chilean workers.

I have come to render accounts to the people. According to the political constitution I am required to inaugurate the regular session of Congress on May 21 and to report to it and to the country on the administrative, economic, social, and political state of the country.

We are breaking in new structures and within one year we shall inform the people in this stadium, or in larger places, dialoguing with the people and telling them that they are the fundamental factor in the Chilean revolutionary process. We attained power in October and on November 3 we assumed the responsibility of governing this country by a popular mandate expressed at the polls and ratified by congressional decision.

Today, I have come to say that slowly but surely we have been gaining power. We have carried out the revolutionary changes of the Popular Unity platform. Chileans have recovered what belongs to them, their basic wealth which was formerly held by foreign capital. We have defeated monopolies and the oligarchy. Both of these advances are essential to break the chains which bind us to underdevelopment, are the only means of destroying the institutionalized violence which exploited the great majorities. That is why we are here to show that we have advanced in the social areas, under the economic program that is fundamental for people's power. We control 90 percent of what was previously private banking. Sixteen banks, the most powerful including the Español, the Suramericano, Crédito de Inversiones, and the Banco de Chile are today the property of the country and the people.

More than 70 strategic or monopolistic enterprises have been expropriated, intervened or nationalized. Today we can speak of our copper, our coal, our iron, our nitrates, and our steel. The fundamental bases for heavy industry are today owned by Chile and Chileans. We have emphasized and extended the agrarian reform process. A total of 1,300 extensive holdings, 2.4 million hectares, have been expropriated. Some 16,000 people now live there and we plan to settle 10,000 more. If it was important to have extended the agrarian reform to make the soil produce in a different manner, and to change its ownership, it was also important to provide seed and fertilizer to those for whom the land is their daily bread. More than agrarian reform, we have made the peasant feel like a citizen and aware of his great task side by side with the workers and the people, so that the people will have more to eat. Your work is spread throughout the country and will represent more health and welfare for all Chileans. That is why we created the Peasant Councils.

Furthermore, we have been striving to change labor relations. Now, the workers are aware that they are the government, that their attitude has to be different. This is why I say to you that the responsibility assumed by the leaders of CUT is exemplary and point out the importance of their agreement with the government. That is also why the national congress has a bill before it which decrees worker participation in the administration of government enterprises; worker participation in mixed enterprises; and participation in private enterprise cooperation committees. That is also why we have created production committees in nationalized and mixed enterprises, and we will have to create them in private enterprises to deeply impress workers with their responsibility in the process of national production.

To us it is very important that the majority, all the workers, understand that they are the government, and therefore, their attitude toward workers' demands, and readjustments, as well as their own personal attitudes should be different. I went to Chuquicamata and spoke to the copper workers. I visited the different sections and held a meeting at each one. In the late afternoon, after the sun had set, I spoke to more than 4,000 workers for three hours. I expounded on the need to revise their list of demands. I asked them, how could they want a copper strike — which the people's enemies very much wanted — at a time when Chile was facing the problem of indemnification to the previous foreign owners? I asked them, how could they conspire to provoke a strike through a list of demands that the enterprise could not grant? I told them that we should write the list of demands in such a manner that the worker, the poor copper worker would be incorporated in the leadership of the enterprise; that the workers assembly would produce administrators; and that according to the CUT-government agreement there would be union-management committees. There would be a readjustment of the minimum salary and a percentage of the firm's surplus profits would go to the union's funds. The balance would be divided between the investment which should be made by the enterprise to achieve technical progress and social investments made to benefit the workers, to pay salaries and wages in relation to the production and productivity, and to lead the worker to productive progress, because the copper enterprises are Chile's wages, and because the copper workers are the owners of these enterprises when they become part of the process.

From here, looking down at other miners, with their helmets, their lighted headlamps, I call on the Chuquicamata workers to assume their responsibility, and tell them that all Chile awaits their answer. I have faith in the copper workers' answer.

I want to point out that the government has been concerned, through the Agriculture Ministry, about a sector of the Chilean people that has been discriminated against, the Mapuches, the Indians, the roots of our race, who are always forgotten. Your government has taken special interest in them. That is why we have intensified agrarian reform in Cautín. That is why we have created the Mapuche Vocational Training Institute and the Indian Development Corporation. We want the Mapuches to have the same rights and the same laws as other Chileans, and we want to improve their cultural, material and political levels so that they can join us in the great battle for the liberation of our country.

There is another group of Chileans, always forgotten, ignored, and in my opinion unknown in the scope of their role. I had the opportunity to see and appreciate their integrity and their value as humans. They are *"afuerinos"* [landless peasants]. They are the 150,000 Chilean outcasts in their own country, without homes, without permanent jobs, without families, walking from village to village, sleeping under bridges, and sometimes persecuted by the police. The Moneda [presidential palace] and the Agriculture Ministry have been opened to them for the first time, and I gave an urgent order to schedule an emergency program so that the landless peasant will be another worker, so that he can till the land, have his own home and so that he can stand beside the Mapuche and the worker in the task we have before us in our country.

That is why we have been gaining power; we have been incorporating deprived groups and sectors. We have been concerned with strengthening democracy and expanding liberties through the redistribution of income and economic liberation.

This government wants an authentic democracy and complete freedom for all Chileans. Democracy and freedom are incompatible with unemployment and lack of housing, the lack of culture, illiteracy and sickness. How is democracy strengthened? By creating more jobs, giving better wages, building more homes, providing the people with more culture, education and better health. Workers, let us see what we have done.

This country has been plagued for more than a century by brutal unemployment. In September 1970, we had 8.4 percent unemployed. By September 1971, we had reduced it to 4.8. In December 1970, there were 87,000 unemployed in Santiago. Now, regrettably we still have 51,000. In December 1970 there were 5,000 unemployed in Puerto Montt, now there are only 300. In Temuco there were 9,000 unemployed last year, there are now only 3,000. In the Bío-Bío, Malleco and Cautín areas we have created 12,000 new jobs. Another important factor in cementing democracy is to balance the possibilities and incomes to lessen the immense differences existing in the capitalist system as far as salaries are concerned.

Let us see what have we accomplished. In 1968, 60 percent of the families received 17 percent of the national income. During that same year 2 percent of the families received 45 percent of the national income. We are correcting this injustice. In 1970, wage earners received 50 percent of the national income. In 1971 wage earners are receiving 59 percent of the national income. We have taken a big step. We have taken a bigger step, however, by increasing the workers', peasants', and government employees' family incomes, bringing them closer to private employees' income.

With compassion and kindness, we have concerned ourselves with pensioners, widows, old people and the poor. For the first time in Chilean history we have not seen in the congressional gardens, or around the presidential palace, old Chileans who gave their life's work and who even in their last hours, were not granted the right to die in peace. Today, your government has taken a basic interest in providing justice for these old people....

Listen well: we have increased by 52 percent the delivery of milk to Chilean children, and the half liter of milk will be a reality for your children, comrades.

We have carried out a campaign against infectious diseases in the provinces affected by the earthquake, and also against endemic diseases, especially summer diarrhea. We have controlled the quality of water and conducted campaigns to eradicate the garbage dumps and clean up the slums. Volunteer work by citizens has been an important factor in these campaigns.

We have democratized the National Health Service to complement the doctor with the personnel working under him to allow workers and their families to really benefit from health services and also to participate authentically in their own health maintenance.

In order to bring democracy to the welfare field we have given social benefits to one-third of the population which did not have them. Some

900,000 have been incorporated into the benefits — merchants, transporters, small and medium farmers, fishermen, craftsmen, dentists, the independent sector and priests, nuns, pastors, ministers of all religious creeds. Some 900,000 Chileans who did not have social benefits will have them thanks to you and the popular government....

We have financed the milk plan for 600 million escudos and contributed to the special mother-child fund which will amount to the considerable sum of more than 1 billion escudos.

...I can say with great satisfaction that in this country we have authentic democracy. There is not one political prisoner in jail here. There are some who abuse their freedom, who deserve to be in jail. [Cheers from the crowd] There is no politician in jail, no student under arrest. University autonomy is respected here. There is not a single banned magazine. Two or three newspapers and five or six magazines have been established since September 4 [1970]. Some of them are poisonous, the likes of which Chile has never seen, but they are there. They print their plots against the government of the people daily, others periodically. Only 20 meters from La Moneda Palace anyone who wants to can purchase papers and magazines which insult the president and his government, but which receive in return the contempt of the people and my own contempt, because I have confidence in your political conscience and faith in your strength for the defense of the government. [Applause]

We have submitted to congress a bill that creates the social area of economy, and in it we have incorporated — as I said before — the participation of the workers. With it we must establish which sectors will be state-controlled and the companies that will become — for the benefit of Chile — part of the social area of the economy. We have provided as a basis 14 million escudos in capital.

In this stage we want to bring under state control between 120 and 150 companies, realizing that in Chile there are 35,000 or more enterprises. The monopolies, the large businessmen, know that their enterprises will be brought under state control in the social area. They will receive compensation. However, 35,000 or more small and medium businessmen and industrialists have nothing, absolutely nothing, to fear from the government of the people. [Applause]

It is appropriate that our nation should be proud of its workers, that there has been an appreciable increase in production in state-controlled industries, in the industries managed by the workers: nitrate production is up 50 percent, cement 7 percent, oil 32 percent, electronics 55 percent — which has made possible the program of popular television sets and you will be able to have television sets in your homes and will see me periodically — Bella Vista Tomé Textile has increased 26 percent, and Caopolicán-Chiguayante 15 percent. That is, all the state-controlled industries have put idle capacity into production enormously increasing their production.

I want to point out that this year 60,000 hectares have been reforested, whereas the average of the last few years was 25,000. I want to say as an example, that the National Oil Enterprise has, in five months, with the help of Chilean workers and technicians, constructed a dock in Quintero for ships of 200,000 tons deadweight, which will save us more than $5 million a year in freight costs.

...The law and order of a revolutionary government is not the law and order of a bourgeois democracy. Our law and order is based on social equality and uses persuasion as its tool. We need order to change structures. It is the law and order of a people's government, of a revolutionary country. We cannot accept the imbalance of isolated individuals who might provoke chaos. The guarantee of order lies in the organized working classes, aware, disciplined, capable of understanding the historic task ahead. That is why we must have the workers participating in all the activities of our life with their class awareness and their revolutionary purpose. That is why we do not accept pressure, why we have said with revolutionary sincerity that we are against the indiscriminate takeover of farms because it creates anarchy in production and the end result is the eviction of the peasants, a result detrimental to the peasants....

We are against the takeover of housing which is detrimental to the workers who have made payments to acquire them. We are against the seizure by workers of small and medium factories. Nationalization, intervention, and requisitioning of enterprises must follow a government plan and not the anarchy of a voluntary impulse of a few.... This year we Chileans did more than the Cubans did during their first year of the Cuban Revolution, and that is not intended to the detriment of the Cubans. When Fidel Castro comes here I am going to ask him and I know what his answer will be. Let it be known for the record that we made our revolution without social cost. I can say that there is no country in the world which has carried out its revolutionary process without social cost. You have seen that the People's Government has done it, we have done it together, and this has a great value in human terms and for the country's economy.

I want to stress that an organized, aware and disciplined people with political ideals, whose workers are organized in unions, and federations, and the CUT, is the political base of the revolutionary process, as are also — and I point this out because this is a process within legality — the armed forces and the *Carabineros* of Chile: I pay homage to the people who wear uniforms, and to their loyalty to the constitution and to the will expressed at the polls by their fellow citizens. I want to emphasize the exemplary discipline of the armed forces and the *Carabineros*, their courage and sacrifice during the sad times of the earthquakes, snowstorms, and volcanic eruptions. I want to point out how they joined the process of defending our economic frontier and are present in the steel, iron and copper industries, and in the atomic energy commission. Chile thereby provides an example which is envied by the whole world....

We have faced serious problems: earthquakes, snowstorms, volcanic eruptions — and the people have marched on — economic problems, a decrease in the price of copper. During the previous administration copper reached a high of 84 cents. The average this year will be no higher than 49 cents. World inflation forces us to pay more for our imports. It is true that we started with $3.4 million in monetary reserves, but we also assumed a foreign debt of $2.56 billion plus $736 million that the copper companies owe.

We are the world's most indebted country. Each of you, hear me well, each one of the 120,000 present here, each one of the 10 million Chileans, owes $300 abroad. Many of you have never seen a dollar and have to realize that you are in debt and that this country is so indebted. Only Israel, a country that is at war, has a higher debt per capita than Chile. During the next three years we must pay, as a result of the commitments of the previous governments, more than $1 billion....

In the political picture we deplore the split in the Radical Party, and we hope that the reunification of that ancient party will soon be possible because we want the political base of your government to be maintained. That is also why we have appealed to the Christian Leftists separated from the Christian Democracy, to join the Popular Unity because we have to strengthen the ties between Marxists, laymen, and Christians which represent the Chilean's revolutionary zeal.

I would like to stress the "ultras" — the pseudo-fascists we might say, those who were involved in General Schneider's murder the pseudo-nationalists, those who never said a word when Chile's copper and wealth were in foreign hands — are now speaking of demagogic nationalism which the people reject. They are the troglodytes and cavemen of an anticommunism called upon to defend the advantages of minority groups. The people will stop them and fascism shall not occur in this country.

There are also, as I have said before, extremist sectors to whom I say that we do not fear discussion or ideological debate, but to begin this discussion it would be well for them to read Lenin's little book which says: "Extremism, the infantile disease of communism."... We cannot disregard the fact that objectively the small and medium bourgeoisie is and must be on our side. Just as we need the small and medium craftsmen, producers, businessmen, technicians and professionals.

That is why more than ever one has to be aware of what Chilean life is and of the path that is authentically ours, which is the path of pluralism, democracy and freedom, the path that opens the doors of socialism.

We have to put an end to centralism and bureaucracy. We want to put an end to the queues at the windows that sell stamped paper and the little phrase "come back tomorrow." We want the public employees to work on Saturday morning. We do not want a "Saint Monday" in the revolutionary government of the people. [Applause]

I would like to point out that voluntary work is something responsible and serious that should be planned.... I had the joy of seeing that the workers of Chuquicamata, the Sunday before last, mobilized 40,000 tons of slag, 36,000 the previous Sunday, and they are going to continue working. This is constructive, planned and organized voluntary work which is a demonstration of the conscientious participation of the people in the great constructive work of the homeland.

We should concern ourselves with the sickness of alcoholics. I have always said that one of the most serious diseases of Chile is alcoholism, and I have said that during the government of the people there would be less and better drinking. We are also going to fulfill that, comrades. [Applause] Don't protest! Don't protest! [Laughter and applause]

We have done a lot for the children but we must do more for the abandoned children and those in unusual situations, for the beggars, for the vagrant children. We have not established a sufficient number of childcare centers and parks. Every town should have a children's library and a children's park. That is the task that we must fulfill.

The people have learned that victory is in unity. Let us not permit the unity of the people to fall apart. Let us not permit extremism which attempts to dislodge the fundamental bases. We have to find, and we will search for it, the language that will unite all revolutionaries because the enemies are too powerful and do not rest. We have to defend the popular victory. The people know that they are the true forgers of victory. The people know that once again, through one of their sons, and the son of a railroad worker, they are on the world stage. The people know that the name of Chile is engraved in history thanks to the verse and song of one of its sons, a man who is one of us, a social fighter, Pablo Neruda, poet of Latin America and the world.

Therefore I said one year ago: Forward, we shall win. We shall win by strengthening our unity. We shall win by broadening the political and social bases of the Chilean revolutionary movement. To the youth: We shall win by studying more. To the workers, technicians, professionals, peasants and employees: We shall win by producing more. We shall win when the Chilean woman learns about our appeal and joins the struggle of her man, her father, her son and her brother.

We shall win when the youth know that their combat post is here, that we have called upon them for the great task of tomorrow.

Forward, comrades, we must win so that we can live as brothers and without hate in our own homeland, improving our morality with the constructive revolutionary force of the people. Forward Chileans, we shall win again for the homeland and the people.

12

Interview with Salvador Allende and Fidel Castro

By journalist Augusto Olivares Becerra, November 1971

Allende's first major foreign policy action was to reestablish relations with Cuba. Fidel Castro visited Chile in the fall of 1971 and was greeted by cheering crowds and scattered acts of violence. In a rare historical moment, the two revolutionary leaders sat down to take questions from journalist Augusto Olivares Becerra in the garden of the Cuban Embassy residence of Cuban Ambassador Mario García Incháustegui. The interview was conducted for a film entitled "The Dialogue of America." The text reproduced here is taken from that film's sound track (the film never received wide distribution in Chile). Journalist Olivares Becerra died during the battle for Chile's presidential palace La Moneda on September 11, 1973, a few hours before Allende himself perished. García Incháustegui survived the machine-gunning of the Cuban Embassy residence that same day. The exchanges between Allende and Castro here reflect much about the situation in Latin America and the world in 1971; the differences — yet similarities — affecting the revolutionary processes in Chile and Cuba; and the nature of fascist reaction in Chile, of great concern to both leaders.

Augusto Olivares Becerra: For a long time now the men of the world have wished to have the opportunity to see the prime minister of Cuba, Commander Fidel Castro and the President of Chile, Salvador Allende, meet face to face. It is interesting that it is Latin America that has produced this phenomenon which today attracts the attention of the whole world. Since Commander Castro arrived in Chile, many journalists have been looking for ways to witness a conversation between these two figures of world politics. And this is the moment and this is the opportunity of having them close and face to face, in an open dialogue about topics that concern all of humanity.

President Allende: the expression "Chilean path" is mentioned not only in Chile but all over the world. How would you define this political process that has come to be called the Chilean path?

Salvador Allende: The people who fight for their emancipation logically have to adapt to their own reality the tactics and strategies that will lead them to transformations. Chile, because of its characteristics, because of its history, is a country where the bourgeois institutions have functioned in plenitude and within this bourgeois legality, the people, with sacrifices, have advanced and achieved gains, increased awareness, and has come to understand that it is not within capitalist regimes nor through reformism that Chile can reach the dimension of a country with economic independence, capable of reaching superior levels of life and existence

Augusto Olivares Becerra: Commander Castro, in relation to what President Allende has stated: there is a permanent interest in an in-depth view into the way the working class is incorporated and how the working class becomes the protagonist in the Cuban revolutionary process.

Fidel Castro: We have defined that problem in this way: the armed guerrilla struggle that was started by a small number of men, was something like a small motor that then started the great motor of history, that being the masses. During the last governments, both the corrupt government of Pergiu as well as the tyrannical government of Batista, the working class movement in Cuba was controlled by official leaders that had taken the trade unions by assault, killing communist leaders and honest working class leaders. In this situation, when the revolution triumphs, there was one special circumstance: there was no official working class leadership but there was total and absolute support from the working class for the revolutionary movement, a movement that was born with workers and peasants. Our guerrilla soldiers were peasants, workers and some intellectuals, that could be called intellectuals because of their origins or because of the fact that they had studied in a university and that was us, some of us, not all.

Augusto Oliveras Becerra: President: the working class, according to your answers, has become the protagonist element within the process. There is another element: the state. Could you speak to us about the Chilean tradition, the tradition of struggle and the style of the country?

Salvador Allende: Well, to answer Augusto Olivares' question I want to tell you, Fidel, that, logically, because of the very characteristics of its regime, Chile had the possibility of the working class organising itself. The working class was born in zones that were controlled by imperialism. This is why it's always had an anti-imperialist conscience. From the nitrate mines, with Luis Emilio Recabarren as the organiser, the guide, the leader of the working class and the struggles of the Chilean proletariat in the trade union movement led many times, as it did in the majority of other countries as well, to violent repression. However, this was overcome and in 1939 it was able to unite into the CUT [Unitary Workers Central]. But before this, the peasants and the workers had formed their own class parties. Thus we have the Communist Party which is the oldest in Latin America, one of the oldest in the world and certainly, in relation to the population, one of the most powerful. Similarly, the Socialist Party, a class-based party, a Marxist party that, despite at times having points of discrepancy on international issues with the Communist Party, has not only kept a dialogue but also an understanding, in order to confront together the essential problems of Chile.

Since 1951, the Socialist Party and the Communist Party began to develop a class process with the aim of enabling a vast and broad movement that would allow the structural changes in Chilean life. That's why today we can say that, aside from small-minded objections, on the basis of the unity of the working class and trade unions and on the pillars of the Socialist Party and the Communist Party, we have succeeded in incorporating sections of the small and middle bourgeoisie, such as the Radical Party, the Unitarian Popular Movement of MAPU, the Christian Left, who have also shaped this process, which logically constitutes a determinant factor in the process of change within Chilean reality. This is more or less a synopsis of what has occurred in Chile and of the combatant organised presence of the workers in the political field and in the trade union movement.

Augusto Olivares Becerra: The motivation of peoples in the struggle to make history is extremely diverse. How would you, Commander, define the motivation for the struggle of the Cuban people?

Fidel Castro: Let's say, at least, according to our concepts, that the great motor of history has been the struggle of the oppressed masses against the oppressors. And this has been thoroughly studied and has been known since the existence of classes in human society. In our country, a double motivation existed: that of a country which was subjugated and humiliated by imperialism and, moreover, within this situation, a great mass of peasants without land, a great mass of working class that was being exploited, appallingly miserable conditions, total lack of medical assistance for the poorer layers of the population, a deficient education system, very high percentage of illiterates, lack of future perspectives for youth, hundreds of thousands of people unemployed. There was a situation of social desperation. We could say that the great motivation for our people was the struggle for life.

Augusto Olivares Becerra: President Allende: The Chilean political experience is followed attentively throughout the world. It's an experience with obstacles. How would you define those obstacles?

Salvador Allende: Do you hear that, Fidel? Three minutes to define the obstacles of a revolution within a bourgeois democracy and its legal channels. Nevertheless, you know perfectly well that we have advanced. Obstacles? From whom? First of all, from an oligarchy with much experience, intelligence, one which defends its interests very well and has the backing of imperialism, within a constitutional framework in which Congress has weight and attributions, and where the government does not have a majority. This means that there are serious difficulties and that the Chilean revolutionary process faces new obstacles every day in its task of implementing the program of the Popular Unity government. You understand Augusto Olivares, that the difficulties we face are related to what? With a freedom of press that is much more than freedom, more like licentiousness. They deform, they lie, they libel, and they distort. They have control over most of the media, which is very powerful. There are journalists linked to foreign interests and the large national financial groups. No. Not only do they not recognize our initiatives but also they deform them. All this, with us having to respect the gains that our people have achieved, and that are now logically being used and misused by the opposition to the Popular Government. This is why, and you have said it yourself, the difficulties that we are faced with are fairly logical.

Fidel Castro: The difficulties are wonderful, I tell you.

Salvador Allende: You can see that.

Augusto Olivares Becerra: President, despite those obstacles it is possible to carry out the process.

Salvador Allende: And we are advancing. I have already said it. The copper is ours, the iron is ours, the nitrate and the steel are ours. In other words, we have conquered the natural riches for our people.

Fidel Castro: I have the impression that that resistance is a result of well-developed classic procedures which we refer to as fascist. They try to increase their following, using demagoguery, among the most backward sectors of the poor as well as the middle strata. Now there is one thing to be demonstrated: if those interests will basically resign themselves to the structural changes that the Popular Unity and the Chilean people wish to put into place. And it is to be expected that, if we are going to do a theoretical analysis, they will resist with violence. This is a factor that cannot be discounted in the current Chilean situation. This is my judgment, which is that of a visitor who comes from a country in different conditions, who might as well be from a different world.

Salvador Allende: You have said it and I believe that it is accurate: revolutionaries have never generated violence. It has been those sectors from the groups overthrown by the revolution that have generated violence in the counterrevolution.

Fidel Castro: They maintained the system through violence and they defend it through violence.

Augusto Olivares Becerra: Commander, you and President Allende have both referred to the obstacles facing the Chilean revolutionary process. Could you speak about the obstacles faced by the Cuban revolutionary process?

Fidel Castro: Look, our struggle began in the midst of a tyrannical and bloody regime that maintained power via a brutal repression, and with political circumstances different from the situation in Chile.

Salvador Allende: Totally different.

Fidel Castro: So a revolutionary war develops, and the people win government through a victorious war. There was struggle of course. There was resistance. But our principal obstacle was a foreign one. Because we immediately clashed with the interests of imperialism, so it was imperialism that became our fundamental opposition. A formidable opposition to our country and which used internal factors: the upper class, the landowners, and the most reactionary elements. It immediately began to organize them for a struggle that, at one stage, was ideological but later became, and remained for many years, violent.

Salvador Allende: Did the imperialists also control the land?

Fidel Castro: The imperialists did control the land. Our copper is sugar cane. And cane is cultivated in the best lands and the best lands belonged to United Fruit Company and to other numerous companies from the United States. So our agrarian reforms immediately meant a clash with imperialist interests.

Salvador Allende: I asked that question because here it's different. Here they controlled the mines. There they controlled the land.

Fidel Castro: Exactly. The difference was that we didn't have these obstacles that the president talked about. Indisputably what we did have was a direct war from imperialism that has lasted these 13 years.

Augusto Olivares Becerra: President, coinciding with the visit of Prime Minister Fidel Castro, there has been a rise of adverse sectors towards your government. What judgment...?

Salvador Allende: Look at the subtle way of calling them "adverse sectors." Do you realize, Fidel? This is the press that you were talking about.

Augusto Olivares Becerra: I have to be objective in asking a question...

Fidel Castro: Do you think it's objective to use such subtle terms to refer to the antithesis of this process?

Augusto Olivares Becerra: That's why I wanted to put forward this question. What do you think would happen in Chile, President, if the counterrevolution were to rise up?

Salvador Allende: In the first place I believe it's useful to highlight, as you have said, Augusto Olivares, that the process has intensified with the presence of Fidel. This is logical.

Fidel Castro: So it's my fault?

Salvador Allende: No. But they know what it means to have the presence of Cuba and the presence of Fidel Castro in Chile. They are aware that it revitalizes the Latin American revolutionary process. They have evidence that the unity of our people is an undeniable factor that strengthens the will and the decision of the peoples to break with dependence. And furthermore, it indisputably contributes to the end of the deliberate isolation of Cuba. That's why it has intensified. And more so Fidel, also because your success hurts them deeply. The fact that miners, peasants, workers, soldiers and priests have had talks with you. The great mass rallies... of course, they have obviously been about fondness and affection for you and the Cuban Revolution. But also, deep down they have been about support for the government, because it is the government of the people that has made your presence here possible, right?

Fidel Castro: It's true, but I'll tell you something. The hand of imperialism is behind all this. Without any doubt. We have enough experience about how it acts. And about a certain acceleration of its attitudes and certain tactics and the way in which these have unfolded, especially during this visit. And how a great part of the world has its eyes fixed on the results of this dialogue between us and the encounter of our peoples and our process. So, they have tried to divert attention towards particular types of problems. I don't have any doubt, not even the slightest doubt, that the hands of imperialism are behind this.

Salvador Allende: The people are in government. If they were to achieve, and they never will, the overthrow of this government, there would be a fall into chaos, into violence, into fratricidal struggle and into fascism. Imperialism, which is and has been behind all the processes to stop the revolution and to criticize the changes and its own defeat, will not be able to disembark in Chile. It will not intervene materially in Chile but it looks for another way. What way? To encourage reactionary groups and to incubate fascist groups that utilize demagogy to mobilize groups with little social conscience. But I have confidence and absolute certainty that the response from the people will be hard and implacable. Personally, I am fulfilling a duty. I am not here to satisfy personal vanity nor honor. I have been a fighter all my life. I have dedicated all my efforts and capacity to making possible the road to socialism. I will fulfill the mandate that the people have given me. I will carry it out relentlessly. I will carry out the program that we have promised to the political conscience of Chile. And those who have always unleashed social violence, who unleash political violence, if the fascists intend to use the same means they have always used to wipe out those who wanted to carry out a revolution, they will meet with our response and my uncompromising decision: I will finish as the president of the republic when I serve out my mandate.

They will have to riddle me with bullets, as I said yesterday, in order for me to stop.

I am not defending something personal, I defend the people of Chile in their just yearning to make the transformations that will allow them to live in dignity, with a different national sense, and to make Chile an independent country, master of its own destiny. I think this is a clear position.

Fidel Castro: I really admire this pronouncement of yours very much. I congratulate you. I am sure this will be an emblem for the people, because where there are leaders who are willing to die, there is a people willing to die, and willing to do whatever is necessary. And that has been an essential factor in all political-emotional processes.

Augusto Olivares Becerra: Commander: both President Allende and yourself have repeatedly referred to imperialism as the main enemy of the revolutionary processes in both countries. The survival of the Cuban process, being 90 miles from the Unites States, is almost inexplicable. How can you define the characteristics of this process?

Salvador Allende with Chilean workers during 1970-73 Popular Unity Government

(top) Allende speaking at public meeting in the Plaza de la Constitución in March 1971; (bottom) Allende at a rally during a factory visit in 1973

(top) Fidel Castro receives Salvador Allende on visit to Cuba in December 1972
(bottom) Salvador Allende with Fidel Castro during visit to Chile, November 22, 1971

Allende speaking at public meeting in the Plaza de la Constitución in March 1971

(top) Fidel Castro speaking in Chile during visit in November 1971; (bottom) Fidel Castro driving Salvador Allende in Matanzas during visit to Cuba in December 1972

(bottom) Allende speaking in los Sauces in 1973

(top) Allende following election as president in 1970
(bottom) Allende defending the Presidential Palace from the military coup led by General Pinochet on September 11, 1973

Fidel Castro: They have used political arms, military arms and economic arms. But we have been able to develop a very united people where there are no divisive factors, there isn't an element of division: we have created a great equality, a great unity: our people, men and women are willing to fight. In our country, men and women are willing to fight until the last drop of blood. And imperialism knows this. And that's why they respect us. And I don't believe they have a remote possibility of crushing the revolution. In any case they would have to crush the country. And in relation to this, we have a saying from Antonio Maceo, who was one of the most courageous combatants of our independence: "He who tries to take over Cuba will see the dust of its soil drenched in blood, if he doesn't perish in the attempt."

Augusto Olivares Becerra: President Allende and Commander Castro: You have met in Cuba many times, but this is the first time that Chile is the stage of this encounter between the two of you as heads of government. The attention of the entire world has been focused on your conversations with Commander Castro and especially Latin America which is still pending. President, what do you think about this encounter of both of you as leaders of peoples who are in the midst of a revolutionary process, in the context of a Latin America suffering exploitation?

Salvador Allende: The truth is that we need to consider that Cuba and Chile constitute the vanguard of a process that all Latin American countries will reach. And I would say more: the rest of the exploited peoples of the world. But Latin America cannot continue to only be the continent of hope. We have to analyze this gap, the distance that separates our countries which are economically dependent and are politically subjugated, from the industrial capitalist countries, from the socialist countries. In Latin America, the brutal differences between a wealthy and powerful minority and the great masses, alienated, deprived of culture, health, housing, nutrition, recreation and leisure, can no longer exist. We have said this many times, and one statistic is sufficient: In Latin America there are more than 20 million human beings who don't have an awareness of currency as a means of exchange. In Latin America there are 140 million semi-illiterates and illiterates. In Latin America there is a need for 19 million homes. 53 percent of Latin Americans are malnourished. In Latin America there are 17 million unemployed. And furthermore, there are more than 60 million people who only have casual work. Therefore, the capitalist regime has proved to be inefficient; its characteristic exploitation of man by man has reached a crisis. Latin America has the opportunity to be present at a time when the world is cracking. Cracks in the economy. Cracks in morality. Cracks in politics. It follows then that the reserves of this continent will have to be remeasured when the people are able to intervene; when the people can govern; when they do away with the old oligarchy, the accomplices of imperialism. And when there is, indisputably, one voice of Latin America, of one continent, as the heroes of our independence wars once dreamt, in every path, in accordance with the characteristics of each country. This vision begins to emerge and is ever present, undeniably, not only in this continent but also other continents. We have said it many times: those who have fallen and fall in Vietnam do so not only for their country. They also fall for the exploited of the world.

Those who fell in Cuba showed a path of effort and sacrifice in order to make the Cuba of today possible. Those who fell years ago in Chile constitute the foundation of this revolutionary process. The exploited peoples of the world are conscious of their right to life. And this is why the confrontation goes beyond our own frontiers and acquires a universal meaning. Latin America will one day be free from subjugation, and have its rightful voice, the voice of a free continent.

Fidel Castro: We believe that this continent has a child in its womb and its name is revolution; it's on its way and it has to be born, inexorably, in accordance with biological law, social law, the laws of history. And it shall be born one way or the other. The birth shall be institutional, in a hospital, or it will be in a house; it will either be illustrious doctors or the midwife who will deliver the child. Whatever the case, there will be a birth.

13

Farewell Address to Fidel Castro

Santiago's National Stadium,
December 4, 1971

Here Allende discusses the differences between the Chilean and Cuban paths to socialism. Emphasizing solidarity among the world's peoples, he notes the similar enemies that Chile and Cuba have had to face. He also denounces the mercenary and seditious nature of the prior day's "march of the empty pots" by women from a "high-class suburb." Allende reiterates that Chile's is the first revolution to include an alliance of Christians and Marxists. He says the Catholic Church is tolerant of his government. (Chile's Cardinal actually went on to back the 1973 coup d'état only to say later that he had been deceived by the military men in charge and now felt obliged to denounce their dictatorship and their notorious violations of human rights.) Allende outlines steps that must be taken to beat back the sinister attempts at counterrevolution by powerful minorities and their foreign backers. Ridiculing threats on his life, he warns, "Only by riddling me with bullets can they stop me from fulfilling the people's programs.... I can interpret your will, but tomorrow other comrades will be at your side, and if one of them falls, another will come, and another and another, and the people will continue in the Chilean revolution."

People of Chile; dear comrade and friend Major Fidel Castro, revolutionary Cuba's prime minister [Applause]; comrade leaders of the political parties and movements that make up the popular parties; dear women comrades; dear young comrades: Fidel Castro's presence in our country signifies the gallant meeting of two peoples, two peoples united by their history, by their desire for justice, by their struggle for true freedom. The two peoples have struggled and are still struggling to break the dependence imposed by the privileged minorities who for so many years wielded power and used that power for their own privilege and profit.

Fidel Castro has come to our country and has traveled from the arid north to the southern areas, from the mountain slopes to the seashore. He came neither to teach nor to learn. He has brought his experience and his words, the words of an authentic revolutionary, who has spoken to peasants, students, soldiers, women and men of our country. He has spoken of the obligations revolutionaries incur. He has pointed out the hardships of the liberating struggle, the effort, the self-improvement required of all levels of people. Furthermore, he has pointed out the vices of the revolutionary process, sectarianism and dogmatism. He did not come to interfere in Chilean domestic politics. He has not said a word that could go beyond our borders to affect rulers of other countries. He has said, in his revolutionary language, what Cuba has been and what revolution is. Revolution has no last name. When he speaks of revolution, he is speaking of Chile and Cuba and all the countries in the world. [Applause]

We were aware that Cuba, because of its history, was different from Chile; therefore, it sought a path according to its own situation. They defeated the Batista dictatorship with arms and started on the difficult task — full of sacrifices — to build a new homeland, where the people's dignity would reach new individual and collective levels. Chile, according to its history and its situation has sought its path, and has traveled this path to achieve within the framework of elections, the creation of a popular, national, truly authentic and democratic government, to enter the broad avenues which will lead us to socialism. [Applause]

Our country had to defeat those who tried to fence it in, isolate it, separate it from the rest of the Latin American countries, as they unjustly and stupidly had done with Cuba. We have helped to break down, to destroy the ideological frontiers created to restrict mankind's thoughts and revolutionary will. As president of the Chilean people, I went to Argentina, Peru, Colombia and Ecuador, and that is why, according to the legitimate right due a revolutionary government, we invited the Cuban people through our friend Major Fidel Castro. [Applause]

We helped to tear down the fence which was put around Cuba 10 years ago, and if anything shows that we interpret the will of the masses and the national majorities. It is the fact that five days after we took office, the first international step we took was to renew diplomatic, cultural and trade relations with Cuba. [Applause]

As I have said before, Cuba and Chile have arrived at a revolutionary process through different paths. We are taking the necessary steps to cement the revolutionary process and advance rapidly toward the goals we have set.

The Cuban and Chilean revolutions contain the best traditions, liberating traditions established by those who set us examples. We can say they are with us, through the examples of their lives, and their thoughts — O'Higgins, Bolívar, San Martín and Martí. They showed us the way to rebellion by the people to make possible our political independence then, and our economic independence now. [Applause] Then, against one empire; now, against another.

The Chilean and Cuban peoples are in the front lines of this new stage of liberation. We expressed our desire for complete sovereignty and our decision to forge our own destinies. Both peoples have rebelled against a social class which was ruling this continent's nations. Both countries have arisen against social violence which still marks Latin America's tragic situation, lack of culture, moral and ideological misery, hunger, unemployment, lack of housing, and lack of sanitary facilities. These are landmarks of the misery and pain of this continent's popular masses.

How often have I said, and we say again, 11 million unemployed — more than 60 million Latin Americans have only part-time jobs. We are lacking 19 million housing units. Some 53 percent of the people in this country are underfed. Our average life-span is shorter than that in industrialized socialist or capitalist nations. The infant mortality rate brutally affects our countries' future. Thousands and thousands and thousands of children die — children who should have lived to be tomorrow's citizens. This contrasts with a minority that lives the pleasures of a consumer society, a minority that denies the people more opportunities and has complacently given away our natural resources. Every year the gap widens between the countries of this continent and the countries that have attained the commercial and industrial revolution and are progressing rapidly into the stage of the technological and scientific revolution.

In the face of this reality emerges the will of the peoples who do not want to live with the pain of hunger, misery, ignorance and backwardness. All the Latin American countries have risen to search for their own independent path that will permit the integral development of the human personality. The drama of Latin America has to be seized by the conscientious will of the popular masses who know perfectly well that they must reject the economic exploitation and the overbearing domination of those who have influenced our lives, limiting our possibilities and subjecting us to be economically dependent countries, impressing upon us a culture that is not ours, denying our past, closing our future, and planning a future of pain and misery for our peoples. Latin America is rising up in revolutionary will to make possible the mandate of our illustrious forefathers — continental unity — and to appear before the world in control of its own destiny. [Applause]

Both revolutionary processes have met and continue to encounter identical enemies, foreign and domestic. Cuba learned years ago about blockade, invasion, and acts of aggression, the daily infiltration and the invasion of Playa Girón. Cuba has defeated the invasion, infiltration and blockade, and is rising up with the conscientious and disciplined effort of its popular masses, and by the will of its revolutionary leaders, to defeat backwardness and rapidly take the path of progress in the collective patriotic task of making Cuba a truly patriotic homeland for all Cubans.

Chile is developing according to our reality, with a revolutionary process that embodies what has been our history and is our tradition. We have repeated this often before the people, and we have said that our path is a new path being constructed by a people who have as their sole guide their own determination and the experience they acquire every day.

Our confrontation is a confrontation which continues every minute and every instant against the minority sectors which had government power before, and against the great foreign interests which warped our economy and which sought to subject us to an implacable yoke of imperialistic penetration. The Chilean people never sought the path of violence. The people of Chile know from the experiences suffered who exercised violence throughout our history, and how we had to learn it in the days between September 4 and November 3, 1970. And that time we experienced the lesson of an arrogant and imposing oligarchy allied with imperialism, which searched for every way to prevent the people from obtaining access to the government. There we learned how implacable its decisions are, decisions which went as far as the murder of the commander-in-chief of the army in order to attack the majority of Chile who wanted to have a popular, national, and revolutionary government.

We have always replied with the complete calm of those who know their strength. We have always repeated that the people do not want violence and that others unleash it, in disguise or shamelessly. We have always warned that we would answer counterrevolutionary violence with revolutionary violence.

We took office, and we have used the paths provided us by our own reality and our own existence, and the revolution has been progressing toward the fulfillment of the Popular Unity program. That is why we recovered our basic wealth from the hands of foreign capital and that is why — within the legal channels and within the constitution itself — we can tell the world, with pride in ourselves as Chileans, that the coal is ours, the nitrates are ours, the iron is ours, the steel is ours, and the copper is ours.

We have intensified the agrarian reform and deeply wounded the *latifundio* [large estate]. We have placed the banks under state control. We have also placed various monopolies under state control to strengthen the social area of the economy. In fulfilling the fundamental aspects of the Popular Unity program we have concerned ourselves fundamentally with the Chilean man and woman, the child, and the old person. That is the reason for the policy of redistributing income, to prevent the perpetuation in our homeland of the brutal differences that distinguish the capitalist system, where exploitation of man by man is the essential thing.

In the progress of our revolution we have hurt the interests of the privileged minorities and we have respected the rights gained by the people. We have progressed and pointed out to the people that the revolution has been made and will be made for the benefit of the majorities. That is why Chile is at this moment experiencing the attack that comes implacably organized from abroad and finds support at home in sectors that yearn for power and would like to stop the progress of your government, the people who have become the government. Domestically we have witnessed a grim, seditious attitude that is becoming more accentuated as we advance in the conquest of economic power for the national majorities.

When I returned from the trip to member countries of the Andean Pact I delivered a speech that surprised many because I was returning after having been treated with deference and hospitality by the governments of Ecuador, Colombia and Peru, as I had been treated previously by the Argentine Government. I delivered a speech that, in spite of the fact that the tour had signified the presence of Chile and recognition from people of those countries, that, I can say with satisfaction, how greatly our revolution and our foreign policy attitude based on the fundamental principles of self-determination of peoples were respected and appreciated — I say that in spite of this success, which had definitively smashed ideological barriers, I spoke to the people pointing out that I could see from a distance how the disaffected sectors were firmly and strongly grouping to stop the accelerated progress of the Chilean revolution. It is not surprising, therefore, that yesterday we witnessed in Santiago a demonstration by women who came from the high-class suburb [shouting and booing] to downtown Santiago. The people should know that that large demonstration was not a women's demonstration. It was preceded by a group of 70 or 80 boys with helmets and masks. They carried clubs with metallic projections, and they were probably armed. The women were flanked by organized groups of men who were similarly attired. A similar group made up the rearguard.

The demonstration was authorized by the government because we will never deny the rights that our laws bestow upon our opponents to walk the streets of Chile. To keep absolute order, however, we put a limit and an end to that demonstration, a demonstration that had, as an expression of protest, the empty pots of the most rotten sectors of the bourgeoisie, of those who never... [loud shouting] of those who have never known the lack of basic foods, of those who came and left in powerful cars, of those who were in Providencia Arriba until 3 or 4 in the morning interrupting traffic, burning tires and endangering homes with the fires. That demonstration definitely had a political content and the people should know this. There was a moment when the men who flanked that column, in the face of protests from the workers, who, with exemplary sacrifice, are constructing the buildings that will house an international conference of extraordinary importance next April, came close to tearing down the doors of those buildings under construction and hurled themselves against them to carry out their aim of burning the buildings to the ground. The workers who are constructing those buildings, with their attitude, with their determination, prevented yesterday's fascists from burning the UNCTAD buildings being constructed by the people.

We must remember that Chile is witnessing an event that is not strange to the processes of peoples who have searched for the path of their emancipation. The latifundists use small and medium farmers, making them believe that the revolution is hurting them. The monopolists use the small producers, the large distributors use the merchants. At this very moment at the Caopolicán Theater [booing], probably hundreds of small and medium producers and merchants are meeting, producers and businessmen who have nothing to fear from the Popular Unity government, who have already received real benefits, but who do not understand what it means for them to serve the interests of those who only yesterday placed the noose around the possibilities of their development.

This is why one must not disregard the fact that a fascist germ is mobilizing certain sectors of our youth, especially in the universities. As I have already said, women are used in protest demonstrations, such as the one held in Santiago yesterday. The events are similar to those experienced by Brazil during the Goulart administration [a reformist government overthrown by the military in 1964]. All that is lacking is the exploitation of religious sentiments to create a deeper emotional atmosphere. They have been unable to do so because it is evident that the people and their government respect the right of every Chilean man and woman to have and to exercise the belief that best agrees with their conviction. And they have been unable to use this resource because they have seen the attitude of detachment and impartiality of the Chilean Church. Those who call themselves Catholics and Christians have not hesitated to insult and slander the cardinal of the Chilean Church himself. [Applause]

This is taking place at the same time that the Christian Left has come to strengthen the Popular Unity. I have pointed out the importance of the fact that Chile is the first country where laymen, Marxists, and Christians make up the solid basis of the popular forces expressed in the parties and movements of the people and fundamentally in the organized conscience of the workers, in the Chilean trade union confederation (CUT). [Applause]

These things that I am pointing out and that the people should not forget, are occurring within our borders, while beyond them arises the attitude of those who believe that these revolutionary peoples do not have the moral strength and the revolutionary determination to defend their revolution and the profile of their own personality. Yesterday the news agencies said that the members of a mission that the U.S. president sent to tour the Latin American countries... [booing] have said that Chile can say little because the Chilean record has no acceptance in the countries which they visited, and that from the talks that they have had with the rulers of these countries it can be deduced that the Popular Government's hours are numbered. [Booing]

This has been reported and published in the newspapers with the largest circulation in the United States. In response to the protest of our ambassador we have received a denial and a clarification. But the fact signaled by the reports still stands, and moreover is tradition. Here I tell those who attempt or who intend to interfere that Chile is not a no-man's-land. Chile belongs to the Chileans. Its people, after years and years of suffering, duty and hope, have come to power, and they have as their president your comrade, who is now addressing you. [Applause]

We are in power to make Chile's development possible, and give a deeper meaning to the word homeland, a word widely mentioned by the reactionary sectors who besmirched themselves when they submitted to foreign pressure or when they gave away our basic resources. The authentic Chilean, the patriot who feels love and affection for the birth land and wants a big and generous country for all Chileans, will be beside the People's Government to defend Chile and Chilean dignity, and to reject foreign threats, insolence and pressures. [Applause]

They are deeply mistaken, those who believe that through threats, through pressures, through restricting our credits or through thwarting our possibilities of refinancing our foreign debt, they can block our path. Those who have decided to continue to defend the control they had over Chile's basic wealth should understand that in pressuring Chile, that there is a new Chile and that Chileans want to own their land, their country's wealth. They are mistaken if they so much as try to prevent us from exercising our right to forge with our efforts and sacrifices the destiny we desire for a great country. [Applause]

That is why this coincidence is suspicious. The people should understand how internal problems and events are brought about. We have observed the coincidence of irresponsible or indiscreet words being uttered, words which could not have been uttered unintentionally because of the high position of those saying them. That is why the people should be aware of the common enemy, they should be aware of what is happening, they should de aware of what has taken place. There was the attack on our comrade, the interior minister. In Valparaíso stones were hurled at the car in which I rode. Knowing that this was the vile and cowardly attitude of those who act in the dark, I got out of the car and walked through Valparaíso's streets, protected only by popular affection and the people's respect. [Applause]

Last night an attempt was made to burn the residence of the comrade health minister, Dr. Concha. Yesterday they tried to attack the Communist Youth headquarters and the Radical Party center. *Carabineros* yesterday battled with those who wanted to go to downtown Santiago and to create even more trouble and to enter the municipal theater, where we, together with the diplomatic corps, were attending ceremonies celebrating the 100th anniversary of our foreign relations ministry. That is why we should not forget these things. That is why it is good to bear these things in mind. That is why the people should understand that as we advance with the program our people want, the opposition becomes more and more obdurate. As president of Chile I tell you people that I will respect the opposition, as long as it is within Chile's legal framework, but that I can tell the difference between opposition and sedition, and that political parties should acknowledge their share of the blame. [Applause]

They are trying to sidetrack us from the path we have charted. They are lying, saying that in Chile there is no freedom, that the right to disseminate information has been suspended and that the press is in danger. They are conspiring to continue spreading deceptions, to gain support in certain sectors. They are the conspirators in the dark plot to oppose the will of the people. I tell you comrades, comrades of so many years, with calm and absolute tranquility, I am not an apostle or a messiah. I am not a martyr. I am a fighter for social rights who is doing his task, the task the people have entrusted to me. Let those who want to turn back history, those who want to ignore the will of the people, know that I am not a martyr, but I will not retreat one step. Let them know that I will leave La Moneda only when I have fulfilled the task entrusted to me by the people. [Applause]

Let them know it, let them know it. [Applause] Let them know it. Let them hear and understand it well. I will defend this Chilean revolution, and I will defend the Popular Government because the people have entrusted me with that task. I have no other alternative. Only by riddling me with bullets can they stop me from fulfilling the people's programs. [Applause]

Let them think this over. There is something which I have helped create. This is a political consciousness among the Chilean masses. As I have so often said, this is not a one-man job, it is the people, organized into parties and labor unions in the slums, in the central union, that are in the government. I can interpret your will, but tomorrow other comrades will be at your side, and if one of them falls, another will come, and another and another, and the people will continue in the Chilean Revolution. [Interrupted by prolonged, thunderous applause]

Comrades, I want to finish. Comrades, comrades, [interrupted by applause] comrades, I want to finish because we all want to hear Major Fidel Castro. I want to point out to you very clearly several things that should not be forgotten. When the people are the government, the public order favors revolution. One must not, therefore, provide pretexts and be provoked. They want to make it appear, as it has been said abroad, that in our country the authorities have lost control and that there is anarchy. They are wrong. I have used and will continue to use the powers the constitution gives the government, and that is why I have declared Santiago an emergency zone, [applause] in order to present the true and clear image of our decision to find a punishment — a decision which has remained within the legal channels. What grieves and might shame many of them, if they have any shame, is that they used young women and boys. At least 60 percent of the 90 persons arrested yesterday are 18 to 20 years old. Boys, sons of their fathers, boys who have never worked and girls who have never washed a pot have let themselves be used to unleash violence.

We say very firmly and very clearly: It was a vain attempt to seek to undermine the unity of the popular parties. It was a vain attempt to accuse the *Carabineros*, as has been done imprudently in today's press. It was a vain attempt, a vain attempt to try to undermine the exemplary discipline and loyalty of the armed forces and *Carabineros* of Chile who respect the constitution and the laws. [Applause]

Every day, every day leaflets, letters, anonymous articles come and go from Arica to Magallanes carrying the miserable contraband of blind criticism, presumption and mystification. This is produced like a controlled torrent in the hope of breaking the fundamental discipline of our basic institutions. They will not achieve this aim. They will not attain it because the Chilean armed forces and *Carabineros* understand perfectly well that this Popular Government is the one that has most concerned itself and will concern itself with giving the armed forces and the *Carabineros* corps what it should as the expression of a development, an effort to make them too participants in the process of transformation and progress of the homeland. [Applause]

But moreover, [applause continues] I also appeal to the parties of the Popular Unity, to all the members and middle-echelon leaders, to understand that unity is not a word without content. To wipe out sectarianism, to end dogmatism, to put an end to partisanship, to set an example in sacrifice, in work, in production, true revolutionaries should conscientiously fulfill these tasks. [Applause]

We have clearly realized who our enemies are. We must understand that they are the lawyers and advisers at the service of imperialism, the great landholders and bankers, and the monopolists. We have to impress upon the sectors that make a living from their own effort and work that they will be the beneficiaries of the process of Chilean economic development. We have to make the people vigilant, we must conscientiously mobilize the masses. A vigilant and mobilized people, a people with a goal, a people knowing what they must do and how they must do it, is the granite base on which the revolutionary process rests.

There can be no worker, peasant, employee, student, technician or professional who does not have a general idea of what Chile wants in this hour, and what the revolution desires. All must understand that beyond the problem of the personal, the union, the enterprise and the economic demands is the Chilean economic development process. All must understand that an excessive wage increase policy would prevent the halting of inflation and the elimination of unemployment. Comrades, we need to have this awareness take root in the will of the Chilean popular masses. They must know how to distinguish between the great revolutionary task and the struggle for petty gains that detract from the prestige of the revolutionary man and the revolution.

To the comrade members of other forces who are not part of Popular Unity, who are revolutionaries, I tell them that what we want with them is discussion, understanding. If there is no understanding, then there should be a public discussion of doctrines to determine who and which way is right and what path we should follow. [Applause]

If I have refused to use strength and violence against my enemies, against the class enemies, how could I have imagined that I should have to use violence against those who are revolutionaries. Comrades, members of the parties of the revolutionary left, understand the significance of the responsibility of the hour through which Chile is living and what the real unity of all revolutionaries represents. [Applause]

Comrade and friend Major Fidel Castro, in the name of the Chilean people, I bid you farewell by saying to you: The image that you must take with you and will take with you is the real image of Chile. It is the man from the nitrate mine, Major Castro, from the coal mine, from the Magallanes farm, the student, the man from the armed forces with whom you talked. It is the Chilean woman who was with you and spoke of her worries and convictions.

I do not have to mention this because I know that neither diatribe nor cunning slander ever touched you. I do so, however, to point out that here in Chile, the visit of Cuba in the person of Fidel broke all the dikes and all the floodgates of evil that have spilled into the radio and press against the revolution and its chief, Comrade Fidel Castro. I know perfectly well that while the people were receiving you with the warmth, respect, and affection that is extended to a brother who brings us brotherly love, the man who brings from Cuba the history of Martí and those who fell in the Sierra Maestra or Playa Girón, I know perfectly well that for Fidel Castro, revolutionary made in revolution and action, here is Chile, represented in this stadium by the people of Santiago, just as it was yesterday in the streets, on the highways, in the mountains, on the coast, to tell the comrade and friend that Chile has been and will continue to be beside Cuba in the desire to walk together to struggle for the free America that our illustrious forefathers envisioned.

14

Here are Assembled
the People of Chile

Speech to citizens' rally in the streets of Santiago, March 18, 1972

Allende sums up how democracy is being carried out fully in revolutionary Chile despite the opposition's attempts to overthrow it. The tens of thousands of people rallying that day shout "No!" to Allende's question if they want the opposition to succeed in its planned constitutional reform to privatize the nationalized sectors of the economy. He counters that the constitutional reforms he is recommending will "consecrate the authentic rights of workers." Allende says there will be no civil war, no repeat of Balmaceda, the reformist president overthrown during a civil war in 1891 at great cost of life. "The people will go on governing," he says, to which the crowd responds with shouts of "Allende! Allende! Allende!" He discusses the interventionist conduct of ITT, a major U.S. corporation and economic power in Chile, and says he will send a bill to Congress expropriating ITT. He reminds people that the year 1972 is focusing on women and youth and that the whole world is watching the Chilean experiment of "constructing a new society in pluralism, democracy and freedom."

C omrades:
Here are assembled the people of Santiago, who represent the people of Chile. Here is the history of our country which has been constructed in these long years with the pain, the suffering, the hope and the revolutionary conviction of thousands and thousands and

thousands of Chileans. Never in our lifetime have we witnessed an act of this magnitude, in this context and with such importance.

Here we find men, women, young and old, from all corners of Santiago, bringing their invincible faith and their confidence in the Popular Unity. Here we have gathered without hatred, with the serene faith of those who know their own strength. Here we are gathered those who triumphed yesterday and who will triumph tomorrow.

Today we have not a formal democracy but an authentic democracy, a democracy in which our opposition can march, scream and protest, they can lie; a democracy steeled and sustained by the unity of the people of Chile. [Applause]

We have consolidated this democracy because we have reduced by half the unemployment we inherited, because we have redistributed income for the benefit of the workers, increasing the percentage received by salaried workers from 53 to 59.6 percent; because we have provided extraordinary benefits to thousands and thousands of pensioners, widows and orphans; more than 54,000 new pensions have been granted by your government; because we have increased the purchasing power of the masses, reactivating the industries that were semi-paralyzed at the start of our term; we have consolidated democracy. We have done this, and the proof is the greater demand which encouraged, in a manner never seen before, a growth of 13 percent in industrial production in 1971.

Today the country produces more cement, more steel, more coal than before. More consumer goods are produced. This Chilean economy is breaking records which had never before been reached. However, and this must be said, there are still social needs that must be met, because the economy that we have inherited, and in particular its capacity of production, is that of an underdeveloped country, where the economic structure is clearly deformed and oriented towards the satisfaction of the needs of only 40 percent of the Chilean population; this is why for some products there are symptoms of partial shortages. Because even though production has increased — despite being in the middle of an expansion program, despite industry working to its full capacity — it is still not enough to satisfy the extra demand which has arisen in this last year. To correct this imbalance means to face this challenge, to exceed the goals set for production, improve the efficiency and allocate resources to expand the capacity of the worker and productivity.

To work and produce more

This is why we have said that only an organized, disciplined and conscious people, who will work and produce more, will make this democracy stronger and consolidate its own revolution.

Past regimes would respond to the challenge of production and demand by increasing prices and containing the purchasing power of the masses, increasing unemployment, keeping salary rises below that of the cost of living, in other words, adapting the weak capacity of production to the necessities of a small privileged group.

The Popular Government has chosen another path, preferring a delay in the supply of some products and not leave hundreds of thousands of workers without work, more than half a million of Chileans without an income, and millions of our compatriots with miserable salaries.

This is why we have redistributed incomes and defended those sectors with less economic means. We have organized the people to consolidate democracy and to avoid speculation. We have formed the People's Supply Committees (JAP's), we have increased the delivery of protein at low cost. People are eating hake (fish) instead of meat, which is so expensive. There you have a type of fish that reaches the working-class suburbs for the first time. There you have an example of inter-national technical cooperation. There you have an example of what hurts the reactionary sectors so much, that they were never willing to provide the people with seafood to consume. [Applause].

To consolidate democracy, we have organized a most ambitious housing plan. We have increased wages to compensate for the rise in the price of essentials. We have restricted the chronic process of inflation, if you consider the last growth index of our economy, which was more than 8 percent in 1971.

Democracy is being strengthened because is the people who are exercising power, from the government to the Supply Committees; the peasants participate in national, as well as local councils, in the agrarian reform process, cooperating in the expropriations and discussing plans for production.

We consolidate democracy, because we have created 3000 new Women's Centers and 1257 new Neighborhood Committees. The youth has been organized into a General Secretariat linked to the government and they have been able to plan their actions in voluntary work brigades, cultural activities and sports. There are 226,000 new places in primary and secondary education, we have strengthened democracy, and now, in some tertiary careers, we have established afternoon and evening courses for the workers for the first time in our history. [Applause]

We have consolidated democracy, and that is why, the workers' union movement has grown by 20 percent. The CUT [Unitary Workers Central] now has legal status; its representatives are elected in a national poll with secret, direct and proportional voting. Seven hundred thousand Chileans have been granted access to welfare services for the first time; now the office workers, the factory workers choose their representatives to their pension funds boards in a direct vote.

We have broadened and consolidated democracy: here in Chile there are elections every day, parliamentary, municipal, of students, of professional colleges, of workers, union delegates, in the workplace, in the industries, in hospitals and in schools. Every day people directly elect their representatives and delegates; this is what the people experience, learn and live: an authentic democracy with its own strength and vitality. [Applause]

We have respected the selection processes and the career paths of public servants.

The national television station reaches almost the whole country and the university stations have expanded. Our old culture, and also a new one, reach millions of Chileans for the first time, making this an authentic democracy.

The struggle for wage increases is expressed in the list of demands and the right to strike; take note, don't forget: in this country, and for the first time in its history, we have not had a strike in strategic areas. Not in the coalmines, steel, nitrate, copper, petrol, the courts, the doctors; this is the great new conscience put at the service of the country. [Applause]

More authentic democracy

In this country we live a most authentic political democracy, a pluralist democracy, in government and opposition; to deny this is to lie blatantly.

Today the people have united to defend this authentic freedom, because we have reaffirmed, expanded and deepened the individual, political, collective and social freedoms. Let this be heard and not forgotten: in this country there is not one political prisoner, in this country there is not one journalist jailed for his ideas. In this country, we have taken to court some so-called journalists, who are really delinquents, but not for their ideas but for the crimes they have committed.

In this country there is total freedom of the press and information and we have the utmost tolerance and respect for all creeds.

These liberties are greater than ever in the history of Chile, they apply to thousands and thousands of Chileans who previously had no notion of their existence. But these liberties, though fundamental, are not sufficient. We also want economic freedom for Chile and each Chilean; in order for our own culture to flourish it is necessary to liberate ourselves from that which is foreign and comes prepackaged and pre-fabricated.

We must develop our own technological capacity and shake ourselves from this dependency.

Here, freedom to work exists because we have more jobs. Chileans will be truly free when we are rid of ignorance, unemployment, exploitation, hunger and moral and physiological misery. [Applause]

But is necessary that this is clear for everyone: with the government of the workers, the freedom to become rich through the exploitation of man by man has ended. The freedom to acquire wealth at the expense of another's work has ended.

The workers of Chile are determined to be truly free. They have assumed the power to resolve by themselves the problems at their workplaces, the regional problems, the national problems. They already manage the nationalized companies. We have not replaced yesterday's boss with insensitive bureaucrats. It is the workers who freely elect their management councils. It is the workers who freely elect their production councils or committees.

We are liberating man: he must cease to see money as the only basis for his well-being. The man free from alienation has other parameters by which to measure life, other values to be considered, and the people sense this, they learn it, they feel it.

We struggle to liberate man from the vices of the consumer society; to liberate women from the additional discrimination imposed on her by the capitalist regime; we struggle to free our youth from escapism, from drugs, from vandalism; women and youth are our central preoccupation and we want true freedom for her and the government of the people will give it to her. [Applause]

Today in Chile, not only do we maintain the traditional independence of the three state powers, but it has also become a real independence. Those who deny this atmosphere of freedom that we breathe in our land, should not forget the words of the bishops of Chile. A few hours ago they said, and those that lie should not forget it: "We are happy that, despite the difficulties, tensions and incidents, we still preserve the necessary freedoms of expression, thought, criticism, dissent, and especially the freedom to follow one's own conscience and to live and act in accordance to one's faith; freedom of spirit is the salt which, according to the Gospel, gives the world its flavor and without which everything would be insipid and colorless." Thus have spoken the bishops of Chile, refuting the attitude of those who deny the reality they are living in: the freedom that is respected and will be respected by your government, the government of the people, the government of Chile. [Applause]

Respect towards the government of the workers

The people must be aware that to bring into effect democracy and freedom, we have destroyed the power bases of the oligarchy; we have recovered the basic wealth from the hands of foreign capital, we have nationalized banks and numerous national monopolies, we have reduced interest of money, democratized credit; we have ended or will eventually end the practice of big-scale land ownership; we have brought import and export commerce under the control of the state; we have established for the first time in history a budget for foreign currency. All this, though important, is not yet sufficient, so we have added to the constitutional reforms the 91 companies that must move into the social area of the economic plan, and we will fight to make this important, definitive, necessary step towards the economic development of our country. [Applause]

They have tried to undermine the constitution with political accusations against government ministers, who are only answerable to the president of the republic, in an attempt to block the Budget Law and include anti-constitutional articles. In both cases, the Constitutional Tribunal ruled in our favor and that is why the courts dismissed the accusations against the Defense Minister José Tohá.

They tried to prevent the president, who has co-legislative powers by constitutional mandate, from exercising his duties. However, the Constitutional Tribunal agreed with us when we presented our legal opinion with regard to the vetoing of the Rental Property Law.

This is why, and it may seem paradoxical, this revolutionary government has endeavored and will endeavor to ensure that the constitution is respected, because I have said it to the people and will go on saying it: Chile's institutionality is open, it allows transformation and change, and as I said, we will proceed in a revolutionary manner, without hesitation, within the framework of the bourgeois constitution; we commit to making changes in Chile respecting pluralism, democracy and freedom.

This we are doing and will continue doing! [Applause]

However, they have gone so far as presenting a constitutional reform. This constitutional reform is intended to make the state incompetent, disabled; it aims to eradicate prerogatives of the president of the republic and state bodies. This constitutional reform aims to establish the so-called worker enterprises, in an attempt to coax the workers into becoming make-believe capitalists, pretending it to be a revolutionary reform and transform the regime, making some companies appear to be autonomous. We have expressed, and I will reassert later on, what our views are on this matter.

This constitutional reform aims at maintaining the capitalist regime; it aims at allowing Congress to bypass the presidential veto and push resolutions through a simple majority, which is an extremely grave situation which I denounce to the people; this constitutional reform is sought in order to return the nationalized industries and banks to their previous owners, and I ask the people whether they are going to accept this. Yes or No? [The people respond: *No!*] Yes or No? [The people respond: *No!*] Besides, we don't accept it because we did it within legal and constitutional norms respecting our prior commitment. [Ovation]

This constitutional reform, which they aim to approve by rejecting the presidential veto through a simple majority, has a further goal beyond what I have already denounced and which some loudmouths have already voiced. Eventually, their intention is to remove the president of the republic; they have already once changed the constitution through a deliberate misinterpretation; they have already once shown anti-patriotic courage to provoke a civil war and the suicide of President Balmaceda. In this country there will be no civil war; we will not tolerate any attempt to cover Chile with blood. In this country, the unity of the people and the conscious obedience of the armed forces to the constitution and the law will crush any seditious activity. We will defend Chile, there will be no civil war and the people will continue to govern! [Applause] [Ovation] [*Allende! Allende! Allende!*]

For the first time in our history we are trying to insert into the constitution the concept of the Social Area of the Economy, and for the first time in our history the genuine rights of the workers will be enshrined into the Chilean Constitution. [Applause]

Their attitude — and the people have to know — has been to refuse to recognize the powers of the Constitutional Tribunal, a tribunal installed during the previous government, and which has already dictated its judgment five times, four of which have favored the position of the Executive. We maintain that it is not up to parliament or the Executive to rule on the competence of the Constitutional Tribunal. Only the Constitutional Tribunal itself can determine its own competence and I declare that my government will respect the resolutions dictated by the Constitutional Tribunal, this being the only way to settle the discrepancies between Congress and the Executive. [Applause]

This is why, what we do is strengthened by our patriotism and a national sense free of chauvinisms in the combats against forces within and outside the country. From outside, because we have nationalized copper and, even though we have done it within the constitution and the law, they ignore this and still combat us. Embargoes, suspension of credits, suspension of technical aid, suspension of credit operations by banks backed by multinationals, the United Nations or by the Organization of American States.

We have suffered other aggressions. We have respected the law; we have not confiscated or expropriated, choosing to negotiate with many foreign-owned enterprises and companies. We negotiated with Bethlehem Steel, with Dupont, with international banks, with RCA, to name only a few. We negotiated with French investors in the Disputada de las Condes creating a mixed venture. Hear this well, people of Chile: I had talks on two or three occasions with the top representative of ITT [whistles] in order to reach a compromise. The people must listen and learn. The minister for the interior, yours truly, expert delegates from Popular Unity, experts from Telecommunications and Technical Services, proposed that a Technical Tribunal, backed by an international body, carry out a technical study in order to fix a compensation amount to be paid to ITT. They flatly rejected our proposal, mainly because they have an insurance policy in the United States which they expect to claim. This company, ITT, is a typical example of a capitalist company; the people must remember the details I am about to provide: in 1930, Congress approved, in its second meeting, 12 votes against two, a 50-year concession to ITT, listen well, from 1930 to 1980 ITT was guaranteed a monopoly. ITT was the only company granted golden status and was granted a fixed guaranteed profit margin of 10 percent. A foreign company was handed responsibility for a key area, compromising national security, and which left our own economy in a vulnerable position. What did ITT leave us? Barely 33,000 telephones for nine million Chileans. There are thousands and thousands of Chileans and hundreds of thousands of localities without telephones. Hear this well: ITT invested $28 million and collected $360 million and have left us with a debt of 1 billion escudos. This is the imperialist penetration and this is the morality of the large transnational corporations. Do you want another statistic? In the world, for every 100 inhabitants there are 7.1 telephones, while in Chile there are only 3.7 telephones.

Well, we have had discussions with ITT, not knowing about the secret documents that a U.S. journalist has since released to the world. We did know and we revealed the events that occurred between September 4 and November 3, 1970. It's important to compare, remember and not forget what occurred during those days and what those secret documents reveal; the conspiracy of foreign and national interests that led to treason, aiming at unleashing political and economic chaos. They intended, without success, to foster conspiracy and sedition and dreamt of a coup d'état. I ordered the publication of the ITT documents, translated by a highly qualified and impartial commission consisting of members of the armed forces. I made sure that our military institutions were involved as a sign of respect and because the documents contained many references to them.

The *Mercurio* newspaper got in before us, but only partially because — and hear this well — they did not publish the full documents and omitted some fundamental points. Once again, this organization, itself named in the ITT documents, hides from Chileans and its people the reality of its own responsibilities.

This afternoon I announce that we will hand over to the courts the records of those named in the ITT conspiracy. I announce that I will send to Congress a project of expropriation of ITT. [Applause]

I announce this afternoon, and not in retaliation but because enough time has passed, that we will take administrative measures within the legal powers of the Banks Administration Act, to end the situation created by some members of a powerful financial clan, specifically the issues revolving around the Edwards Bank. This has been damaging to us. What has happened there has done extraordinary damage to Chile's credit rating and has been used as a pretext for the closure of several lines of credit, bringing, as a consequence, difficulties in the supply of consumables, raw materials and spare parts. We will end this situation, within legal and administrative norms, but we will do so in a clear and definite manner, saving the depositors and also guarding the job opportunities of the workers of these institutions, who bear no responsibility in what has occurred. [Applause]

Comrades, I have already said it at the National Stadium: this year must be the year of care for the women and youth of Chile.

We have to care for the daughter, the mother, the sister and the partner. There is no revolution without participation of women in this process. Each day, her presence alongside the revolutionary man becomes more necessary. This is why, this year we will sign a public commitment, a formal letter of agreement, with legal, economic and social content, with the women of Chile, and even beyond the women of the Popular Unity. Similarly, we will sign a commitment with the youth of our country. The Popular Unity youth, or those that don't belong to the Popular Unity, who need opportunities for work, sport and education, must understand that this time it is true, that the workers' strength will open a different horizon. The preoccupation for this year will be our women and our youth, the seeds for the progress of the Chile of tomorrow. [Applause]

I would also like to tell you that we are aware of the hardships that affect the everyday life of the people and that we intend to deal with them. Bad public transport; I have said it once before, we can divide the people into those that have drinkable water and those that don't; those that have access to transport and those that don't. The government is about to finish in a few months the first stretch of the underground railway system. We have already imported 1,000 chassis, 1,000 buses and 1,000 taxis. It is not enough! We need to and will bring more chassis, more buses, because when I drive my car, it hurts to see my compatriots standing on corners waiting endlessly for public transport. We have allocated 50 buses to ensure that children in small towns can go to school but we need 100 more. [Applause]

We need to mobilize the specialists in the public administration areas to install drinking water in all the suburbs. We need to develop the most audacious plan to bring electricity to the darkened shantytowns, for the distribution of essential articles, mainly food. We need people to understand, and I have partly explained this, that shortages occur when there is a breakdown in the relationship between produce and need, between offer and demand.

I have pointed out how absurd it is to have money and use it to push prices or foster the black market and trafficking.

Finally, I tell you: we have halted in our task in order to meet today, in the most dense, combative and massive rally, not to sow hate but to sow faith and hope, faith in Chile, in its people, the peasant and the university professor, faith in the teacher and the doctor, faith in the worker, the craftsman and the bricklayer, faith in the old, who stimulate us with their hope despite so many years of misery and pain, faith in the young who strengthen with new vitality the endless chain of our joint endeavors.

Comrades of Santiago, people of Chile: return to your humble homes and illuminate our tomorrow with the faith of your revolutionary convictions. What Chile has done and is doing attracts the attention of the world because we are constructing a new society based on pluralism, democracy and freedom.

Let us be people with a sense of history and the responsibility to write it. We will say that we are our homeland's past, Chile's patriotic tradition; let's raise the Chilean flag in our hands, let our people be the flagpole and our flag the emblem for victory, emblem for progress, emblem for a socialist future.

15

Address to the Third United Nations Conference on Trade and Development UNCTAD

Santiago, April 13, 1972

This famous speech calls attention to the increasing economic power and corrupting influence of transnational corporations. It deals with trade, debt and related issues in a manner remarkably appropriate for today. Prophetically, Allende warns of the intentions of Japan, the United States, and the European Economic Community to use the General Agreement on Tariffs and Trade (GATT) as a tool for the expansion of their own corporations' economic interests by means of "free trade," wiping out "at a stroke of the pen the advantages of the general system of [tariff] preferences for the developing countries." Foreign debts, he observes, "constitute one of the chief obstacles to the progress of the Third World." They are "largely contracted in order to offset damage done by an unfair trade system, to defray the costs of the establishment of foreign enterprises in our territory, [and] to cope with the speculative exploitation of our reserves." Rejecting Latin America's decades-long strategy of "import-substitution" dependent on foreign investments as one that leads to "recolonization," he urges a new technology development policy that will relate "to our own needs" and will be "prompted by a humanistic philosophy which sets up the human being as its major objective." Noting that moneys gained from disarmament "would be more than enough to start shaping a solidarity world economy," Allende concludes: "Progress and the liberation of the vast underdeveloped world depend on the urgently needed transformation of the world economic structure, on the conscience of countries, on choosing a path of cooperation based on solidarity, justice and respect for human rights."

L adies and Gentlemen: Let me begin by thanking you, on behalf of the people and the government of Chile, for the great honor you have done us by choosing Santiago as the venue for this third session of the United Nations Conference on Trade and Development. We appreciate it all the more as you will be discussing the world's most serious problem: the sub-human condition of more than half its population. You have been convened to rectify the unfair international division of labor, based on a dehumanized concept of mankind.

The presence of so many leaders of economic affairs from every part of the world, including ministers and high-ranking officials, enhances the significance of this honor. It is encouraging that all the organizations of the United Nations system are represented here, besides the intergovernmental and nongovernmental bodies concerned with development problems, and the information media of all five continents.

With me are the representatives of the Chilean nation: the presidents of the Senate, the Judiciary and the Chamber of Deputies, comrades ministers of state and members of parliament and civil, military and ecclesiastical authorities, accompanied — in representation of the people — by workers and students.

Accordingly, in the name of our people and of its representatives present at this ceremony, I offer our guests a very warm welcome, and wish them a pleasant stay in a country that receives them with cordial friendship and understandable anticipation. I also extend my respectful greetings to the resident diplomatic corps.

To you, Mr. Kurt Waldheim, secretary general of the United Nations, we owe a very special debt of gratitude. In taking the trouble to attend this opening meeting so soon after assuming your high office, your intention has doubtless been to show that you accord this conference the priority it deserves; that for you the development of the Third World and the expansion and improvement of trade are matters of as much urgency and importance as the most explosive political questions; and that you fully realize that economic stability and development are, as established in the charter, essential and interdependent factors of international peace, security and goodwill.

To my good friend, Mr. Manuel Pérez-Guerrero, secretary general of UNCTAD, I should like to express our deep appreciation of his selflessness and efficiency in the discharge of his functions, and of the outstanding quality of the preparatory work for the present meeting.

Lastly, to Professor Langman, Minister for Economic and Financial Affairs of the Kingdom of the Netherlands, I would offer the sincere gratitude of the government and people of Chile for his country's generous contribution of the transmitting and amplifying equipment for the conference rooms in this building.

UNCTAD and the future of the Third World
In UNCTAD III, I hail an assembly of the world community of nations — in effect, of almost all mankind. Unfortunately, not yet quite all. For us, the peoples of the Third World, UNCTAD should constitute the chief and most effective of the instruments available for negotiation with the developed countries.

The basic mission of this third session which is starting today is to further the replacement of an outdated and essentially unjust economic and trade order by an equitable one based on a new concept of man and of human dignity, and to promote the reformulation of an international division of labor which the less advanced countries can no longer tolerate, inasmuch as it obstructs their progress while it favors only the affluent nations.

From the standpoint of our countries this is a crucial test. We refuse to go on giving the name of international cooperation for development to a mere travesty of the concept enshrined in the Charter of the United Nations. The results of the conference will show whether the commitments assumed in the International Strategy for the Second Development Decade reflected a genuine political will or were simply delaying tactics.

Preliminary observations
If the analyses and decisions of UNCTAD III are to be realistic and pertinent, we must face the world as it is, defending ourselves against illusions and mystifications, but at the same time throwing wide the gates of imagination and creativeness to new solutions for our old problems.

The first point to be recalled is that our community is not homogeneous, but divided up into peoples who have grown rich and peoples who are still poor. Yet more important is it to recognize that among the poor nations themselves there are, unfortunately, some that are even poorer than others; and many that exist under unbearable conditions. Their economy is dominated by foreign powers; outsiders hold all or part of their territory; they still endure the yoke of colonialism; or a majority of their population is exposed to the violence of racial prejudice and of apartheid. Worse still, in many of our countries deep social disparities oppress the masses and benefit only the privileged few.

Secondly, the toil and the resources of the poorer nations subsidize the prosperity of the affluent peoples.

Manifest, too, is the validity of the declaration signed in Lima by the ministers of the Third World. Between 1960 and 1969, our countries' share in world trade dropped from 21.3 percent to 17.6 percent. During the same period, our annual per capita income increased by only $40, while that of the affluent nations rose by $650.

Over the last 20 years, the ebb and flow of foreign capital into and out of the Third World has meant a net loss for us of many hundreds of millions of dollars, besides leaving us in debt to the tune of nearly $70,000 million.

Direct investment of foreign capital, often presented as an instrument for progress, has almost proved negative in its effects. For example, between 1950 and 1967, according to data furnished by the Organization of American States, Latin America received $3.9 million and disbursed $12.8 million. We paid out $4 for every dollar we received.

Thirdly, this economic, financial and trade order, so prejudicial to the Third World precisely because it is so advantageous to the affluent countries, is defended by most of these with bulldog tenacity, through their economic might, through their cultural influence, and, on some occasions, and by some powers, through almost irresistible forms of pressure, through armed interventions which violate all the commitments assumed in the Charter of the United Nations.

Another development of unquestionably vital importance, which cuts across and embraces the present structure of international economic relations, and which in practice makes a mockery of international agreements, is the expansion of the great transnational corporations.

In economic circles, and even at meetings like this, trade and development facts and figures are often bandied to and fro without any real attempt to measure how they affect the human being, how they affect his basic rights, how they strike at the right to life itself, which implies the right to full self-realization. The human being should be the object and the goal of all development policies and of all desirable forms of international cooperation. This is a concept which must be borne in mind in every discussion, in every decision, in every policy measure which aims at fostering progress whether at the national or at the multilateral level.

If the present state of affairs continues, 15 percent of the population of the Third World is doomed to die of starvation. Since, moreover, medical and health services are seriously deficient, the expectation of life is only half as long as in the industrialized countries, and a high proportion of the population can never make any real contribution to the progress of thought and creative activity. Here I may repeat something of which our people are painfully aware. In Chile, a country with about

10 million inhabitants, where levels of diet, health and education have been higher than the average for developing countries, there are 600,000 children who, for want of proteins in the first eight months of their life, will never attain the full mental vigor for which they would have been genetically fitted.

There are more than 700 million illiterates in Asia, Africa and Latin America, and as many millions more have got no farther than the stage of basic education. The housing deficit is so colossal that in Asia alone there are 250 million persons without a proper roof over their heads. Proportional figures are recorded for Africa and Latin America.

Unemployment and underemployment have soared to a terrifying pitch and are still increasing. In Latin America, for example, 50 percent of the economically active population are out of work, or have jobs which are nothing but forms of disguised unemployment, their earnings from which, especially in the rural areas, fall far short of their vital needs.

This is the logical outcome of a well-known fact: the developing countries, in which 60 percent of the world's population is concentrated, have at their disposal only 12 percent of the gross product. There are scores of countries in which annual per capita income does not exceed $100, while in several others it amounts to about $3,000 and in the United States it reaches $4,240.

Some can look forward to a livelihood which will bring everything within their reach. Others are born to starve. And even in the midst of plenty, there are millions who lead a handicapped and poverty-stricken life.

It is incumbent upon us, the underprivileged, to strive unflaggingly to transform an archaic, inequitable and dehumanized economic structure into one which will not only be fairer to all, but will be capable of counteracting the effects of age-old exploitation.

Ways out of underdevelopment
The question is whether we poorer nations can meet this challenge from our present subordinate or dependent positions. First we must acknowledge long-standing weaknesses on our own part which have done much to perpetuate the disparate trade patterns that have led the peoples of the world to develop along equally disparate lines, for example, the connivance of some national ruling groups with the causes of underdevelopment. Their own prosperity was based precisely on their role as agents of foreign exploitation.

No less important has been the alienation of the national consciousness. It has absorbed a view of the world worked out in the great dominant centers and presented in scientific guise as the explanation of our backward state. Such theories ascribed the inevitable stagnation of the developing continents to supposed natural factors such as climate, race or racial mixtures, or attachments to autochthonous cultural traditions. But they paid no heed to the real causes of backwardness, such as foreign colonial and neocolonial exploitation.

Another respect in which we are to blame is that the Third World has not yet achieved full unity, unconditionally backed by every single one of our countries.

The correction of these mistakes must be accorded priority. The same view is expressed in the Charter of Algiers and in the Declaration of Lima drawn up by the Group of 77.

The internal effort of the developing countries themselves

The governments of the countries of the Third World have now formulated a philosophy much more consciously in keeping with the realities of today. For example, the Declaration of Lima, besides endorsing the emphatic assertion in the Charter of Algiers that the primary responsibility for our development is incumbent upon ourselves, pledged its signatories to carry out the reforms in their economic and social structures required to ensure the full mobilization of their basic resources and to guarantee their people's participation in the process of development and in its benefits. The declaration likewise condemned dependence in any shape or form which may help to aggravate underdevelopment.

Not only do we support this philosophy in Chile but we are putting it fully into practice. We are doing so with profound conviction, consistently with our socio-economic and political situation.

The people and the government are committed to a historical process designed to bring about fundamental and revolutionary changes in the structure of Chilean society. We want to lay the foundations for a new society which will offer all its members social equality, welfare, freedom and dignity.

Experience, often a hard task-master, has taught us that in order to meet our people's needs and provide each one with the means of full self-realization, it was essential to leave behind the capitalist regime of dependence and forge ahead along a new road. This new road is the socialism we are starting to build.

In line with our history and tradition, we are conducting this process of revolutionary change while taking steps to make the system more truly democratic, with due respect for the pluralism of our political organization, within the legal order and using the legal instruments with which the country has equipped itself; not only maintaining but extending the civic and social, individual and collective liberties. In Chile there is not a single political prisoner, nor the least restriction on oral or written freedom of speech. All creeds and forms of worship are unconditionally permitted and are treated with the greatest respect.

In this country the forces of the opposition can exercise the right granted them by the law and the constitution to voice their protests and organize marches; and it is precisely on its legal substantiation that this attitude is based. Moreover, the government guarantees the right in question through the security forces dependent upon it.

Chile's process of change has been launched under a multiparty regime, with a highly developed body of law and judicial system that is absolutely independent of the other state powers. The opposition holds the majority in parliament.

By releasing pent-up dynamic forces in the economic system, we propose to do away with the traditional growth model which was based almost entirely on the expansion of exports and on import substitution. Our strategy implies assigning priority to popular consumption and relying upon domestic market prospects. We do not advocate economic self-sufficiency, but utilization of the immense potential represented by our people and our resources as active agents of development.

One of the primary objectives of the People's Government is the recovery of the country's basic sources of wealth for its own use.

We have nationalized iron, steel, coal and nitrates, which now belong to the Chilean people. We are nationalizing copper through a constitutional reform that has been unanimously approved by a parliament in which the government does not hold the majority. We have taken charge of the copper industry and have achieved a high production figure, overcoming immense technical and administrative difficulties, and remedying serious deficiencies imputable to those who were drawing the profits of these mines.

The recovery of our basic resources will now enable us to use for our own benefit the surpluses formerly sent abroad by the foreign companies. Thus we shall improve our balance of payments.

The nationalization of copper was an inevitable step which could brook no delay. To assess the harm that was being done to our economy, suffice it to quote only a few figures: according to their book values, the copper-mining companies made a net initial investment of $30 million in Chile 42 years ago, and since then, without having subsequently brought in any fresh capital, have withdrawn the enormous sum of over $4,000 million — an amount almost the equivalent of our current external debt. They have also bequeathed us credit commitments totaling over $700 million, which the state will have to pay off. According to the 1968 balance sheet, the Anaconda Company had placed only 17 percent of its total world investment in our country. Yet it obtained 79 percent of its profits from Chile.

I will refer to only two other aspects of my government's socioeconomic action: one is its policy of broad and radical income redistribution, and the other the speeding-up of the agrarian reform, with the aim of ensuring that by the end of this year not a single *latifundio* will be left in Chile. This reform includes a dynamic and realistic agricultural development strategy. Thus, in but a few years we hope to make up the food deficit which nowadays compels us to import food-stuffs to a value of over $300 million, a sum out of proportion to our resources.

The regional effort

All that has been done at the national level has been complemented by a determined policy of economic integration with the Latin American countries. In particular, the Andean Pact (whose members are Bolivia, Chile, Colombia, Ecuador and Peru) is a living example of the immense possibilities that exist for cooperation between underdeveloped countries, when there is a firm political will to take action.

In less than three years we have trebled our reciprocal trade, and we are applying instruments for coordinating the economic strategies of the individual countries. To this end, we have agreed upon a Common Treatment for Foreign Investment, which puts an end to our suicidal competition to tap external resources and corrects unfair practices that have long been in current use. We are fully convinced that integration among countries like ours cannot derive solely from the mechanical interplay of market forces; joint planning must be undertaken for the key sectors of the economy, with a view to determining the lines of production that each country will be called upon to undertake.

The Andean Pact — authentically Latin American — is of vital importance not only because of the technical pragmatism with which we are tackling problems as they arise, but also because we are conducting an autochthonous experiment in integration, based on the most absolute respect for ideological pluralism and for each country's legitimate right to adopt whatever internal structures it may deem most appropriate.

The structure of international economic relations and under-development

The task assigned to the third session of UNCTAD is to design new economic and trade structures, precisely because those established in the postwar period, which are seriously prejudicial to the developing countries, are on the verge of complete collapse.

The concepts formulated at Bretton Woods and Havana, which brought into being the International Bank for Reconstruction and Development (IBRD), the International Monetary Fund (IMF) and the General Agreement on Tariffs and Trade (GATT), were characterized by exchange, trade and development financing systems based on the interests of a few dominant countries. They evolved at a time when war between the industrial countries of the West and the socialist world was deemed inevitable. As always, economic interests and political interests joined forces to overbear the countries of the Third World. The systems in question established the rules of the trade game. They closed markets to the products of the Third World through the establishment of tariff and non-tariff barriers, through their own anti-economic and unfair production and distribution structures. They set up pernicious financing systems. Furthermore, they determined shipping practices and norms, fixed freight rates and thus secured a virtual monopoly of cargo. They also left the Third World countries to watch the march of science as outsiders, and exported to us technical know-how which in many cases simply constituted an instrument of cultural alienation and of increased dependence. We poorer countries cannot allow this situation to continue.

Moreover, the systems conceived at Bretton Woods and Havana have proved incapable of raising the level of living of more than half the human race, or even of maintaining the economic and monetary stability of their own creators and administrators, as has been demonstrated by the dollar crisis which precipitated a collapse.

New world conditions facilitating the work of UNCTAD III
Since the second session of UNCTAD at New Delhi, which was so great a disappointment to the developing countries, world events themselves have transformed the whole political and economic scene, and today there are better possibilities for UNCTAD III to take important steps in the direction proposed.

It is clear to all that the financial conceptions of the postwar period are tottering; that the new or strengthened centers of political and economic power are generating striking changes among the industrialized countries themselves. Peaceful coexistence between the capitalist and socialist countries has finally carried the day. After 20 years of injustice and violation of international law, the exclusion of the People's Republic of China from the world community has come to an end.

Furthermore, in our countries the growing resistance to imperialist supremacy and likewise to internal class domination is daily increasing in strength; a healthy nationalism is gaining renewed vigor. Possibilities are opening up, embryonic as yet although promising, for the less developed countries to make their efforts at self-improvement under a milder degree of external pressure and at a less heavy social cost. Among these hopeful signs is the awareness which the poorer nations are acquiring of the factors responsible for their backwardness. On occasion, their conviction is so profound that no foreign power and no native privileged group can sway it, as is shown by the invincible heroism of Vietnam. Few still dare to expect all the countries of the world to adopt the same socio-economic models. What is compulsory, on the other hand, is the mutual respect which makes it possible for nations with different socio-political systems to live side by side and trade with one another. The present time is witnessing the emergence of specific possibilities for constructing new international trade patterns, which may at last open up prospects of equitable cooperation between rich and poor nations.

These prospects rest upon two bases. Firstly, the decisions which substantially affect the destiny of mankind are increasingly influenced by world opinion, including that of the countries which uphold the status quo. Secondly, conditions are arising which make it advantageous for the central countries themselves (although not for all their enterprises) to establish new patterns for their specifically economic relations with the peripheral countries.

Obviously, the forces of restriction are not yet beating a general retreat. The new hopes that promise liberation may lead only to new forms of colonialism. They will crystallize in one shape or the other according to our clarity of thought and capacity for action. Hence, the exceptional importance and timeliness of this third session of UNCTAD.

Just as in the last century the forces unleashed by the Industrial Revolution metamorphosed the customs, ways of life and modes of thought of all countries, so today the world is being swept by a tide of new technical and scientific discoveries which have the power to bring about still more radical changes, in conflict with preexisting social systems.

We should make sure that the march of pure and applied science is not so conditioned by inflexible social and political structures — both national and international — as to militate against the liberation of mankind. We know that the Industrial Revolution and the wave of change it brought represented for many countries a mere transition from colonial to neocolonial status, and for others, direct colonization. For example, in the international telecommunications system a formidable danger is implicit: 75 percent of it is in the hands of the developed countries of the West, and of this proportion more than 60 percent is controlled by the big United States private corporations. Both to you, Mr. Secretary General, and to the delegations present, I wish to point out that in less than 10 years our community institutions and our homes will be flooded by information and publicity which will be directed from abroad by means of satellites of high transmission power, and which, unless counteracted by timely measures, will serve only to increase our dependence and destroy our cultural values. This danger must be averted by the international community, which should demand that control be exercised by the United Nations.

Another factor that should be regarded as more favorable stems from the increasingly obvious conflicts between the interests of the wealthy nations (those which are of real benefit to their peoples) and the private interests of their great international corporations. The overall cost (military, economic, social and political) of operating through transnational enterprises exceeds their contribution to the central economies and becomes more and more burdensome to the taxpayer.

We should also take into account the depredations of these consortia, and their powerful corruptive influence on public institutions in rich and poor countries alike. The peoples affected oppose such exploitation, and demand that the governments concerned should cease to leave part of their external economic policy in the hands of private enterprises, which arrogate to themselves the role of agents promoting the progress of the poorer countries, and have become a supranational force that is threatening to get completely out of control.

This undeniable fact has profound implications for the proceedings of the present conference. There is a serious risk that even if we arrive at satisfactory understandings among the representatives of sovereign states, the measures upon which we agree may have no real impact, inasmuch as de facto these companies handle quietly the practical application of the agreements in conformity with their own interests.

We spend our time at international meetings discussing the visible features of the Third World's structure of dependence, while its deeplying determinants slip by us unseen, like the submerged three-quarters of an iceberg.

UNCTAD should look very carefully into this threat. This flagrant intervention in the internal affairs of states is more serious, more subtle and more dangerous than that of governments themselves, which is condemned in the Charter of the United Nations. The corporations actually seek to upset the normal functioning of the governments and institutions of other nations, to start worldwide campaigns against the prestige of a government, to make it the victim of an international boycott and to sabotage its economic relations with the rest of the world. Recent and well-known cases, which have shocked the world, and by which we are directly affected, sound the alarm for the international community, which is under an imperative obligation to react with the utmost vigor.

Reflections on some crucial problems

I now want to turn to other problems. It is for the delegations attending this conference to put forward whatever solutions they may deem appropriate. Not only is there abundant documentation prepared by the United Nations, but also — and of particular importance — the Lima Declaration, Principles and Program of Action. This document constitutes "the unified expression of the shared hopes and aspirations of mankind, as expressed by the ministers of 96 developing countries, who represent the vast majority of mankind," which should "go a long way in evoking favorable response from the international community and, in particular, from the peoples and governments of the developed world." It is for you to meet all the legitimate demands which the Action Program embodies.

They are all of vital importance. I would stress the problems relating to primary commodities because they are of basic interest to the great majority of the participants.

For my own part, I only want to place before the meeting some of the points that concern me, as chief of state of one of the Third World countries, with respect to certain items on the agenda.

It is impossible for all the industrialized countries to respond alike. Their resources and means of action are different, nor have they all had the same share of responsibility in the creation and maintenance of the existing international order. For example, neither the socialist countries nor all the small and medium-sized countries have contributed to the generation of this irrational division of labor.

Reforms of the monetary and trade systems
The first of my anxieties relates to the danger that the restructuring of the international monetary and trade systems may once again be carried out without the full and effective participation of the countries of the Third World.

In connection with the monetary system, and particularly since the crisis of last August, the developing countries have recorded their protest in all world and regional meetings. They had no responsibility whatever for the breakdown of monetary and trade machinery in whose management they had taken no part. Time and again they have urged that a monetary reform must be jointly prepared by all the countries of the world; that it must be based on a more dynamic concept of world trade; that it must recognize the new requirements of the developing countries and that never again must it be handled exclusively by some few privileged countries.

It is of vital importance that the conference should unhesitatingly and unreservedly reaffirm these objectives.

True, the details of a new system can be completed in other more specialized gatherings. But so close is the connection between monetary problems and trade relations, as the crisis of last August testified, that it is the duty of UNCTAD to discuss the subject in depth and to see that the new monetary system, studied, prepared and administered by the whole of the international community, will also serve to finance the development of the Third World countries, alongside the expansion of world trade.

In respect of the indispensable trade reform there are some grounds for alarm. A few weeks ago the United States and Japan, on the one hand, and the United States and the European Economic Community, on the other, sent respective memoranda to GATT. These two almost identical documents declare that the sponsors pledge themselves to launch and actively support the conclusions and implementation of integral agreements under GATT as from 1973, with a view to the expansion and liberalization of international trade. They add that, furthermore, their aim is to improve the level of living of all peoples, and that ways of achieving this include, among others, the progressive lowering of trade barriers, and endeavors to improve the international framework within which trade is carried on.

It is, of course, satisfactory that three great centers of power should decide to subject their international economic relations to a through overhaul, taking into account the improvement of the levels of living of all peoples. It is also laudable that they should mention the need to reorient trade policy through international or regional agreements making for market organization. But it does not escape our observation that the liberalization of trade among the industrialized countries of the West wipes out at a stroke of the pen the advantages of the general system of preferences for the developing countries.

And what we find most disquieting is that the three great economic powers are proposing to implement this policy not through UNCTAD but through GATT. The General Agreement on Tariffs and Trade has always been essentially concerned with the interests of the powerful countries; it has no reliable linkage with the United Nations and is not obliged to adhere to its principles, and its membership is at odds with the concept of universal participation.

I think that the developed countries should put an end to these continual onslaughts against UNCTAD, which is the world community's most representative body in this field, and affords exceptional opportunities for negotiating major economic and trade questions on a footing of legal equality. The developing countries, in contrast, wish to perfect the existing institution and broaden its authority. It is essential that UNCTAD should acquire full autonomy and become a specialized agency of the United Nations system, so that it can exercise greater freedom of action, greater influence, greater capacity to solve those crucial problems which fall within its province. We peoples of the Third World, who did not speak out at Bretton Woods or at the later meetings where the financial system now in force was drawn up, who do not participate today in the decisions of the Ten on the financial strategy of the great Western powers; we who have no voice in discussions on the restructuring of the world monetary system; we need an efficacious instrument to defend our threatened interests. At the present time, this instrument can only be UNCTAD itself, converted into a permanent organization.

The overburdening of the developing countries by debt

My second concern relates to the external debt. We developing countries already owe more than $70,000 million, although we have contributed to the prosperity of the wealthy peoples from time immemorial, and more particularly in recent decades.

External debts, largely contracted in order to offset the damage done by an unfair trade system, to defray the costs of the establishment of foreign enterprises in our territory, to cope with the speculative exploitation of our reserves, constitute one of the chief obstacles to the progress of the Third World. The Lima document and Resolution 2,807 of the most recent General Assembly of the United Nations dealt with the question of indebtedness. The latter resolution took into consideration, inter alia, the increasingly heavy burdens imposed by debt servicing on the countries of the Third World, the weakening of gross transfers of resources to the developing countries and the deterioration of the terms of trade. It emphatically requested the competent financial institutions and the creditor countries concerned to give sympathetic consideration to requests for rescheduling or consolidation of their debts with appropriate periods of grace and amortization, and reasonable rates of interest. It also invited the same countries and institutions to examine more rational ways of financing the economic development of the Third World. All this is highly satisfactory for us.

I believe it is indispensable to make a critical study of the way in which the Third World's external debt has been contracted and the conditions required to rescue it from this position without impairing its efforts to combat underdevelopment. Such a study might be undertaken by the secretary general of UNCTAD and presented to the General Assembly of the United Nations.

At the present time Chile exemplifies the seriousness of the situation. Our total annual income is $1.2 billion. This year we are due to pay $408 million. It is inconceivable that out of every $100 that flow into its coffers a country should have to earmark $34 for the servicing of its external debt.

Pressures to prevent the exercise of the right to dispose freely of natural resources

My third concern is directly connected with the second. It relates to the real and potential pressure exerted to restrict the sovereign right of peoples to dispose of their natural resources for their own benefit. This right has been proclaimed in the Covenants on Human Rights, in several resolutions of the General Assembly and in the First General Principle adopted at the first session of UNCTAD.

In the Lima Declaration the Group of 77 very clearly formulates an additional principle for the defense of our countries against threats of this kind. We need to raise it from the status of a principle to that of a ruling economic practice. It reads as follows: "The recognition that every country has the sovereign right freely to dispose of its natural resources in the interests of the economic development and well-being of its own people; any external, political or economic measure or pressure brought to bear on the exercise of this right is a flagrant violation of the principles of self-determination of peoples and of nonintervention, as set forth in the United Nations Charter, and, if pursued, could constitute a threat to international peace and security."

Why did the developing countries wish to be so explicit? The history of the past 50 years abounds in examples of direct or indirect coercion, military or economic — cruel for those who suffer it and degrading for those who inflict it — designed to prevent the underdeveloped countries from making free use of their basic resources which represent the daily bread of their inhabitants. Mexico, Central America and the Caribbean have known it. The case of Peru, in 1968, elicited an uncompromising retort from the Latin American countries at a meeting of the special Committee on Latin American Coordination (CECLA) — witness the Consensus of Viña del Mar.

Chile has nationalized copper, the basic resource which accounts for over 70 percent of its exports. Little weight has been carried, however, by the fact that the nationalization process, with all its implications and consequences, has been the clearest and most categorical expression of the will of its people, and has been conducted in full accordance with the exact dictates of provisions established in the nation's constitution. Little weight has been carried by the fact that the foreign companies which exploited the mines have drawn profits many times greater than the value of their investments. These companies, which amassed huge fortunes at our expense, and assumed that they had the right to burden us indefinitely with their presence and their abuses, have stirred up forces of every kind, including those of their own state institutions, in their country and elsewhere, to attack and injure Chile and its economy.

I am unwilling to leave this unpleasant subject without singling out, among the forms of pressure to which we have been subjected, two whose impact transcends the violation of the principle of non-intervention.

One is designed to prevent Chile from obtaining new terms and new time limits for the payment of its external debt. I imagine our creditors will not countenance it. Friendly countries are not likely to lend themselves to forcing down still farther our people's low level of living. It would be an injustice, a tragic injustice.

The other type of pressure seeks, by virtue of a law on foreign aid adopted by one of the biggest contributors to the International Bank for Reconstruction and Development (IBRD) and to the Inter-American Development Bank (IDB), to make those banks' financial assistance to Chile conditional upon our applying policies which would infringe constitutional principles governing the nationalization of copper. Of these two banks, one is linked to the United Nations and the other to the Organization of American States, whose official principles and objectives forbid them to accept terms such as these.

If policies like these were implemented, they would deal a death-blow to international cooperation for development and would destroy the very basis of the multilateral financing systems to which many countries, in a cooperative effort contribute as far as they can. Such policies imply the downfall of conceptions which embodied a sense of worldwide solidarity, and spotlight the naked fact of ulterior motives of a strictly commercial order. This would set the clock back 100 years.

Remarks on access to technology

I would also draw the attention of this meeting to the urgent need for the Third World to have access to modern science and technology. The obstacles we have encountered hitherto are determinants of our underdevelopment.

Industrialization, as an essential part of the overall development process, is closely related to a country's scientific and technical creative capacity, whereby industrial development can be adjusted to the real characteristics of each region, whatever its present stage of economic growth.

Today, our capacity for the creation of technology is far from adequate, as the result of our history of dependence. For example, our research projects follow the theoretical models of the industrialized world. They are inspired more by the real conditions and needs of the developed countries than by those of our own. And with steadily increasing frequency, thousands of scientists and professionals leave their native lands to work in the affluent countries. We export ideas and skilled personnel; we import technology and dependence.

To find a solution for this basic problem that would enable us to finish with technological subordination is a difficult, slow and costly process. We are faced with two possibilities.

On the one hand, we can continue to base our industrial development on foreign investment and technology, intensifying more and more the dependence which is threatening to turn us back into colonies. Latin America has enjoyed a long period of buoyant optimism deriving from the policy of industrial development through import substitution. In other words, the installation of factories for local production of what had formerly been imported, an operation which was subsidized with costly fringe benefits: exchange facilities, customs protection, loans in local currency and government guarantees for financing from abroad. Experience has shown that this type of industrialization — promoted mainly by international corporations — has proved to be a new instrument of recolonization. Its harmful effects include the establishment of a technician-manager stratum which has grown increasingly influential, and has become a defender of the foreign interests which it has identified with its own. Still more serious have been the social effects. The big industrial plants, using advanced techniques, give rise to serious unemployment and underemployment problems, and bankrupt small- and medium-scale domestic industries. We should also mention the tendency to concentrate on industries producing consumer goods which are of use to only a limited group of privileged persons, and indirectly create conspicuous consumption tastes and patterns to the detriment of the values characteristic of our culture.

The other possibility consists in creating or strengthening our own scientific and technological capacity, resorting in the meantime to a transfer of knowledge and methods firmly supported by the international community, and prompted by a humanistic philosophy which sets up the human being as its major objective.

At present, this transfer takes the form of trade in a merchandise which appears under different guises: technical assistance, equipment, production processes, etc. This commerce is conducted on certain explicit and implicit terms which are extremely unfavorable to the buyer country, especially if it happens to be underdeveloped. In 1968, for instance, Latin America disbursed over $500 million under the head of purchase of technology alone.

These conditions must be abolished. We must be able to select technology in relation to our own needs and our own development plans.

Towards solidarity in the world economy

What can be done in these circumstances? The world as it is, with all its injustice towards the underdeveloped countries, cannot be changed overnight. We have no choice but to continue the struggle to mitigate the negative effects of this state of affairs and lay the foundations for constructing what I would call a solidarity world economy.

The present international conjuncture is favorable for endeavoring to change the economic order. Perhaps this is an over-optimistic appraisal, but the truth is that international events in the last few decades have resulted in a gradual accumulation of factors which have finally crystallized into a new opportunity. The most striking feature is the possibility offered to the world of more self-respecting international relations, free from submission and despotism alike. There is understanding between the capitalist world powers; there is coexistence and dialogue between these and the socialist countries.

Could something similar develop between the former colonizing and imperialist countries on the one hand, and the dependent peoples on the other? The future will tell whether we peoples of the Third World will gain recognition for our rights through the restructuring of international trade and the establishment of relations that are fair to each and all. The latter, it must be emphasized, may be the more delicate and thorny question.

It is for the delegations present at the third session of UNCTAD to ask themselves on what bases it would be possible to organize a new form of human coexistence, founded at last on solidarity, after the long-drawn-out history of oppression we have lived and still are living through.

Let me say, however, that in my own opinion one of these bases might be disarmament on lines that would lay the foundations for a solidarity economy on a world scale, although some believe that this is beyond the bounds of possibility.

For the socialist economies, the prospect of peaceful development is their fundamental historical aspiration. Once peace has been firmly established, they will be able to play a more active part in multilateral cooperation and to supply the world market with technical and productive resources which would play a decisive role in their own prosperity and would make an effective contribution to the success of the Third World in overcoming the distorting effects of centuries of exploitation.

In view of the experience of recent years, I do not think that the capitalist countries should seek to perpetuate such ideas as colonialism and neocolonialism, and to persist in the maintenance of an economy for war in order to ensure full employment. Only the Third World, with its immense needs, can constitute a new economic frontier for the developed countries. Only such a new frontier is capable — more so than a war economy — of absorbing the production capacity of the large companies and giving employment opportunities to the whole of the labor force. I should like to believe that enlightened leaders, aware of the radical changes that lie ahead, are beginning to give serious thought to new solutions, in which the Third World and the socialist countries will participate fully.

Fund for homogeneous human development

It is essential to make a determined search for an economically viable equation between the vast needs of the poorer nations and the immense production capacity of the richer countries. The solution might be found in a strategy of pacification, through a disarmament plan under which a high percentage of the expenditure hitherto allocated to munitions and warfare would be assigned to a fund for homogeneous human development. This fund could be available primarily for long-term loans to enterprises in the same countries that set it up.

As the amount spent every year on war and armaments nowadays exceeds $220,000 million, potential resources exist that would be more than enough to start shaping a solidarity world economy.

The objectives pursued would be to turn a war economy back into a peace economy and, concurrently, to contribute to the development of the Third World. The fund would finance major projects and programs for these countries, of a kind such as would absorb the manpower released by the reduction of expenditure on armaments, would produce enough to cover their costs, and, above all, would be set up as autonomous national companies capable of sustained growth. At the same time, it would launch a new era of continuing economic development; of full employment of the factors of production, including the whole of the labor force; and, above all, of progressive bridging of the gulf between the prosperous nations and the despoiled peoples.

This is not a utopia. In the world of today, which must cooperate or perish, new ideas, prompted not only by justice but invariably by reason, may result in worthwhile solutions for the human race.

To the delegations here present I would say that I wish them every success in their work. Chile will do all it can to contribute to that end, taking advantage of all the opportunities afforded it by its position as host to facilitate contacts and create a climate favorable to understanding. Its delegates will not seek unnecessary clashes of opinion, but fruitful agreements.

The passionate fervor that an entire people has put into the construction of this building is a symbol of the passionate fervor with which Chile desires to contribute to the construction of a new humanity, so that in this and in the other continents, hardship, poverty and fear may cease to be.

I dare to believe that this conference will give positive answers to the anguished questionings of millions of human beings. Not in vain has the long journey to this distant country been made by the most distinguished economic leaders of almost all the countries of the world, including those that have most power to turn the course of events.

Of one thing at least you can be certain: as was said at Lima, the peoples of the world will not allow poverty and affluence to exist indefinitely side by side. They will not accept an international order which will perpetuate their backward state. They will seek and they will obtain their economic independence and will conquer underdevelopment. Nothing can prevent it: neither threats, nor corruption, nor force. Progress and the liberation of the vast underdeveloped world depend on the urgently needed transformation of the world economic structure, on the conscience of countries, on choosing a path of cooperation based on solidarity, justice, and respect for human rights. Otherwise, on the contrary, people will be forced to take the road of conflict, violence, and suffering precisely in order to impose the principles of the Charter of the United Nations.

16

Interview with Chilean Journalists

On the radio show "The Great Inquiry,"
September 10, 1972

On the well-known Radio Portales program "The Great Inquiry," Allende dialogues for one-and-a-half hours with the show's journalists. He repeatedly denounces small fascist groups like the "ill-named" Fatherland and Liberty and the illegal and violent destabilizing tactics of big U.S. corporations like Kennecott Copper and ITT. He comments on the subtlety of imperialism's tactics, including its "invisible blockade" and disinformation campaign that are becoming more powerful every day. He answers questions on topics ranging from food shortages (rationing and hoarding) to incidents of violence and threats by ultra-rightist and ultra-leftist groups. He says how deeply moved he is by recent peaceful pro-government street marches incorporating hundreds of thousands of Christian Democrats and members of other groups outside the governing Popular Unity coalition. In the face of growing demands from different sectors, however, Allende warns of the dangers of violent confrontation and stresses the importance of finding peaceful political solutions to the problems facing the country. He criticizes the Christian Democrats for breaking earlier agreements but reiterates his invitation to dialogue with all the political parties of the opposition. Finally, he speaks to the rights of Chile's middle classes, including small shopkeepers, in whose interests the revolution is being made, and to the rights of women, children and youth.

Q uestion: The past 15 days have been marked by violence. Many events in several cities of the country have disclosed a panorama that, to say the least, causes concern and unrest among Chileans. Because of this, we thought it would be interesting to devote this program to talking freely with the president.

Chileans know that Dr Allende is the president of Chile who talks most with his people, who travels most and who is in the closest contact with the masses. A foreign journalist has said of you, Dr Allende, that you have set up your office in a plane and in the back seat of your car. This means that you are constantly on the go throughout the country. However, you do not talk with a group of reporters often. This is the first time since you became president that you have granted an interview to a radio program.

We would like to talk with you about the most important and urgent Chilean problems, such as the economic problem. I think we will talk about that. But the most recent news is about the situation created in the country by a U.S. firm that used to exploit our copper mines. Would you prefer to begin with this topic?

Salvador Allende: As you wish, but first let me clarify that I have been meeting and I will continue to meet frequently with national and foreign journalists. It is true that this is the first time that I have talked with a regular radio program since the time I spoke when I was president-elect. I take advantage of the microphones of Radio Portales and of the "Great Inquiry Program" to greet the listeners of Radio Portales, to greet my compatriots and to tell them that I am prepared to talk about any topic that you might suggest.

You have brought up the Kennecott matter, and I believe that there is good reason for every Chilean to be concerned and indignant over the decision of that foreign company. It is trying to embargo Chilean copper production and our copper shipments to get even — according to them — for our not paying indemnity.

It is necessary to again emphasize that the government has only applied a constitutional amendment that was unanimously approved by the Congress — where the government is in the minority, a marked minority. It is not only paradoxical but unbelievable that a firm should reject the verdict of a court to which it has taken its case. How legal can this be, what can this attitude mean?

I think that all of Chile, not just the political parties that approved the government's proposal in Congress, all of Chile should react with the dignity of a country — with nationalism and patriotism. There is an international awareness about these transnational companies. Chile already knows how ITT acted, how it practically led us to a civil war. And now we have an aggression by these big firms that thrust their exploiting claws into many hemispheres, that crushed our countries.

This is why, Leonardo Caceres [presumably radio reporter] I am convinced — and I am pleased that you have asked this question — that Chileans, regardless of their ideological position, regardless of whether they have an ideological position, will support their government in this matter of defending Chile — its tradition, dignity and future.

Question: President, for a long time now there has been talk abut Chile being the victim of an invisible blockade by big foreign powers. This is no longer an invisible blockade, it is an actual blockade. Does this mean that this is an aggression?

Allende: It means a much clearer attitude, an effort to block the popular government's economic progress. You understand that they are going to embargo the copper shipments, that is, the production of copper which has been already sold. Furthermore, an international campaign has been waged saying that Chile will not be able to meet its commitments. Can you imagine that, comrade reporters of "The Great Inquiry"? On the international banking level, the copper contracts have been handled the same way that any bank in Chile handles bank documents — drafts for example. We have all had drafts with the banks at one time or another, I probably more often than you, right? If you draw against an unbacked draft, but if you have had an account and honored the payments, the bank will give you an advance on this document, right — a percent that is quite high — 50, 60, even 80 percent. This is what was happening with the copper contracts. They are real documents and were given to the banks for collection by them. Therefore, there was a certain interest on them.

But also foreign currency in dollars was advanced. Why? Because the accounts are in dollars. An international atmosphere has been created with the campaign waged in Chile about great faults and deficiencies, that we will not be able to meet our commitments, that three, five reverberating furnaces burst, and so on and so forth. Then what about these drafts sent to the banks? These documents are no guarantee for the banks today because they are not going to be backed by copper production; they are just pieces of paper. This embargo has enormously harmed Chile. Go ahead.

Question: President, from your words one can see that the basic problem is, one could say, the following: For us, for the Chilean process, the form of imperialism was more sophisticated, more concealed, than in the case of other peoples and experiences. This, maybe, is the biggest problem today as far as achieving internal unity. I do not know if this is your opinion.

Allende: Of course, you are right Fernando Reyes, [presumably another reporter] because in this country nobody would accept a direct intervention, nobody would accept what happened in Santo Domingo [Dominican Republic, invaded by U.S. Marines in 1965]. Chile is a country that has great nationalism, and everybody has reacted, I think everybody, even the government's most stubborn opposition, has reacted. But then, the people do not see this concealed, veiled way of acting. The people are unaware of this. Furthermore, what does the peasant know, what, for example, do many comrade workers — including employees and even professionals — know? Since we have not indemnified the copper companies, they think we have taken the mines without taking over any commitments.

No, the companies have a $726 million debt which they must pay the Chilean Government. But since we did not indemnify the companies because we applied the constitutional reform, they have cut off our short-term credits in the American banks. Even though we renegotiated Chile's bank debt with them — and this was under good terms, I would say with understanding from the banks — yet they have not reopened the lines of credit. Chile had $230 million in U.S. lines of credit. We do not have a penny. Just think what it means — besides all this, the price of copper has gone down extraordinarily.

In 1970, during Mr. Frei's administration, the price of copper was 59 cents a pound. In 1971 it was 49 cents a pound, or $175 million less in income. We produced more copper because the Exótica and La Andina mines began operating. This year we are going to produce more copper because production is really going to increase. Now that the Exótica and La Andina are operating, we are going to produce more than in 1971. However, our income is going to be less because the price of copper will not even reach 49 cents. It will be 48 cents. Go ahead, Comrade Gana.

Question: President, I would like to ask a question on this matter. The truth is that the Kennecott affair, besides being serous, is critical. You say that the people must support their government, something which I consider to be absolutely logical because after the unanimous approval of the constitutional reform it has become obvious that there is a consensus of opinion in the country, that there is a unanimous opinion on copper matters. But, what will the government do to defend itself against the Kennecott attack, because as far as people can see, it is not only the problem but the manner of defending the country? Your decision can strengthen support.

Allende: First of all create awareness. To insist on this and explain why what I have referred to as Chile's paycheck — copper — is steadily decreasing, but not for the reason the opposition is giving — not because of less production but because of lower prices and threat of embargoes. It is really important that the people positively know why, because now we have at our doorstep other conflicts that are also a result of

Congress's approval of the executive branch's proposal. You know, comrades of "The Great Inquiry," and Raúl Tarud had better not forget this — I can tell that he is interested in what I am saying — do not forget that we have submitted a bill to nationalize ITT. It has been unanimously approved by the Chamber of Deputies. It is back in the Senate now. Undoubtedly we are going to have problems, difficulties, because they expect us to pay indemnification to this firm which practically led us to a civil war. This firm intervened, spent money, used its influence, practically determined which the Chilean groups should be, from the armed forces to the politicians. It had influence on the murder of General René Schneider. Well, the nationalization if ITT is coming.

ITT is supported by a big insurance company for which the United States is responsible. They say that to pay ITT this insurance when it is nationalized, the United States will have to tax the American taxpayer. This then will create several problems that the people are unaware of — in other words, problems which they do not realize exist. As Fernando Reyes Matta was saying, this is a much more concealed way, but it is extraordinarily harmful, and this is why the people must be made aware, we must tell this to them. Furthermore, excuse me just a moment Comrade Caceres, in reply to Juan Gana, I say that, in juridical terms, we must conduct more serious and in-depth studies.

We must also appeal to international awareness, if some markets are closed to us. El Teniente production, for example, nearly 70,000 tons — of special significance in copper production — is basically earmarked for England. We do not believe that England will fail to demand the fulfillment of the long-term contract. But we also have the possibility of placing this copper in other areas where they will be unable to embargo it.

But it interests us very much that there is a great demonstration of national protest and also that internationally it is being noted how these companies operate. It was clearly established in the UNCTAD III meeting. In the United Nations also, the secretary general, and especially the under-secretary, condemned the Geneva meeting. Our delegate Hernán Santa Cruz obtained a unanimous agreement which I never thought would be approved — get this, unanimously. In other words, an international condemnation exists, and this is favorable to Chile's position.

Question: There is a latent subject in all that we have discussed which we have called the people's unity. I would like to speak of this a little, perhaps Hernán Rodríguez...

Question: Mr. President: I would like to ask a question about that because in recent days I have been speaking with a U. S. reporter who is a *Washington Post* correspondent in South America. He has served in Buenos Aires for approximately two years, and very often visits Chile. He is extremely interested in the Chilean situation and was deeply impressed by last Monday's march. He was impressed, he said, because of the great support the government enjoys after two years in office — especially on the part of the working class. Because, he said to me, "the people who produce are the ones who marched there." The results of the Coquimbo elections also impressed him deeply, where Amanda Altamirano, a Popular Unity worker managed to defeat all the united opposition forces — an extraordinary feat. At least, this had not happened in Chile for many years. This undoubtedly demonstrates great popular support. Moreover, he commented on the CUT, how the CUT was operating, and how he did not understand much of the Chilean process. In this regard, he asked me why, within the CUT, the Christian Democrats were working beside the Socialists, Communists, and other parties of the UP [Popular Unity]. And later — forgive me for expanding on this — he would comment that in the nitrate refineries, as an example, in the Pedro de Valdivia offices, the head of the voluntary tasks elected by votes of the UP is a Christian Democrat. And undoubtedly all of this is also difficult to explain to the *Washington Post* readers.

Allende: What is significant is that the U.S. reporters attempt to explain it. The problem is that there is not much interest in telling it, in explaining it — at least according to what I see in the press clippings from U.S. dailies. There are also reporters with an ethical attitude who at least state what they see. In this case the reporter is understandably surprised. I have stated this. It is possible that some people do not believe it, but that is the truth. You yourself have just stated something that I want to emphasize. It is the first time during this government — and I believe it may be twice or three times at the most in the past 30 years — that the opposition and the government have confronted each other in a special by-election and the government has won. Recall the case of the by-elections during the Pedro Aguirre Cerda government. I refer not to the presidential elections, but to the parliamentary by-elections.

This victory at Coquimbo is therefore very significant. We obtained 53 percent of the votes. Furthermore, I have told Chile that this is the government with the greatest support. No government, after 20 months in office, has obtained such support at the polls against a united opposition as the government which I lead.

Without taking into account the municipal elections where we won, where the government obtained 50 point something votes, without considering those elections, but considering the by-elections lost by the government and those at Coquimbo which we won, the average is 47.8

percent. The PDC on the other hand, obtained 43 percent of the votes in the elections after 20 months in office.

Then there are the workers' social forces. Despite what happened, despite everything that was said, we obtained more than 70 percent of the votes in the CUT. They mobilized from Arica to Magallanes, in the provincial capitals and in several departments. According to reports I have received — and I believe them — more than 1.5 million Chileans were mobilized. And you must have heard about the rallies organized in Valparaíso, Antofagasta, Concepción, Los Angeles and Puerto Montt. In Los Angeles they lived through the drama of the three murdered peasants as was also the case in Valparaíso with the death of a young man from the Communist Youth..

Never, never has such a large mass mobilized — almost 100 percent of the population. I said that this had only occurred in France when De Gaulle had to return to France in connection with the May events because of the problems that had arisen.

Not only did the people take to the streets, but the large industries, the copper, coal, and nitrate installations, the railroads, the hospitals, schools, and stores symbolically stopped their activities. They were demonstrating the great social force possessed by the people. But what is more important is to meditate on what I said before.

Here in Santiago no one has dared to talk about the figures which were released in order not to alarm the foreign reporters: they were 600,000 or 700,000 persons. But, when did all these people mobilize? They mobilized as the price increases began to hit their homes the hardest. They mobilized as the cost of living reached such high levels — levels which we ourselves had not imagined — when the readjustments were not in effect.

For this reason I was extraordinarily moved, I was deeply affected and became aware of what the people stand for. And I became fully convinced of what the people can do when they have faith and confidence, and that the workers know that this is their government. I became aware that they understood the mistakes and that at last they have admitted them and are ready to suffer. For this reason a worker carried a sign which said "I prefer to eat bread standing up than to eat chicken on my knees." I think this is the symbol of dignity, a dignity we had not seen before. And this is the force of the people, their awareness that they are a factor in history and that this is their government. They became aware that this is their government and therefore also became aware that the errors are theirs — the errors of the workers — since this is the government of the workers.

Question: In line with this subject, what importance do you attach to the joint statement issued by the Socialists and the Communists? I ask this question because there has been a lot of talk about the division existing within the UP.

Allende: Leonardo Caceres, I would not call it division. I would call it a lack of united, centralized thinking, a lack of a similar tactical concept since we must assume that there is a common strategy to attain socialism. Furthermore, I have already said this publicly.

I sent a letter to the UP parties and they answered independently. Who has responded? MAPU, the Christian Left, API, the Communists. However the Radicals and my own party have not yet answered.

The response of the four parties whose letters I have received does not represent united thinking, there are discrepancies. In all the world discrepancies occur, but here they are harshly criticized. Like what happened in Concepción when all the UP parties except the Communists participated with the MIR. What I have condemned in the strongest possible terms is what happened last Wednesday—the incidents during which one *carabinero*, Corporal Aroca, was killed and two others were wounded. And I said that it is inconceivable that anyone could think that one of the ruling parties could have deliberately, through one of its members, caused the death of a *carabinero* under circumstances in which public order — the order which the government needs — is maintained by the *Carabineros*. These actions were carried out by a provocateur or a degenerate who might have infiltrated the ranks of the popular parties. Naturally, such things do happen. Then the people must understand that they must take utmost care and avoid provocation. I have had to use my influence to hold back strong groups of workers, like the group in Cordón [industrial belt] Cerrillos, for example. Fifteen thousand workers could come to downtown Santiago to sweep away 300, let's say 600, insolent fascists, provocateurs, and I have told them no. No, that is what they want, a confrontation, that's what they want. The government has the public order force that allows it to guarantee order. Outside of that there is the Emergency Zone if matters get out of hand, or the state of siege, and so on. I say no more...

Question: In that context, one notices the importance of a phrase you used in the National Stadium: "To overthrow this government is to make this country explode; to try to overthrow it — because you are not going to overthrow it — is to destroy this country." Consequently, behind that affirmation, one notices that President Allende governing this country is the best guarantee of peace today in Chile. So it is, and why?

Allende: I think it is this way because, in essence, there exists the broadest democracy that we are all living. Here there are not only by-elections, municipal elections, there are elections every day. Moreover, citizens' rights have not only been preserved, they have been broadened by us. So far as freedom goes, do you believe, for example, that in other countries a president would submit himself to this conversation? You ask whatever you want, whatever occurs to you.

I believe freedom of information here is the broadest anywhere; press liberty at times has the characteristics of libertinism, not liberty. I have seen opinions about these relations, from other countries, that have admiringly stated: "Mr. President, how can press freedom arrive at such an extreme in Chile that ethical lines are crossed every day when the press misinforms, when obvious and clear facts are denied?" For example, a few dailies said that everyone was amazed by the Santiago march, right? That speech that you are commenting on, Fernando Reyes, in it you have read a sentence; very well, I have seen it twisted beyond recognition in the majority of the opposition dailies. No one, for example, no one notes that I welcomed the statements issued by Cardinal Raúl Silva Henríquez with fervor, respect and affection.

I said with a clear conscience that I welcomed this appeal because as you can see there has been no difficulty, no friction, no incident between the government and the various churches. I am speaking of the Catholic, Orthodox, Seventh Day Adventist, Protestant and Evangelical churches. There are the ecumenical congresses. In what countries have these congresses taken place as they do here?

I have stated — in fact I have made the accusation and demonstrated how — for example that when 700,000 persons mobilized in Santiago not a single window pane was broken, not a single car was scratched, no one was hurt. Yet when 600 or 700 persons mobilized, unfortunately a group of young students and hoodlums who were directed by others took the lead and burned tires, bales of paper, broke windows and store windows and even fired stones with slingshots. These are strictly fascist actions that are of a rather secondary character, but still efficient in this sort of urban confrontation. This has never before occurred in Chile, and this also applies to the banging of empty pots.

We have all seen the front page headlines: "Accumulate Rage." As I was saying, in certain speeches, what if the people were to accumulate rage? And what if that rage were to explode some day? Could anyone morally criticize the people, when it is they [presumably the rightists] — who have been telling Chileans to accumulate rage? We ourselves have been telling the people. "No, we do not want that path which leads to violence. We reject it." When I hear certain people speak of civil war, for example — I will not say that people blame me personally but it does worry me deeply.

There is such maturity in this country, the workers have such force, manage such a high percentage in the economy — they have political influence, not only in the industrial unions but also in the agricultural unions. Imagine what would happen if passion exploded here. What would happen to our economy?

Apart from that about which we do not wish to speak, which would mean a true genocide. So, comrade, I tell you, I have listened to the cardinal, I have looked with great satisfaction at what is being suggested by certain PDC members — Tomic's statement, what I have heard regarding Leighton, even the president of the Senate's suggestion. I think that 90 percent of the Chileans do not want a confrontation. I am well aware that we have hotheads amongst the leftist sectors but no one can deny that the government has been rough on them. In Curimóm we arrested and brought before the military courts the so-called national liberation army, another myth. In jail — the lamentable Las Ventanas affair, in jail. An absurd thing has just happened in the central post office — in jail.

We have never covered up for nor will we ever cover up for a leftist, because if he is a leftist and if he is a member of the Socialist Party, he is doubly guilty, because we have committed ourselves to using certain tactics in keeping with our own conscience and the country's wishes.

Question: What you are saying is highly positive, because if we call it as it is, there are persons [who worry about] certain kinds of action which do not seem to be sufficiently clear. Things are said, much thinking is done, speeches are made, and there are problems which rebound indirectly here in the government. So, speaking frankly, there are people who think that there is a bit of authority lacking, Mr. President. I have said, and I am going to repeat it to you here, that you are somewhat like a conductor leading an orchestra which is off-key because certain musicians do not pay attention to the baton or because they all play the music their own way. Therefore I think that what you have said is really positive because it is an answer to the people who are uncertain, who have doubts. This idea seems fine to me.

Allende: Not only have I said it but I am asking you: When has this government supported or left an incident of this kind in the shadows? We have turned the guilty persons over to the courts, most of them for violating the state's internal security law. All right, we have gotten that far. I know, for example, that certain people criticized me when I went to the Lo Hermida Campamento [shantytown]. All right, I myself have said before the country that I have a different concept of how to exercise authority, and I do not think I have degraded authority. I think it's my duty, in the first place out of conviction and secondly because I am a man elected by the people, by the workers, by the shantytown dwellers. If there was a shantytown dweller dead in an incident which I consider unfortunate and which should never have occurred, my obligation was to go confront things.

They say: "But the president loses authority because a document that was disrespectful to him was read there." No one has been disrespectful to me. Besides, I went there and I told them: "This morning you sent a document demanding that I publicly and in writing accepted your points, and that if do not I should not come to the camp." I have not accepted your points and I am here and I am here alone, with the military aide-de-camp and also with the acting director of investigations. In this way I was defending the military and showing that I respect the armed forces. Since the Investigations Department was questioned, I went with only two persons, but one of them was the acting director of investigations. And I can tell you that I spoke very clearly to the shantytown dwellers.

I said in language they could understand that I was the highest authority, because in a country the president of the republic is the person responsible for the administrative and economic march of the nation, and that I, of course, was going to take measures with regard to the case, to investigate. At the same time I told them that I am not a man who can put anyone in jail or take anyone out of jail and that there are national powers here, that there are norms to be respected, that an institution cannot be judged here as to whether its action is fair or unfair by the attitude of one or two people. This is what I told the shantytown dwellers, just as I have told them that they cannot demand of me more than I can do. That is my concept of authority, what the government is going to do....

Question: Regarding what the inhabitants of Lo Hermida have said. They said they were never again going to attend a rally called by the government, and yet they all went, they carried placards, they attended in an organized manner.

Allende: I have again been invited to Lo Hermida. I am going to go talk with them. There I was interrupted by a man who is not a shantytown dweller — a man named Moore. This same man has now occupied the university, and since we respect the university's autonomy, we can do nothing. But, in my opinion, that is... well, out of respect for the people and for you I am not going to say anything. But Mr. Moore's attitude is not that of a normal political leader, and he already exhibited this attitude blatantly and the shantytown dwellers themselves taught him a good lesson. Now it is said that the vice rector of the university at Osorno is heading the takeover of the local campus of the university. Well, we respect university autonomy. I hope the student organizations will react and highlight the attitude of this group, which I think is staging a provocation, because it is not going to solve any problems, it is not going to mark out any path of just claims, it is not going to be supported. This gentlemen was a candidate for secretary general of the university and obtained an incredibly small, super-small, number of votes. Nevertheless he dares to do these things. Well, too, like Juan Gana was saying — that it is lack of authority — no, if these things happen, and the people have bad memories. Remember when Caldera was President of Venezuela and Bernardo Leighton was interior minister — a disgraceful incident occurred which I profoundly regretted.

Remember, too, the takeovers of different university campuses during the governments of Alessandri and Frei, such as occupations, etcetera. In this connection, remember the strikes, how long did the teachers' strikes last? They lasted three months or so — the copper strikes, the health workers strikes, the coal strikes and all those things which many people have already forgotten about because they purposely want to forget. They magnify certain incidents which should not occur, and especially should not be caused by the left. Yes indeed, I have been very hard, precisely on the members of the UP, and I have been still harder on the members of my party. But we have never covered up for anyone, and we will never do so. Much less for people who are playing with gunpowder. No, never.

Question: You just spoke of provocation. I think that at present there is in Santiago an atmosphere of provocation, especially in popular sectors because organized groups of ultra-rightists are making seizures, are harassing the shantytown dwellers — obviously in Las Condes, in La Granja, around Maipú — and certain conflict situations have been arising. Now, you also spoke of the state of emergency...

Allende: Those are isolated incidents. From where did the 700,000 demonstrators come? From the shantytowns. There is where our strength lies. Why then? Because they are mercenaries. You have the statement from a boy who says they paid him, as they say, "10 bucks," to come provoke incidents here, downtown — and his mother confirmed it.

Question: I am speaking, Mr. President, of organized ultra-rightist groups — which are not popular, which park their cars in front of the camps, which threaten their inhabitants, which are hostile to them, which turn their lights on the camp dwellers when they threaten to burn their dwellings down, and which shoot at the shantytown dwellers.

Allende: Of course, that is the clearest image of fascism. Those are incidents which are absolutely alien to the norm in our country. That is something thought out, organized. I would say there are advisers with considerable international experience in this kind of incident. Whoever reads the ITT documents finds, esteemed comrades of "The Great Inquiry," that the entire plan for provocation is laid out there. They either do not study it or do not read it or do not wish to recall it. But here there are obvious facts which demonstrate corruption. There is a foreign mentality here. The Chilean's idiosyncrasies, his attitude, his way of acting is very alien to what has taken place — very alien to what has taken place.

When, for example, have the houses of ministers ever been surrounded? During what government? Not even during González Videla's government, when there was a concentration camp in Pizagua, did the opposition people act this way. When did that ever happen in the case of Alessandri? When were there any dead in José María Caro's time? When did such things occur during Mr. Frei's government — despite what happened in Pampa Irigoyen? When was a mother with three children ever beseiged, as in the case of the wife and the children of Minister Matus? Then the leftist political leaders, then the leftists themselves — employees, professionals, who live in the Providencia sector, in the Las Condes sector. When has the country ever seen a more delicate incident than the attack on Mireya Baltra, basically because she is a woman, besides being a minister of state? They almost destroyed her car. I am not going to speak to you of family things because I know I, too, have daughters. The youngest of my daughters lives in what has always been my home and which is the home to which I am going to return when I leave Tomás Moro, which is not a private residence but rather is the residence of the president of Chile, in Guardia Vieja.

Night after night hearing pans being beaten in the street—and it is not the neighbors doing this. They know us too well. Why, we have been living there for 20 years. Many people do not share our ideas, but I never saw a poster of any of the candidates who opposed me — neither during Alessandri's campaign nor during Frei's, nor now — in the two-and-a-half blocks of Guardia Vieja.

During Alessandri's other campaign, in the two-and-a-half blocks from Providencia to my house, 80 to 90 percent of the people were not on my side, but why did they not put up posters? Out of respect for the neighbor, for the family head who led a normal life, with his wife and children — people who walked through the neighborhood like everybody else and who never bothered or provoked the neighbors, either.

Now two, three, five consecutive nights — not just banging on pans, but firing in the air and yelling all sort of things.

So, these are things to contrast with the mobilization of thousands and thousands of people without a single piece of broken glass. There is fascism — there it is — that should be a warning. Those people are capable of using as their argument clubs, iron bars, Hondas, revolvers — to sum it up, violence. Those people stop at nothing, and fascism is the negation of life, freedom and democracy.

Question: Mr. President, may I invite you to take a look at the other side of the coin?

Allende: But of course, this is a conversation.

Question: Thank you, Mr. President. You highlight, and justifiably so — fully justifiably so — the popular support which has been shown concretely during the latest rally. I would like to tell you something— something modest, if you like, or if you like, domestic. The radio gets many letters from all over the country — from Futalefu, from Lonquimay, from Marchigue, from all over. And I am telling you that the majority of the letters carry messages for Comrade [Denson] — messages which, I am going to say here, are messages having to do with domestic life, Mr. President—messages of concern, of anguish, over economic problems. They are not criticisms, and they say: Please tell the Comrade President.

So I am telling you: You cannot be everywhere, but someone must contain those who commit abuses. For example, a kilogram of onions is officially priced at four escudos and some pence, and the market sells it at 15 to 20 escudos a kilogram. Therefore, those people who support you honestly and faithfully are at the same time encountering this kind of problem — and it must be pretty difficult, Mr. President.

Allende: You are perfectly right, Juan Gana, but we have to go to the root of the problem, and those comrades who write — those modest, humble lady comrades who miraculously still say tell Comrade Allende that prices have risen, that there is speculation here — they cannot find an explanation. But you and I can give them one.

I can bring you loads and loads of statements from ministers of all the governments in which they speak of the prohibition of meat sales. Besides, you went through it. You went through it with Frei, with Alessandri and with Ibáñez, right? We are even going to surpass some of the months of highest inflation during the Ibáñez government — but there are other setbacks — the readjustments. We have just launched a readjustments bill. It is still not out of the Senate. We have just sent another one, because we realized that we fell short, that we must intensify our efforts. So we have anticipated the people's just demand. We have defended, basically, who? Those who live off salaries or wages.

But what has happened in this country? What happened is that this country was not prepared for the consumption by those who have to consume. In the first place, there was a 25 percent idle status in the industries. We put it to work. Internal purchasing power is greater. And besides, as you well know, there is organized contraband.

This country has one of the lowest costs of living in the world — food. Frei, Alessandri, González, Videla, all the presidents used to buy $160, $180, $200 billion worth of meat, wheat, fat, butter and oil. I wonder in how many Chilean homes butter was eaten or in how many butter is eaten?

So, what has happened? We redistributed the income. We gave buying power to thousands of Chileans who did not have it before. We have run up against an industrial production which, despite the fact that work is being performed and despite the fact that the businesses are making it produce to full capacity, does not satisfy the demand. There is greater demand than there is supply. Furthermore there is the fact that contraband is not negligible and in the case of foodstuffs, even importing, I say to you that when 42 percent of his food was imported the Chilean still ate badly. If we have given work to 220,000 Chileans, this means that 600,000 or 700,000 people had nothing to buy, nor anything to buy anything with. Now they have been able to buy.

So, logically, we have to import more foodstuffs, and we have done so, but we found that the prices of foodstuffs and spare parts on the international market have risen a lot. Why? Because of the devaluation of the dollar. For example, many people — and I have said this, many people say: oh imagine, Mr. Allende might (with a certain derogatory tone) lead us to rationing. And I tell you honestly, for example, if I could, or if there were a way to ration certain things here — certain articles, for example meat — I would do it. Is it not much fairer for you, Juan Gana, or you, Hernán Reyes — who are heads of household and who have three or four people in your home — to receive enough meat per week for four persons? On the other hand, people who are two, sometimes five at home, buy not for two or for five but for 15 or 20 persons and for several months. And for several months. Why are such measures taken during wartime? Because the danger is there, right? Because you can hear the cannon roaring, but are we not at war against hunger, against the unemployment which some people feel in this country? However, we are not yet living a revolution, a revolutionary conscience. I have said it before, we cannot suppress the purchase of beef overnight because we do not have enough fish, because we have still not been able to develop a good policy as regards the poultry industry or pork production. The storms, for example, ruined most of the chances of radically increasing poultry production. We find that we lack materials. We lack roofing for many — let us say it simply — chicken coops — places to raise poultry. We lack roofing. Why? Because we do not produce enough perlite and other materials used for roofing, just as we do not produce enough cement to build. Chile should double its production of cement. We are setting up a cement factory, a factory to produce good cement. The credit, the feasibility, the water, the site where it will be installed, the machines, where they will be purchased— all this will take two years. But we will begin producing cement in Antofagasta around the end of next year.

Then all of this is correct and these things must take place and have always taken place. John Kennedy said: "In this country two million persons go to bed each night hungry." Where did he make this statement? In the powerful capitalist country. The U.S. secretary of agriculture said three years ago: The decade of the 1970s will be called the decade of superhunger in Latin America.

These things have been repeated, but, naturally, they are now blown up, increased, magnified. Is this our fault? How is it possible that in 35 years a cattle industry has not been developed? It is not our fault, a herd of cattle cannot be created in one or two years, and the same could be said about any two things in our country.

Look, 35 percent of the railroad cars need repairs. There are steel plates in Huachipato to repair these railroad cars, but we do not have the means to transport them. Then this is a vicious circle. For example, what has happened with the beets for the processing plants, what about the conflicts with the truckers? The people will ask for health care and we cannot provide it because we lack doctors, midwives, nurses.

Comrades, I am going to tell you something that I am sure you do not know. The Chilean laboratory, in order to meet the nation's need for medicines has increased its production by 596 percent — 596 percent — and today many more persons are demanding their right to health care. As I have told the country, there are in some maternity hospitals two or three persons in a single bed.

True, it could be said it is not possible to solve problems faced by the developing countries. Has there, perhaps, not been a great national effort, a great awareness of the masses which support us? On the other hand, for example, the same understanding has not existed among labor sectors so far as the cost of living goes. If the cost of living has increased by 40 percent, by 80 percent, what good will it do to have more currency? Then you have the problem of the private social service employees fund arising from an error made by the *Carabineros* fund vice-president.

Question: I would like to return to a subject which has been mentioned several times: the people's unity, the unity of the rank and file. Specifically, what do you think of the Price and Supply Boards, the unity committees, the self-defense committees proposed by the CUT in a Santiago CUT plenary meeting chaired by a Christian Democrat during which a decision was made regarding the creation of the unity committees?

Allende: If we demand the unity of the UP we must be perfectly clear, then we are fighting for the unity of the workers. The needs of the Christian Democratic worker are the same as the needs of the socialist or communist workers. The needs of a worker — when I say worker I mean the laborer, the peasant, the employees, the small and middle level businessman and professional people — are the same. We are not implementing a policy for Popular Unity, for the members of Popular Unity. We ask them to understand, to be ready to make sacrifices so that the policy of the workers' unity may advance. This is the problem. Any more questions? It is becoming late.

Question: Regarding unity, there are certain phrases — excuse me for referring to your last speech — which parenthetically, I believe, marks a second stage in your government. There was a phrase which said that outside the confines of Popular Unity — you were then speaking about rejecting confrontations — they [presumably the opposition] have a political sense which indicates to them that they must seek a political solution.

You also said that the people, who are the majority, must indicate the path toward these solutions, and the people must clearly understand how this path can be reached.

It appears to me that at this point you somewhat opened the path which runs beyond the boundaries of Popular Unity and that you have set the basis for something which is not clearly discernible yet but which represents a political opening.

Allende: Logically, but first what is the solution? I believe the question interests you, Fernando Reyes, who have asked it. I want to answer the question, but if you want to interrupt, go ahead.

Question: What Reyes says somewhat coincides with statements made yesterday by Bernardo Leighton and with statements made by Tomic in his letter of explanation to the dailies.

Allende: This is a hard, difficult moment when fascists are in the streets, when the fascists are acting insolently in the streets, when provocations are taking place in the shantytowns. We are living through an abnormal stage. What is the proper thing to do during this stage? Confrontation? This I reject overwhelmingly and categorically. You understand — I have said this before — referring to what happened when hoodlums and some obstinate fascists — approximately 600 persons — mobilized and when 10,000 or 20,000 workers marched in the center of Santiago in support of their government. Well, this is not the problem. This then is not a question of repression or of deploying the public forces. Neither must there be an attitude of violent repression which could lead to the use of weapons, because quite frequently the instigators and those responsible for disorders run away and innocent people die. Then, what political solution is available? Regarding a political solution which interests all the Chilean people, we have, for example, a goal: March. You understand that if in March the electorate — the will expressed in the ballot box — is drastically against the government, then I will understand and will become aware of the serious problems we have caused. When the people do not vote for us, I will have to ask myself seriously: Well, what is happening in this country? And, lastly, I will say: I am the one who has been wrong. Otherwise, if a high percentage of the people vote for us — or, a strong possibility, if the forces almost balance — we will have to reach the conclusion that the great majority stands for changes. If we analyze what Tomic has stated during his campaign, what the Christian Democrats are saying, this means that not 50 percent, but 70 percent of the Chilean people desire the changes. Well, let us seek a way to implement these changes in such a way that peoples' will and desires are not violated. Then we have the case of Congress, for example. I have always maintained that it is possible to open the path of socialism with pluralism, democracy and freedom, so long as the Chilean constitutional system is flexible. I was referring to the Congress where we lack a majority. But it is a Congress which has rejected the Sea Ministry, a Congress which has delayed for two years and has not yet approved the organization of the Family Ministry. Why? When one of the best moves they could make is to create the Family Ministry so that we may provide services to the children, the youth, adults and the aged.

What we seek is to promulgate a family code. What we seek is that there be equality of rights among the children. What we seek is to fundamentally defend the woman. When I see, for example, that as a result of that initiative by this government, there are people who combat the service of women calling it compulsory.

But, how can there be no understanding that if there is no children's nursery, there is perhaps no service. Because 1.2 million children, one person per 10 children presupposes a service of 120,000 persons. How many millions and millions would have to be paid in salaries? On the other hand, there are thousands and thousands of young girls who do nothing and it would be good for them to understand that someday they will be mothers; it would be good for those bourgeois girls to go to the shantytowns in order to become aware of where our people live and how difficult it is for them to bathe a baby because they have no water. And how useful it is for the town girls to acquire knowledge, since otherwise later they will become mothers without having had the possibility of attending a school to learn. However, now they learn because of the initiative of this government.

Then, there is political passion which reaches such extremes that one asks, well, what to do. I favor dialogue on national problems with clarity. We have sought it. We invited Mr. Renán Fuentealba to my house. I told him we should seek a solution to a vote so that a confrontation between the executive branch and Congress is avoided in the interpretation of their insistence on a simple majority. This is true and I do not want to give details, but we were not reluctant on this. I can tell you that as a first fruit of this conversation, Justice Minister Jorge

Tapia and Under-Secretary General of Government Sergio Inzunza brought to me the projects they had drafted as an agreement based on a letter that came from the Senate. The only thing I had to do was to sign, and when they returned to the Senate the voting had already taken place and the talks had ceased. And I signed, but I remained quiet. I could have told them that this is a snub of the president. They demand projects of agreement; they accept them; we study them for a week, and when the time comes for the justice minister and the under-secretary of government to physically walk four blocks — which takes 10 minutes — the panorama of talks maintained for a month-and-a-half changes completely.

Question: Mr. President, you have spoken of the moral decomposition of the adversaries to Popular Unity.

Allende: No. As a matter of fact, no. That would be unjust, that would be harsh. I do not want to go into detail about this aspect. There could have been many reasons. You should know that when I refer to moral decomposition, I am referring to other people who lie, to the people who use defamation and slander, to the people who know perfectly well that some problems connected with the serious ones — such as the copper case — should not be raised. To say that we are not going to produce copper to fulfill our contracts is to hurt Chile in the most savage way that can be done. It is to deceive Chile to say emphatically that gold has disappeared from the vaults of the Central Bank. And a magistrate of the judicial branch had to testify that the gold is there. This is hurting Chile. I believe it is very serious, extraordinarily serious. When a senator speaks about civil disobedience and when the National Party youth distribute leaflets saying: "Civil disobedience is on," we then look for the location of those who propose things that can undoubtedly bring serious or dramatic consequences for the country and I am determined to avoid it. For this reason I have publicly proposed a call, I have extended my hand. I have said that, if we are interested in avoiding this, I know that there is in certain sectors in this country — even in the sectors strongly opposed to the government — the understanding to prevent a social and economic incident that could create conditions for Chile we never imagined, and a civil war that, in the aftermath of animosities between families, groups and members of the same family, sometimes lasts two or three generations instead of days. And the economy of a country, that interests everyone... Imagine, here with a labor force leading the economy of the nation, it is not enough to say the words. One must think them, feel them, realize them. That call of mine is honest and that opening of mine is clear. To seek a political solution, but a political solution, let's say, that undeniably permits a consolidation of gains and a path toward what the majority of people in the country want.

The PDC [Christian Democratic Party] has said it in their program. They say it in their declarations; they say it in their speeches, people of the PDC who deserve the respect of many Chileans and fundamentally on my part, because I have known them for many years. It is good to be in a position like this. I am not going to speak with them, I am not disposed to speak, no one can prevent me, is that it? But I want to speak about a certain possibility: to reach agreements and hold to them, not spend a month-and-a-half discussing only to undo in five minutes everything that has cost so much to believe could be agreed upon.

The political solution is in March, so there is no time for a plebiscite. They have been talking about a plebiscite for a long time. We did not oppose it, but we said that we would call a plebiscite when the circumstances force us into it and on matters we consider proper, but that is a presidential prerogative. Now, there is no political confrontation other than the elections, because I tell you: I will drastically prevent every possibility of a confrontation. I will clip the wings of the pseudo-leftist or feverish leftist hotheads, just as I have demonstrated to the ultra-rightists. No one can tell me that a leftist man who has committed a crime, or has gone out of line, has not been sent to the courts by us. Well then we have the authority to do it.

Question: Mr. President, a problem arises. For example, there is the impression that last Monday's march, among other things, was a reply to all this street uproar. There are small children who say they are hungry, who live in the upper-class neighborhood and come downtown to cause disorders. Then, how is it that the people are spouting off, if you will pardon the expression?

Allende: My obligation is that they not spout off too much [laughter], because if they do they will do whatever they want and take justice into their own hands, and that is the definite beginning of chaos. The people must have confidence in the government and in the measures this government takes, and that is fundamental. The people — and by this I am referring to the entire country, the armed forces; the air force, navy, army, *Carabineros*, investigations police — must have the confidence that the government will not accept ultrarightist and ultraleftist armed groups. It is my obligation to eliminate them, wherever they are. I have been doing this. But it turns out that they are using new tactics. If sometimes I order raids on the offices of the morally unhealthy Fatherland and Liberty Movement, what will I find inside? Posters, paint cans. And, where do they keep the implements they use in marches? In their homes. That is the problem. That is why organization of the people is required — in other words, not only Popular Unity wants to defend democracy. Look here. For example, I have been the first to condemn the death of Corporal Aroca and a *Carabineros* legal adviser is investigating the death.

But the exploitation made of that death shows moral laxness. When has a Senate session been suspended for the other deaths? For the 10 or 15 *carabineros* killed in recent days. A week earlier a *carabinero* was slain by criminals. Did any right-wing congressman attend the funerals at which a minister was present? When previously has there been disrespect toward a minister and even toward a deceased member of the *Carabineros*? The *Carabinero* corps itself was forced to make a public statement protesting the political exploitation of the *carabinero* corporal's death. And the three peasants killed in Frutillar? Have you seen the government opposition press devoting articles to them protesting or implacably questioning their deaths? No, sir. And the dead peasant?

We undoubtedly have committed mistakes, many mistakes, above all in the economic area and we recognize it. I have concisely explained the mistakes in some aspects of supply, distribution and transportation. But, politically you are a newspaperman.

It is said that there is no democracy here, no freedom of the press, no freedom of assembly. But a short time ago some 300,000, 250,000 people — I do not know, cite whatever figure you wish — gathered. I never argue with figures. They are going to gather on Tuesday and we have given them authorization. I have told the Santiago intendant to call the Christian Democratic leaders and tell them: these are the government's plans; this is what we intend to do to avoid any confrontation. Furthermore, the Popular Unity parties and I will tell our people not to come out into the streets to provoke but to come out instead so the city may not be deserted, since this hurts the image of Chile abroad, which is the [opposition's] objective.

In the first place, if 700,000 persons march in a city, the city will not be deserted. But to close other streets and business establishments and to force the people from the upper-class neighborhoods to keep their Venetian blinds closed for eight hours would create a sort of psychosis. But the people do not do this if we leaders tell them not to. I will tell them through the intendant: Look, we are going to deploy so many uniformed *Carabineros* as well as so many plainclothes *Carabineros*, so many members of the Investigations Department, and you deploy people in such and such buildings in such places, contribute, help because a provocation could come from anywhere. It is true, there can be 100,000, 200,000, 300,000 people in one street. From how many buildings or roofs can a provocation come that is intended to create problems for us and to bring blame upon us?

Then, they must assume the responsibility; they know in what atmosphere they are acting. Logically, I set the concentration area in the Torres de Tajamar, instead of separately on Providencia with Pedro de Valdivia, because it was also possible that a provocation could come — I am not referring to people from the right — from provocateurs. And a provocateur is a mercenary. He can be at the service of a small group, an internal fascist group, at the service of alien and foreign interests — the ones which today have felt hurt by government measures, the ones which have been at the verge of creating a civil war, the ones accustomed to corruption, the ones accustomed to making threats, those who have always thought that the small countries are simply a source of unlimited wealth for them. This is the problem.

Question: In the face of this, what you are calling an atmosphere...

Allende: Listen, do not press me any more....

Question: No, but I believe that this last question will interest the people. Is it not true that there has been a tense climate full of difficulties, a series of elements concerning the economic problem that have been diagnosed, etcetera?

Then, let us speak of the average man — to give an abstract image — and you ask yourself, well, is it worthwhile living through all this — since all the problems we face, the problems abroad, the imperialist compulsion over a country, are clear from explanations you have given? The people ask: Is it worthwhile to live through this and why is it worthwhile? What explanation would you give the people?

Allende: No! It is worthwhile.

Question: Who is the average man?

Allende: The average man is the employee, the technician, the professional, the soldier, the military man — it is the Chile that works. I ask you: Can a man feel satisfied, having become an architect and knowing that he will never be able to work in a country where 500,000 housing units are needed? Can a doctor feel satisfied knowing that he can apparently or really improve the health of thousands of children with summer diarrhea only to see them released from the hospital and again become ill? Can a regimental commander feel satisfied knowing that at the gates of his headquarters an extremely high percentage of the people are rejected because they do not meet the proper physical conditions? Can the commander-in-chief of any of our institutions feel satisfied knowing that in order to be efficient, not only good physical condition is needed; but also the necessary mental development? Can the doctor, the professor, the military man, the seaman, the pilot or the *carabinero* feel satisfied if he knows that in Chile there are 600,000 mentally retarded children because they have not received proteins? Can you newspaper reporters feel satisfied? No.

It is those sectors of the middle class that must understand that at a given time their situation could seem unimproved, but that the struggle to progress is, in the end, essentially for them, so that, for example, there will not be the separation between manual worker and intellectual worker, so that, for example, there will not be contempt for the domestic employee, and the people will understand that the world has another dimension.

Moreover, I believe that the income of middle class sectors has not been hurt. I can tell you that I believe that shopkeepers in this country have never earned more. They sell everything. Whatever you want to sell, you sell. What happens is that people are not apt to think generously about their neighbor, and sometimes they do not consider even their own family. This is the problem. Therefore, I think that the middle class sectors — the small craftsmen, the shopkeeper, the industrialist and the farmer — must understand that in the capitalist system the concentration of economic power is slowly being produced in very few branches. Thus, there are the big monopolies which have strangled the middle level and small shopkeepers. We want security and guarantees for them, and we have proposed legislation to this effect. Regrettably, the bills have not been processed in Congress, but we want to impart confidence in them because we have nothing against them.

For example, it is said that retailers will be suppressed. There must be... How many 180,000, 240,000 in Chile? Can you imagine suppressing them? What work can we give those people? It is impossible to imagine. We need these people. The people must understand that retailers are indispensable.

We can locate people's warehouses nearby, we can create national distributors. But retailers serve; they are needed; they fulfill a function and they themselves can find backing in the consumers in their district, and they can be assured that the products they really need be delivered to them. If they proceed correctly, they will be helped by the consumers themselves. The problem is organization, people's awareness. And that is the struggle in which we are involved.

Now, it is very difficult to implement a revolution based on pluralism, democracy and freedom with such a dramatically violent opposition. It is difficult when they deny everything and are not willing to help in anything.

Question: Mr. President, we had planned on speaking for an hour and we have been at it for one-and-a-half hours. Undoubtedly there are many subjects in mind. I would like to ask you one last thing. In this entire conversation we have been speaking about what the country can be, of what it must be in the future. The children, that is, the youth of this country, are the ones who will construct what is envisaged — the entire world you imagine — which many of us in this country are trying to construct. What do you have to say to the young, to the youth in secondary schools and to the youth in primary schools?

Allende: I must tell them that they are the future and that it is fundamental to have a profound patriotic and national feeling to understand that man's basic obligation is to work for the future of this homeland and people. This is a country of young people and I tell the young people that they must understand that there is a need to work more, study more and produce more to be able to make a country progress. I am not impressed by vocal revolutionaries who are poor students, poor workers, poor leaders. I believe that the first lesson for a revolutionary is to show, by his example, the possibility for others to follow. For this reason I have many times repeated how fine was the phrase written by a student on the wall of a University in Paris: "The revolution is begun by people rather than by things." And that is very serious and profound.

Well, you have exploited me enough. I have been very pleased. I hope that not too many months pass before we talk again. I repeat my regards to the listeners of Radio Portales and "The Great Inquiry."

17

Address to the United Nations General Assembly

December 4, 1972

In perhaps the greatest and most famous speech of his life, as appropriate today as the day he delivered it, Allende becomes the first world leader to explain at length the sinister importance of transnational corporations (TNCs) for people everywhere. He gives a full and clear explanation of how fairly, even generously, Chile is treating the foreign copper companies that it has nationalized with compensation. Yet, "my country is the victim of serious aggression.... suffering from yet another manifestation of imperialism, one that is more subtle, more cunning and more terrifyingly effective.... We are having to face forces that operate in the half-light, that fight with powerful weapons, but that fly no identifying flags and are entrenched in the most varied centers of influence." He hammers at the international sabotage and blackmailing of Chile, the "economic and trade aggression." He denounces the "financial blockade" and "strangulation" of Chile by major U.S.-based TNCs, noting how "what is happening in Chile is opening up a new stage in the battle between imperialism and the weaker countries of the Third World.... Imperialism exists because underdevelopment exists, underdevelopment exists because imperialism exists." Citing recently publicized ITT internal documents as irrefutable proof, Allende accuses ITT of "attempting to bring about civil war in my country.... That is what we call imperialist intervention." He quotes John F. Kennedy: "Those who stand in the way of peaceful revolution make violent revolution inevitable." After a special plea for the world's "2,000 million underprivileged," Allende calls for peaceful resolution of world tensions. He observes that Latin Americans are standing up to shout "Enough — no more dependence," "An end to intervention," and he concludes that "the great values of humanity will prevail."

T**he President** [interpretation from French]: On behalf of the General Assembly, I have the honor of extending a welcome to His Excellency Mr. Salvador Allende, President of the Republic of Chile, and I have the great pleasure of inviting him to address the assembly.

Mr. Allende (President of the Republic of Chile) [interpretation from Spanish]: I am very grateful for the high honor of being invited to speak from this rostrum, the most representative in the world and the most important forum in all matters concerning mankind. I should like to greet the secretary general, whom we were honored to welcome to our country during his first few weeks of office, the representatives of more than 130 countries composing the General Assembly, and you, Mr. President, who come from a country with which we have friendly ties, and whom we have known personally since you presided over the delegation of the People's Republic of Poland at the third session of the United Nations Conference on Trade and Development (UNCTAD).

I come from Chile, a small country but one where every citizen is free to express himself as he sees fit, where there is unlimited cultural, religious and ideological tolerance, and where racial discrimination has no place; a country whose working class is united in a single trade union federation, where universal suffrage and the secret ballot are the cornerstones of a multiparty system; a country whose parliament has been active without interruption since its creation 160 years ago, whose judiciary is independent of the executive, and whose constitutional charter, which has practically never ceased to be applied, has been amended only once since 1833. I come from a country where public life is organized around civic institutions; a country whose armed forces have demonstrated their professional vocation and profound democratic spirit; a nation of close to 10 million people which, in one generation, has produced two Nobel Prize winners for literature, Gabriela Mistral and Pablo Neruda, both children of modest workers; a land whose history, soil and people have merged in a great sense of national identity.

Chile, however, is also a country whose backward economy has been subjected to, even taken over by, foreign capitalist enterprises and whose external debt has swollen to over $4,000 million, the annual service of which represents more than 30 percent of the value of its exports; it is a country with an economy extremely sensitive to outside events, chronically stagnant and inflationary, where millions of people have been forced to live in circumstances of exploitation, misery and open or covert unemployment.

I come here today because my country is confronted with problems that, because of their universal importance, are the object of the permanent concern of this assembly of nations: namely the fight for social liberation, the struggle for well-being and intellectual progress, and the defense of national identity and dignity.

The prospect that faced my country, as in the case of so many other countries of the Third World, was the familiar model of adopting an alien pattern of modernization, which technical studies and tragic reality have both shown to have the inevitable effect of excluding more and more millions of people from all possibility of progress, well-being and social liberation, and of relegating them to a subhuman existence — a pattern destined to lead to still greater housing shortages and to condemn an ever-increasing number of citizens to unemployment, illiteracy, ignorance and physical want. In a word, this same prospect before us has kept us in a state of colonization or dependency and exploited us in times of Cold War as well as in times of open conflagration and of peace. We, the underdeveloped countries, are asked to agree to being condemned to a second-class, eternally subordinate status. This, then, is the pattern which the working class of Chile, upon becoming arbiter of its own future, has decided to reject, striving instead for a rapid, self-determined and independent development and the revolutionary reorganization of traditional structures.

The Chilean people has won for itself the reins of government, after a long period of noble sacrifice and it is now fully engaged in the task of establishing economic democracy so that the country's productive activities will meet its social requirements and expectations and not be exploited for private gain. Through a well-planned and coherent program, the old structure based on the exploitation of the worker and the domination of the principal means of production by a minority is being superseded. Its place is being taken by a new structure directed by the workers which, in serving the interests of the majority, is laying the foundations for a pattern of growth which spells genuine development, which involves all the inhabitants of the country and which does not relegate vast sections of the people to poverty and social banishment.

The workers are replacing the privileged groups politically and economically, both in the centers of work and in the communes and the state itself. This is the revolutionary content of the process being experienced by my country today: the rejection and replacement of the capitalist system and the opening of a way towards socialism.

The need to place all our economic resources at the service of the people's tremendous unsatisfied requirements had to go hand in hand with the recovery by Chile of its national dignity. We had to put an end to the situation where we Chileans, struggling against poverty and stagnation, were forced to export huge amounts of capital for the benefit of the most powerful market economy in the world. The nationalization of our basic resources constituted a historic act of reclamation. Our economy could no longer tolerate the state of subordination implied in the concentration of more than 80 percent of its exports in the hands of a small group of large, foreign companies that have always placed their own interests before the needs of the countries in which they were making exorbitant profits. Neither could we accept the vicious effects of the *latifundia*, of the industrial and commercial monopolies, of credit restrictions in favor of only a few, or of brutal inequalities in income distribution.

The change we are effecting in the power structure; the progressive management role which the workers are assuming; the nation's recovery of its basic resources and the freeing of our country from its subordination to foreign powers constitute the culmination of a long, historic process of efforts to win political and social freedoms and of heroic struggle by several generations of industrial and rural workers to organize themselves as a social force in order to conquer political power and oust the capitalists from economic power.

The Chilean people's traditions, personality and revolutionary consciousness have enabled them to push forward towards socialism while strengthening civic freedoms, both collective and individual, and respecting cultural and ideological pluralism. Ours is a continuing struggle for the institution of social freedoms and economic democracy through the full exercise of political freedom.

Our nation's democratic will has taken up the challenge to carry through this revolutionary process within the framework of a state of highly institutionalized legal precepts, which has been flexible to change and today faces the need to adapt to the new socio-economic reality.

We have nationalized our basic resources. We have nationalized copper. We have done so by a unanimous decision of parliament, in which the government parties are in the minority. We want everybody to understand this clearly: we have not confiscated the great foreign copper mining companies. In accordance with constitutional law, however, we have put right a long-standing injustice by deducting from the amount of compensation the profits over 12 percent per annum which those companies have obtained since 1955.

The profits which some of the nationalized companies had obtained over the previous 15 years were so exorbitant that, in applying the limit of a reasonable profit of 12 percent per annum, the companies were affected by significant deductions. Such was the case, for example, with a branch of the Anaconda Company, whose annual profits in Chile between 1955 and 1970 averaged 21.5 percent on its book value, while Anaconda's profits in other countries were only 3.6 percent per annum. The same applied in the case of a branch of the Kennecott Copper Corporation, which over the same period made an average annual profit of 52.8 percent in Chile, even reaching such incredible rates as 106 percent in 1967, 113 percent in 1968 and over 205 percent in 1969. Kennecott's average profits in other countries during that period amounted to less than 10 percent per annum. In other cases, however, the application of the rules established in line with the constitution has meant that other foreign copper companies have not been subject to deductions under the heading of excessive profits since the reasonable limit of 12 percent per annum had not been exceeded.

It should be stressed that in the years immediately preceding nationalization the large copper companies initiated expansion plans. However, those plans — which were unsuccessful for the most part — were not financed from their own resources, despite their huge profits, but by means of external credits. In accordance with legislative provisions, Chile has had to take over responsibility for those debts, which amount to the enormous sum of more than $727 million. We have begun to pay those debts, including one which one of those enterprises had contracted with Kennecott, its own parent company in the United States.

Those same enterprises exploited Chile's copper for many years, in the last 42 years alone taking out more than $4,000 million in profits although their initial investment was no more than $30 million. In striking contrast, let me give one simple and painful example of what this means to Chile. In my country there are 700, 000 children who will never be able to enjoy life in a normal human way because during their first eight months of life they did not receive the minimum amount of protein. Four thousand million dollars would completely transform Chile. A small part of that sum would ensure proteins for all time for all children of my country.

Copper mining has been nationalized not only with scrupulous regard for domestic legislation but also with respect for the norms of international law — which does not exist, of course, simply to serve the interests of the great capitalist enterprises.

That, in brief, is the process through which my country is living and which I have thought it appropriate to describe to this assembly — a process backed by the authority we enjoy by virtue of the fact that we are complying strictly with the recommendations of the United Nations and basing our economic and social development on our own internal efforts. This assembly has advocated transforming outmoded institutions and structures; mobilizing national resources both natural and human; redistributing income; allocating priority attention to education and health and also to special treatment for the poorer sectors of the population. All these are essential components of our policy and are being implemented to the full. In view of what I have said, it is all the more painful for me to have to come here to this assembly to denounce the fact that my country is the victim of serious aggression.

We had foreseen that there would be external difficulties and opposition when we began to make changes, particularly as regards the nationalization of our natural resources. Imperialism and its cruelties have had a long and ominous history in Latin America; and the dramatic and heroic experience of Cuba is still fresh in our minds, as is that of Peru, which has had to suffer the consequences of its decision to exercise its sovereign rights over its petroleum.

After all the innumerable agreements and resolutions adopted by the world community recognizing the sovereign rights of each country to dispose of its natural resources for the benefit of its people; after the adoption of the International Covenant on Economic, Social and Cultural Rights [resolution 2200 A (XXI)] and the International Development Strategy for the Second United Nations Development Decade [resolution 2626 (XXV)], which solemnly confirmed all these instruments, here we are, well into the 1970s, suffering from yet another manifestation of imperialism, one that is more subtle, more cunning and more terrifyingly effective in preventing us from exercising our rights as a sovereign state.

From the very day of our electoral triumph on September 4, 1970, we have felt the effects of large-scale external pressure against us which tried to prevent the inauguration of a government freely elected by the people, and has attempted to bring it down ever since. An attempt has been made to cut us off from the world, to strangle our economy and paralyze trade in our principal export, copper, and to deprive us of access to sources of international financing.

We are aware of the fact that, when we denounce the financial and economic blockade applied against us, it is somewhat difficult for world public opinion, and even for some of our fellow citizens, to understand what we mean. This aggression is not overt and has not been openly declared to the world; on the contrary, it is an oblique, underhand, indirect form of aggression, although this does not make it any less damaging to Chile. We are having to face forces that operate in the half-light, that fight with powerful weapons, but that fly no identifying flags and are entrenched in the most varied centers of influence.

There is no embargo against trading with us. No one has stated an intention to fight us face to face. On the surface it would appear that the only enemies we have are our natural political adversaries at home. But this is not true. We are the victims of virtually imperceptible activities, usually disguised with words and statements that extol the sovereignty and dignity of my country. We know in our own hearts, however, the distance that separates these words from the specific activities that we have to face.

I am not talking about vague matters; I am referring to specific problems that burden my people today and that will have even more serious economic repercussions in the coming months.

As is the case with most of the developing countries of the Third World, the external sector of Chile's economy is highly vulnerable. Chile's exports amount to a little over $1,000 million a year, but over the last 12 months the slump in the price of copper on the world market has meant a loss to my country of income of about $200 million, whereas the products which the country has to import — both industrial and agricultural — have risen sharply in price, in some cases by as much as 60 percent. Thus, as nearly always, Chile is obliged to sell cheap and buy dear.

Moreover, at this very time, which is itself so difficult for our balance of payments, Chile has had to face, among others, the following concerted actions apparently designed to take revenge on the Chilean people for its decision to nationalize its copper.

Until my government took office, Chile received a net inflow of resources of approximately $80 million per year in the form of loans granted by international finance organizations, such as the World Bank and the Inter-American Development Bank. This source of finance has now been cut off abruptly.

In the last decade, Chile was granted loans worth $50 million by the Agency for International Development of the United States Government. We do not expect that these loans will be continued. The United States, in its exercise of sovereignty, may grant or withhold loans in respect of any country it chooses. We only wish to point out that the drastic elimination of these credits has resulted in sharp restrictions in our balance of payments.

When I became president my country had short-term credit facilities from private United States banks amounting to about $220 million to finance our foreign trade. Within a short space of time, however, these credits were suspended and about $190 million of this total credit was withdrawn and we had to pay this sum as the credit was not renewed.

Like most Latin American countries, Chile is obliged, for technological and others reasons, to acquire substantial amounts of capital goods from the United States. Now, however, both the supplier credits and those normally granted by the Export-Import Bank in respect of this type of transaction have also been denied to us, so that we are in the anomalous position of having to pay in advance to obtain such goods. This places our balance of payments under extraordinarily severe pressure.

Disbursements under the terms of loans contracted with United States agencies in the public sector, and already in operation before my government came to power, have likewise been suspended. Consequently, in order to go ahead with the projects concerned — for which it had been confidently expected that financing would be provided by

United States Government bodies — we have been obliged to make cash purchases of goods on the United States market, since it is impossible to change the source of the imports in question in the middle of the execution of the projects.

As a result of the actions directed against the copper trade in the countries of Western Europe, our short-term transactions with private banks of that area, mainly involving the collection of payments from sales of copper, have been very seriously obstructed. Thus, credit facilities in respect of over $20 million have not been renewed, financial negotiations involving over $200 million which were on the point of coming to a favorable conclusion have been broken off, and a climate has been created which hampers the normal course of our purchases in Western Europe and seriously distorts all our activities in the field of external financing.

This financial strangulation, which has had an immediate and a violent effect because of the nature of the Chilean economy, has led to the severe limitation of our ability to secure the equipment, spare parts, manufacturing inputs, foodstuffs and medicines which we need. Each and every Chilean is suffering from the consequences of these measures, because they affect the daily life of each citizen, and naturally his internal political life.

What I have just described to the assembly amounts to a perversion of the fundamental nature of international agencies, the utilization of which as tools of the policies of individual member states is legally and morally unacceptable no matter how powerful such states may be. Such misuse represents the exertion of pressure on a economically weak country, the infliction of punishment on a whole nation for its decision to recover its own basic resources, and a premeditated form of intervention in the internal affairs of a sovereign state. In a word, it is what we call imperialist insolence.

As members are well aware and are scarcely likely to forget, that kind of action has been repeatedly condemned by United Nations resolutions.

We not only are enduring a financial blockade, but also are the victims of downright aggression. Two companies belonging to the hard core of the great transnational enterprises, namely, the International Telephone and Telegraph Corporation [ITT] and the Kennecott Copper Corporation, which had driven their tentacles deep into my country, proposed to manage our political life.

A gigantic corporation whose capital is larger than the national budgets of several Latin American countries put together, and bigger even than that of some of the industrialized countries, the ITT launched a sinister plan to prevent me from acceding to the presidency just as soon as the people's triumph in the September 1970 elections became known.

Between September and November of that year in my country terrorist activities took place which were planned outside our frontiers in collusion with internal fascist groups. Those activities culminated in the assassination of the Commander-in-Chief of the Army, General René Schneider Chereau, who was a just man, a great soldier and a symbol of the constitutional attitude of Chile's armed forces.

In March, 1972, documents revealing the link between those dark designs and the ITT came to light. The ITT has admitted that in 1970 it even suggested to the United States Government that it should intervene in the political events in Chile. The documents are authentic, and no one has dared gainsay them.

In July the world was shocked to learn the details of a new plan of action which the ITT itself presented to the United States Government, a plan aimed at overthrowing my government within a period of six months. I have in my briefcase the document, dated October 1971, which contains the 18 points of that plan. The objectives of the plan included strangling the country's economy, diplomatic sabotage, sowing panic among the population and fomenting social disorder so that the government would, it was hoped, lose control of the situation and the armed forces would be impelled to break the democratic system and impose a dictatorship.

At the very moment when the ITT was putting forward that plan, its representatives were pretending to negotiate with my government a formula for the purchase by the Chilean state of the ITT's share in the Chilean Telephone Company. From the earliest days of my administration we had, for reasons of national security, started conversations to purchase that telephone company, which was controlled by the ITT.

I myself had two interviews with senior executives of the enterprise. My government acted in good faith in those discussions, but the ITT refused to accept a price fixed on the basis of an assessment made by international experts. It placed difficulties in the way of a rapid and fair solution, while surreptitiously it tried to bring about a chaotic situation in Chile.

The refusal of the ITT to accept a direct agreement and the knowledge of its sly manoeuvres have compelled us to place a nationalization bill before Congress.

The determination of the Chilean people to defend the democratic system and the progress of the people's revolution, and the loyalty of the armed forces to their country and its laws, foiled the sinister designs of the ITT.

Before the conscience of the world I accuse the ITT of attempting to bring about civil war in my country, the greatest possible source of disintegration of a country. That is what we call imperialist intervention.

Today Chile is threatened by another danger, the removal of which depends not only on the national will, but also on a wide range of external elements. I refer to the action taken by the Kennecott Copper Corporation.

The Chilean Constitution provides that nationalization disputes should be resolved by a tribunal which, like all tribunals in my country, has complete independence and sovereignty in the adoption of decisions. Kennecott accepted that jurisdiction and for a year it pleaded its case before that tribunal. When its appeal was rejected, however, it decided to use its great power to rob us of our copper export earnings and to bring pressure to bear against the government of Chile. It was so bold, in September last, as to request the courts in France, the Netherlands and Sweden to place an embargo on payments for those exports. It will no doubt attempt that in other countries too. The grounds for this action could not possibly be less acceptable, from whatever legal or moral standpoint they are viewed.

Kennecott wants the courts of other nations, which have nothing to do with the problems or affairs between the Chilean state and it, to declare invalid a sovereign act of my government undertaken by virtue of the highest mandate, namely, that given by the country's constitution and backed by the unanimous will of the Chilean people.

Such pretensions run counter to fundamental principles of international law, according to which a country's natural resources — particularly when they are its very lifeblood — belong to it and can be freely utilized by it. There is no generally accepted international law or, in this case, any specific treaty that can justify Kennecott's action. The world community, organized in accordance with the principles of the Charter of the United Nations, does not accept that international law can be interpreted in a manner which subordinates it to capitalist interests so as to induce the courts of law of any foreign country to protect a structure of economic relations designed to serve capitalism. Were it to do so, it would be undermining a fundamental principle of international life, that of nonintervention in the domestic affairs of states, as explicitly recognized by the third session of UNCTAD.

We are governed by the principles of international law that have been reaffirmed repeatedly by the United Nations, particularly in General Assembly resolution 1803(XVII), and were recently restated by the Trade and Development Board specifically in relation to the denunciation which my country formulated against the Kennecott Copper Corporation. In addition to reaffirming the sovereign right of all countries to dispose freely of their natural resources, the board's resolution states in paragraph 2 that:

in the application of this principle, such measures of nationalization as states may adopt in order to recover their natural resources are the expression of a sovereign power in virtue of which it is for each state to fix the... procedure for these measures, and any dispute which may arise in that connection falls within the sole jurisdiction of its courts, without prejudice to what is set forth in General Assembly resolution 1803.[1]

General Assembly resolution 1803 (XVII) provides that, in exceptional circumstances, disputes may be settled through international adjudication provided there is "agreement by sovereign states and other parties concerned."

This is the sole thesis acceptable to the United Nations. It is the only one which conforms to its philosophy and principles. It is the only one that can protect the rights of the weak from the abuse by the strong. As is only right in view of the foregoing, we have succeeded in the Paris courts in securing the lifting of the embargo affecting the proceeds of the sale of a consignment of our copper. Notwithstanding, we shall continue with undiminished determination to maintain that only the Chilean courts are competent to pass judgment in any dispute concerning the nationalization of our basic resources. For Chile, this is not merely an important problem of juridical interpretation; it is a question of sovereignty. Indeed, it is far more than this — it is a question of survival.

The aggression perpetrated by Kennecott is causing serious damage to our economy. The direct difficulties that it has posed for the marketing of copper alone have meant the loss of many millions of dollars for Chile in two months. But that is not all. I have already referred to the effect that it has had in obstructing my country's financial operations with Western European banks. Quite clearly, there is also a desire to create a climate of uncertainty among the purchasers of our principal export product, but that shall not happen.

Such are the designs of that imperialist enterprise at the present time. It cannot hope, however, that any political or juridical power will in the long run deprive Chile of what is legitimately its own. It is trying to force our hand, but it will never succeed!

The aggression of the great capitalist enterprises is intended to prevent the emancipation of the working classes. It represents a direct attack on the economic interests of the workers, in this specific case, leveled against Chile.

Chile is a nation which has attained the political maturity to decide by majority vote to replace the capitalist economic system by the socialist. Our political system has shown that it possesses institutions

---

[1] See Official Records of the General Assembly, Twenty-seventh Session, Supplement No. 15, Part One, annex I, resolution 88 (XII).

that are sufficiently open to have brought about the expression of this revolutionary will without violent upheavals. It is my duty to inform this assembly that the reprisals and economic blockade that have been employed in an attempt to produce a chain reaction of difficulties and economic upsets represent a threat to domestic peace and coexistence. But they will not achieve their evil intention. The vast majority of the Chilean people can resist this threat with dignity and patriotism. What I said at the beginning will always be true: the history, the land and the people of Chile have combined to produce a great feeling of national identity.

At the third session of UNCTAD I referred to the phenomenon of the transnational corporations and drew attention to the staggering increase in their economic power, political influence and corrupting effect. It is not surprising, therefore, that world opinion should react with alarm in the face of this reality. The power of these corporations is so great as to transcend all frontiers. The foreign investments of United States companies alone, which today amount to $32,000 million, grew by 10 percent annually between 1950 and 1970, while United States exports rose by only 5 percent. The profits of such companies are fabulous and represent an enormous drain on the resources of the developing countries.

In one year those enterprises repatriated profits from the Third World representing net transfers in their favor of $1.723 billion: $1.013 billion from Latin America, $280 million from Africa, $366 million from the Far East and $64 million from the Middle East. Their influence and sphere of action are rudely transforming traditional practices in international trade, the transfer of technology, the transmission of resources among nations, and labor relations.

We are witnessing a pitched battle between the great transnational corporations and sovereign states, for the latter's fundamental political, economic and military decisions are being interfered with by world-wide organizations which are not dependent on any single state and which, as regards the sum total of their activities, are not accountable to or regulated by any parliament or institution representing the collective interest. In a word, the entire political structure of the world is being undermined. "Merchants have no country of their own. Wherever they may be they have no ties with the soil. All they are interested in is the source of their profits." Those are not my own words; they were spoken by Jefferson.

The great transnational enterprises are not only undermining the genuine interests of the developing countries, but their overwhelming and uncontrolled force is felt too in the industrialized countries in which they are based. This fact has been denounced in recent months in Europe and the United States; it has in fact given rise to investigations in the

U.S. Senate. In the face of this danger the developed countries can feel no more secure than the developing world. This disturbing phenomenon has already prompted the growing mobilization of organized labor, including the world's great trade unions. Once again international solidarity among the workers of the world must face a common adversary: imperialism.

This is basically why the Economic and Social Council, as a result of the complaint submitted by Chile, unanimously adopted in July of last year resolution 1721 (LIII) calling for the appointment of a study group of eminent persons to study "the role of multinational corporations and their impact on the process of development, especially that of the developing countries, and also their implications for international relations... and to submit recommendations for appropriate international action."

Ours is not an isolated or unique problem: it is simply the local manifestation of a reality that goes beyond our frontiers and takes in the Latin American continent and the whole Third World. In varying degrees of intensity and with individual differences, all the peripheral countries are exposed to something of this kind.

As for the developed countries, the concept of human solidarity should cause them to feel repugnance at the fact that a group of corporations can with impunity interfere in the most vital workings of the life of a nation, even going so far as to disrupt it completely.

When the spokesman of the African group of States in the Trade and Development Board announced the position of the African countries a few weeks ago regarding Chile's complaint about the aggression of the Kennecott Copper Corporation he said that the group was in complete solidarity with Chile because the issue was one that did not affect only one country, but represented a potential threat to the entire developing world. Those words are highly significant, for they indicate that a whole continent recognizes that what is happening in Chile is opening up a new stage in the battle between imperialism and the weaker countries of the Third World.

The battle to protect their natural resources is part of the broader struggle being waged by the countries of the Third World to overcome underdevelopment. There is a clear-cut dialectical relationship: imperialism exists because underdevelopment exists; underdevelopment exists because imperialism exists.

The aggression that we are suffering makes it seem illusory to give any credence to the promises that have been made in recent years regarding large-scale action to bring the nations of Africa, Asia and Latin America out of their backwardness and want. Two years ago this General Assembly, celebrating the 25th anniversary of the founding of the United Nations, solemnly proclaimed the International Development

Strategy for the Second United Nations Development Decade. Under it, all states members of the organization pledged themselves to spare no effort to change, through specific measures, the existing inequitable international division of labor and to bridge the enormous economic and technological gap separating the affluent countries from the developing nations.

It is now clear that none of those pledges has become a reality. On the contrary, we have moved backwards. Thus the markets of the industrialized countries have remained as firmly closed as ever to the commodities of the developing world — especially agricultural commodities — and the level of protectionism is on the rise. The terms of trade continue to deteriorate; the system of generalized preferences for our exports of manufactures and semi-manufactures has not been implemented by the nation whose market, given its volume, offered the best prospects; and there is no indication that the country concerned will implement it in the immediate future.

The transfer of public financial resources, far from reaching 0.7 percent of the developed nations' gross national product, has dropped from 0.34 to 0.24 percent. The indebtedness of the developing countries, already enormous at the beginning of this year, has risen in a few months from $70 to $75 billion. The heavy debt service payments, which are an intolerable drain on those countries' resources, are largely attributable to the types and terms of the loans. Those payments increased by 18 percent in 1970, and by 20 percent in 1971, which is more than twice the average rate for the 1960s.

That is the tragedy of underdevelopment and the tragedy of our countries, which have not yet been able to claim our rights and, through vigorous concerted action, protect the prices of raw materials and commodities and withstand the threats and aggressions of neo-imperialism.

We are potentially rich countries; yet we live in poverty. We go from place to place seeking credit and help; yet — a true paradox in keeping with the capitalist economic system — we are major exporters of capital.

Latin America, as a component of the developing world, forms part of the picture I have just described. Together with Africa, Asia and the socialist countries. Latin America has fought many battles over the last few years to change the structure of economic and trade relations with the capitalist world and to replace the unjust and discriminatory economic and monetary order created at Bretton Woods at the end of World War II.

It is perfectly true that there are disparities in national income between many countries in our region and those of the other developing continents, and such disparities exist, too, within our region — a region which includes several countries which may be considered as relatively less developed among the developing nations. But these disparities — which become almost insignificant in comparison with the national product of the industrialized world — do not exclude Latin America from that immense sector of humanity which is underprivileged and exploited.

The Latin American Consensus of Viña del Mar, approved in May 1969, affirmed these common characteristics and typified, defined and quantified the region's economic and social backwardness and the external factors responsible for it, stressing the tremendous injustices committed against our region under the guise of cooperation and help. For the much-admired great cities of Latin America conceal the tragedy of hundreds of thousands of people living in shantytowns, the result of fearful unemployment and underemployment, hiding the gross inequalities between small privileged groups and the broad masses, whose nutrition and health standards are no higher than in Africa, and who have practically no access to culture.

It is easy to understand why Latin America has such a high infant mortality rate and such a low life expectancy when it is realized that it lacks 28 million dwellings and 56 percent of its population is undernourished, that there are more than 100 million illiterate and semi-literate persons, 13 million unemployed and over 50 million underemployed. More than 20 million Latin Americans do not even know what money is, even as a medium for trade.

No system, no government, has been capable of making good the dramatic deficiencies in housing, work, food and health. On the contrary, these get worse year by year with the natural growth of population. If this situation continues what will happen at the end of the century when the population of Latin America will be over 600 million? The situation is even worse in Asia and Africa, with their lower per capita income and weaker development process.

It is not always realized that the Latin American subcontinent, with its enormous potential resources, has become the main field of action of economic imperialism in the past 30 years. Recent data from the International Monetary Fund reveal that for Latin America the private investments account of the developed countries showed a deficit of $9,000 million between 1960 and 1970. In other words, this amount represents a net capital contribution to the richest countries in one decade.

Chile feels a deep sense of solidarity with all the countries of Latin America, without exception. It therefore advocates and strictly observes the policy of nonintervention and self-determination, which it applies at the world level. We ardently promote closer economic and cultural relations. We support greater dovetailing and integration of our economies. Hence, we are working enthusiastically within the Latin

American Free Trade Association and, as a first step, we are striving for the formation of a common market for the Andean countries, linking us with Bolivia, Colombia, Peru and Ecuador.

Gone are the days when Latin America simply protested. Statistical data and the continent's needs contributed towards strengthening a sense of awareness. Ideological barriers have been broken down by realities. Plans designed to divide and isolate us have not succeeded. What has come to the forefront is a desire to coordinate the defense of the interests of all nations of the hemisphere and of those of all developing nations. "Those who stand in the way of peaceful revolution make violent revolution inevitable." Again, those are not my words; I agree with them. They were spoken by John F. Kennedy.

Chile is not alone. No one has succeeded in isolating it from Latin America or from the rest of the world. On the contrary, it has received infinite demonstrations of solidarity and support. The growing repudiation of imperialism, the respect merited by the efforts of the Chilean people, and the response to our policy of friendship with all nations of the world have combined to defeat the attempts to erect a hostile barrier around us.

In Latin America all the systems of economic and cultural cooperation and of integration to which Chile belongs at the regional and subregional level have continued to gain vigor at a rapid pace, and within this context our trade, particularly with Argentina, Mexico and the countries parties to the Andean Pact, has increased considerably.

There has been no split in the concerted stand adopted by the Latin American countries at world and regional meetings in support of the principles of self-determination in respect of their natural resources. In the face of the recent threats to our sovereignty we have received fraternal demonstrations of complete solidarity. To all we offer our sincere thanks.

Socialist Cuba, which is enduring a rigorous blockade, has always unreservedly given us its revolutionary support.

At the world level, I must say in particular that right from the start the socialist countries of Europe and Asia have been at our side in an attitude of absolute solidarity. The large majority of the world community honored us in choosing Santiago as the site for the third session of UNCTAD, and it has displayed interest in our invitation — which I hereby repeat — to hold in Chile the forthcoming United Nations Conference on the Law of the Sea.

In September, the conference of foreign ministers of Nonaligned Countries, held in Georgetown, Guyana, last August, publicly expressed its firm support for us in our fight against the aggression practiced by the Kennecott Copper Corporation.

The Intergovernmental Council of Copper Exporting Countries, the coordinating body established by the main copper exporting countries — Peru, Zaire, Zambia and Chile — recently met at the ministerial level in Santiago at the request of my government to take up Kennecott's aggression against my country. At the meeting the council adopted various resolutions and recommendations of great significance. These constitute unreserved support for our position and an important step taken by Third World countries to defend the trade in their raw materials.

No doubt there will be an important debate in the second committee on those resolutions. I merely wish to stress the categorical assertion that any action likely to hinder or curtail the exercise of a nation's sovereign right freely to dispose of its natural resources entails an act of economic aggression. The action of Kennecott Copper Corporation against Chile indeed constitutes economic and trade aggression. Furthermore those resolutions call for the suspension of all economic or trade relations with Kennecott, and provide that disagreements on questions regarding compensation for nationalizations are within the sole jurisdiction of the very states exercising such rights.

But of paramount importance is the decision taken to establish permanent machinery for protection and solidarity regarding copper. Such machinery and that of the Organization of Petroleum Exporting Countries on oil form the nucleus of what should be an organization of all Third World countries to protect and defend all their commodities, mineral and hydrocarbons as well as agricultural.

The vast majority of the countries of Western Europe, from the Scandinavian countries in the north to Spain in the south, have increased their cooperation with Chile, and their understanding has been of great support to us. Thanks to that, we have renegotiated our external debt.

Lastly, we have been touched to see the solidarity of the workers of the world, expressed through their major federations and trade unions and made manifest in such deeply significant acts as the refusal of the stevedores of Le Havre and Rotterdam to unload Chilean copper, payment for which had been arbitrarily and unjustly placed under embargo.

I have concentrated my statement on the aggression against Chile and on Latin American and world problems which are connected with the origin or effects of that aggression. I now wish to refer briefly to other matters of interest to the international community.

I shall not mention all the world problems on the agenda of this session. I do not pretend to have solutions for them. This assembly has been working hard for over two months in defining and adopting appropriate measures, and I am confident that this work will bear fruitful results. My comments will be of a general character and will reflect some concerns of the Chilean people.

The picture of the international political scene in which we have lived since the last world war has changed very rapidly, and this has resulted in a new correlation of forces. Centers of political and economic power have grown in number and strength. The socialist world, whose influence has increased significantly, is playing an ever more important role in the adoption of vital international policy decisions. I am convinced that the reform of world trade relations and the international monetary system — a change that is desired by all nations of the world — will be impossible unless all countries in the world, including those in the socialist area, participate fully in the process. The People's Republic of China, which contains nearly one-third of the world's population, has finally, after a long period of unjust ostracism, recovered its place in the forum of multilateral negotiations and has initiated diplomatic and trade relations with most countries of the world.

The European Economic Community has been enlarged with the entry of the United Kingdom and other countries, which now have a bigger say in decision-making, particularly in the economic field. Japan's economic growth-rate has reached prodigious proportions.

The developing world is daily becoming more conscious of the realities which surround it and of its own rights. It demands justice and equal treatment and recognition of its rightful place on the world scene.

As always, the motive force behind these changes has come from the people, who are making history in their progressive struggle for freedom. Man's intelligence has pushed science and technology forward at a giddy pace. The persistence and vigor of the policy of peaceful co-existence, economic independence and social progress which the socialist nations have promoted has helped decisively to ease the tensions that divided the world for more than 20 years, and it has been a determining factor in the acceptance of new values in international relations and society.

We welcome the changes which bring promises of peace and prosperity to many nations, but we demand that the whole of mankind be able to share in them. Unfortunately, these changes have brought only meager benefits to the developing world, which continues to be as exploited as before and indeed is becoming increasingly remote from the civilization of the industrialized world. The noble aspirations and the just rebellion now seething in it will continue to find expression in an increasingly forcible manner.

We are gratified to see the virtual end of the Cold War, and other heartening developments: the negotiations between the Soviet Union and the United States on both trade and disarmament; the conclusion of treaties between the Federal Republic of Germany and the Soviet Union and Poland; the imminence of the European security conference; the negotiations between the two German states and their almost certain entry into the United Nations; and the negotiations between the governments of the Democratic People's Republic of Korea and the Republic of Korea, to name some of the most promising. There is no doubt that the international situation is now marked by truces, agreements and an easing of the previously explosive situation.

There are still too many unresolved conflicts, however, that call for a stronger will by the parties to reach agreement and for collaboration between the world community and the major powers. Aggression and friction continue unabated in several parts of the world: the Middle East conflict, the most explosive of all, for which it has not yet proved possible to find the peaceful settlement advocated in resolutions of the principal organs of the United Nations, among which is resolution 242 (1967) of the Security Council; the blockade and persecution of Cuba; colonial exploitation; the ignominy of racism and apartheid; the widening of the economic and technological gaps between rich and poor countries.

There is as yet no peace in Indochina. But it has to come. There shall be peace for Vietnam. It must be so, because nobody now has any doubt regarding the futility of this monstrously unjust war that is still pursuing the totally unobtainable objective of imposing on peoples with revolutionary consciousness policies which they cannot accept because they run counter to their national interests, their genius and their personality. Peace will come. But what will this war — so cruel, so long and so unfair — leave behind it? After all these years of bloody fighting, the only outcome is the torture of a remarkably dignified people; millions of dead and orphaned; entire cities wiped out; the ecological destruction of hundreds of thousands of acres of land, devastated without any possibility of future vegetation. The people of the United States themselves are touched by grief; thousands of homes have been plunged into sorrow by the absence of their loved ones. The path that was laid out by Lincoln has not been followed.

This war has also taught many lessons. It has taught the world that the abuse of power saps the moral fiber of the country that misuses it and produces profound doubts in its own social conscience; whereas a people defending its independence can be raised to heroic heights by its convictions and rendering capable of resisting the physical violence of the world's mightiest military and economic machine.

The new political framework offers favorable conditions for the community of nations, in coming years, to make a major effort to give the world order a new lease on life and a new dimension. That effort must be founded on the principles of the charter, and on others, such as those of the third session of UNCTAD, which the world has added to it. As we have already said, the United Nations should be guided by three concepts that are fundamental to the responsibilities entrusted to it:

collective political security, collective economic and social security, and universal respect for basic human rights, including economic, social and cultural rights, without any discrimination whatsoever.

We attach particular importance to the need to ensure collective economic security, on which Brazil and the United Nations secretary general have recently placed so much stress. As a major step in this direction, the world organization should implement as soon as possible the Charter of Economic Rights and Duties of States,[2] a valuable proposal which the President of Mexico, Luis Echeverría, brought before the third session of UNCTAD. Like this great leader of a fraternal country, we too believe that a just order and a stable world are impossible so long as no set of commitments and rights has been established to protect the weaker states.

Future action by the community of nations must place emphasis on a policy in which all nations will play an active part. After all, the United Nations Charter was conceived and presented in the name of "We, the peoples of the United Nations."

International action must be directed towards serving the man who enjoys no privileges but who suffers and toils: the miner in Cardiff and the *fellah* in Egypt; the cocoa farmer in Ghana or the Ivory Coast, and the peasant of the plateaus of South America; the fisherman in Java and the coffee farmer in Kenya or Colombia. International action must reach the two billion underprivileged, those whom the community has the obligation to bring up to the level of the modern world and to reaffirm the "dignity and worth of the human person," to use the words of the preamble to the charter.

The international community must not wait a moment longer to secure the implementation of the Strategy for the Second Development Decade and to bring that instrument into line with the new realities of the Third World and the burgeoning awareness of its peoples.

The slackening of tension in international relations and the process of cooperation and understanding make it not only possible but essential to divert all the enormous efforts that have been devoted to making war to activities that will try to cross new frontiers and meet the truly vast and varied needs of more than two-thirds of humankind. Thus, the more developed countries must increase their production and employment in line with the real interests of the less developed countries. Only when that is done will it be possible to say that the international community really exists.

This assembly is to decide upon the arrangements for holding the United Nations conference which is to establish what is termed the Law

---

[2] See *Proceedings of the United Nations Conference on Trade and Development, Third Session,* vol. I, Report and Annexes (United Nations publication, Sales No. E.73.II.D.4), annex I.A, resolution 45 (III).

of the Sea — namely, a set of standards to regulate, on a worldwide basis, everything connected with the use and exploitation of the vast areas represented by the sea and the sea-bed, including the subsoil thereof. This is a major task of great promise for the United Nations, for the problem is one of which humankind in general has only recently developed an awareness, and even many existing situations may be perfectly compatible with the general interest. I should like to recall that just 20 years ago the countries in the southern-most part of Latin America — Ecuador, Peru and Chile — were responsible for beginning that process which will culminate in the adoption of a treaty on the Law of the Sea. It is essential that that treaty include the principle approved at the third session of UNCTAD on the rights of coastal states over the resources of the sea-bed and the subsoil thereof coming within the limits of their national jurisdiction,[3] and that instruments and machinery be established to ensure that the sea-bed area beyond the limits of national jurisdiction is the common patrimony of humankind and is exploited for the benefit of all by an international authority.

I should like to reaffirm our confidence in the mission of the United Nations. We know that its successes and its failures depend on the political will of the states of the world and on its ability to interpret the wishes of the vast majority of humankind. Whether the United Nations is simply a forum for debates or an effective instrument depends on the will of those states.

I have brought to this assembly the voice of my country, a country united in the face of pressure from outside, a country that asks for, and deserves, understanding, for it has always respected the principles of self-determination and complied strictly with the principle of non-intervention in the internal affairs of the other states. My country has never failed to comply with its international obligations and is now actively cultivating friendly relations with all the countries of the world. Admittedly, we have differences of opinion with some of them, but there is no country with which we are not prepared to talk matters over, using the framework of the multilateral and bilateral instruments to which we are parties. Our respect for those treaties is unswerving.

I have tried to reaffirm most emphatically that a desire for universal peace and cooperation is one of the dominant characteristics of the Chilean people. That is why they will resolutely defend their political and economic independence and the implementation of their collective decisions, which have been democratically adopted in the full exercise of their sovereignty.

Events that have taken place within less than a week strengthen our conviction that soon victory will be with us in the struggle to attain these

---

[3] Ibid, resolution 46 (III).

objectives: the candid, direct and friendly exchange of views with the distinguished President of Peru, General Juan Velasco Alvarado, who publicly restated the full solidarity of his country with Chile in the face of the hostile actions I have already exposed, the resolutions of the Intergovernmental Council of Copper Exporting Countries I have mentioned, and my visit to Mexico.

It is difficult, indeed almost impossible, to describe the depth, the force, the spontaneity and the eloquence of the support given us by the government of Mexico and the Mexican people. I received such expressions of support from President Luis Echeverría, the Congress, the universities and the people, all speaking with one voice, that I am still under the spell of their boundless generosity.

I come here reassured, for after such an experience I am absolutely certain that the awareness of the Latin American peoples of the risks facing us all has acquired a new dimension and that they are convinced that only by unity can they defend themselves from this grave peril.

When one has witnessed, as I have in the past few days, the enthusiasm and warmth of hundreds of thousands of men and women crowded in the streets and squares and crying slogans such as, "We are all for you; do not give up," all our doubts are dispelled and all our anxieties are erased. It is the peoples, all the peoples south of the Rio Bravo, that stand up to shout, "Enough — no more dependence," "An end to intervention"; to affirm the sovereign right of all developing nations freely to dispose of their natural resources. This is something that is embodied in the conscience and determination of more than 250 million human beings who demand that they be listened to and respected.

Hundreds of thousands of Chileans wished me Godspeed with fervor and warmth when I left my country and gave me the message which I have offered to this world assembly. I am convinced that you, representing the nations of the world, will understand and assess my words. It is our faith in ourselves that increases our confidence in the great values of humanity and our confidence that those great values will prevail. They cannot be destroyed.

The President [interpretation from French]: On behalf of the General Assembly, I wish to thank His Excellency the President of the Republic of Chile for the important statement he has just made.

18

For Democracy and Revolution, Against Civil War

Third Annual Message to the National Congress, May 21, 1973

In the concluding section of this constitutionally required presidential address to the new legislative session of Congress, President Allende builds upon the unprecedented gains by the Popular Unity governing coalition in the mid-term elections of March 4, 1973, caused in part by an incredibly huge voter turnout, a reflection of Chile's deepening democracy. "In such an unfavorable economic moment like the one we are facing, it is the popular decision to advance toward socialism," he observes. Allende calls for a nationwide discussion of reforms to the constitution in order to democratize the judiciary; overcome bureaucratization; broaden citizen rights and duties; increase local and regional grassroots democracy; democratize social security; develop culture and technology; and increase the armed forces' participation in the new socio-economic programs. He denounces those domestic and foreign elements who are trying to create economic chaos in order to generate a political crisis and "impose fascism." Calling once more on worker unity, Allende asserts that "lack of understanding and divisions over partisan motives have no place in our struggle against imperialism and reaction."

The March 4 elections hold a profound significance that I don't want to leave unmentioned. The new Congress emerges from an electoral consultation carried out in a lively and creative manner, showing the dynamic nature of our democracy. It puts to rest the claims of those who had anticipated the end of citizen participation in public matters and a suppression of political rights of the opposition once the workers were in power, and it also ridicules those who invented imaginary electoral frauds to hide their own historical dismissal. The Electoral Tribunal has ratified the clean nature of the process.

It makes me proud, and I am sure that the majority of Chileans share this pride, to see that since 1970 there is a new trend in our political environment: the vast increase of popular participation in public affairs. In less than three years, our countrymen have been called to exercise their right to vote on seven occasions. There have been two national elections. The number of citizens who have directly participated in the election of their political representatives has gone from 2,954,000 in 1970 to 3,660,000 in 1973.

But, in proving that civic rights are alive, it would be insufficient to only refer to its current massiveness. In this country, where each day there are dozens of elections — in trade unions, communities, professional groups, student unions, neighborhood groups, etc. — a phenomenon of qualitative significance is taking place which will mark in the country's history the efforts made during these years. For the first time, large sectors of the population can exercise their political rights, which had been previously denied, through having concrete means to guarantee them the right to expression and association. For the first time, economic democracy is a reality. For once, the decisions which most affect each person, influencing his creative dimension, his job and well-being, have ceased to be a privilege for the powerful or select minorities, and are adopted by the organized masses in their job centers or residences. A new era has begun for Chilean democracy.

The parliamentary elections of March 4 have demonstrated, equally, something which throws some of our adversaries into desperation and confusion: the regular functioning of the political-institutional mechanisms through which popular will is expressed. In contradicting the designs of those who have not ceased in their intent to destroy them, because they saw the elections as an "end without destiny," March 4 was a clear manifestation in defense of the democratic regime.

On the other hand, the significance of the electoral result is reflected in the historical context in which it took place. The government's policies have been vindicated by the massive support received by the political parties that sustain it, the highest that any government has received in the last 20 years after 27 months in office. On March 4, the Chilean road to socialism has been reaffirmed.

While the privileged sectors become exasperated by the deterioration of their hegemonic status and by the relative decrease in the comfort and well-being they enjoyed at the expense of the great mass, the latter perceives the revolutionary sense of the transformations being carried out.

This is why, in the national consultation of March 4, not only was the result supportive of the government but it also reaffirmed the revolutionary will. It's something more than a simple wish for change. In economic circumstances as unfavorable as the ones we are experiencing, the popular decision is to advance towards socialism.

At the same time, in the March 4 result the government notes the need to introduce some modifications in the current policies, which have not found support of certain groups of workers and middle class areas, despite our actions being oriented in their favor.

The constitutional regime must adapt to the new reality
The government aim that the state should serve the workers and the great majority of the country is powerfully counteracted by the rigidity of our legal and administrative structures. Each day their inadequacy in dealing with the urgent necessities of economic and political life becomes more apparent. For example, when speculation has acquired proportions never before seen, the state is practically devoid of any legal tools to sanction hoarding and black market practices. Now that the decision-making powers achieved by the workers are a reality, promising firm development, the state apparatus appears close-minded and resistant to recognize and organize it. The dynamic nature of a revolutionary process frees up repressed energies, hurts dominant interests, generates new social phenomena able to be guided and which the government has endeavored to control. But, for this to have a satisfactory outcome, it needs a flexible institutional regime.

In other words, the new situation taking shape in the last years requires legal and administrative measures, which cannot be delayed any longer. Both to improve its positive dimensions and also to correct its negative aspects. The delay in their adoption can only be detrimental. Only if the state apparatus acquires a popular character, can we avoid the progressive worsening of its inadequacies to the real Chile, a maladjustment that is behind many of the political and economic conflicts.

One year later, I cannot but reiterate with greater urgency what I stated at the beginning of the last term: "A whole regulatory system must be modified and a set of administrative measures must be put into practice in order to deal with the new needs. The banking system, financial system, the labor regime, social security, planning systems, the state's own administration structure, the political constitution itself, are not in tune with the demands created by the new changes. This program, which concerns and belongs to the whole of the people, must be debated by the people, and then acquire legal validity."

Today I reiterate once more that we do not see the road of the Chilean revolution in the violent collapse of the state apparatus. But the current legislation constitutes a confusing and inconsistent system of norms, lacking the necessary conditions to adapt to the new circumstances.

Chile requires a simple, clear, flexible and systematic legislation. Only by abolishing a considerable part of the current precepts, revising others and dictating new ones, will we achieve a legislative system reflective of an egalitarian, just and fluid organization, intent on resolving the current social contradictions.

A difficult task, impossible to tackle all at once or in the short term, only progressively and with the firm will to replace the current legislation, oblivious to the reality it is supposed to govern. The way this is done will depend, to a large extent, on this new Congress. It will require that we are conscious of the need to give the country a new political constitution and of the required laws.

The government has elaborated a draft of a constitution, which will be subject to a comprehensive national debate at every level to collect criticisms and suggestions before its presentation to Congress. I will now mention only some of its relevant aspects.

a. Democratization of the judicial body and precautions against bureaucracy

The justice administration must be democratized in its methods of generating its senior ranks and be in touch with the problems of coexistence of the people. It also requires modernization. It is necessary that a tribunal be established to deal with cases involving the administrative authorities and staff members or other private citizens. On the other hand, respect for the constitution and the strengthening of the principles of legalities call for an expansion of the faculties of the Constitutional Tribunal, assigning it the power to rule on jurisdiction disputes between the political-administrative authorities and the Justice Tribunals, and also the issue of laws being inapplicable due to their anti-constitutional character.

An increase in the functions of the state heightens the risk of increased bureaucracy and demands legal instruments able to avert it in time. The risk that a civil servant might distort his task of serving the community, and subject it to the interest of particular groups or, what's worse, for personal benefit, demands the adoption of a regime where the conduct of civil servants comes under supervision in order to impose sanctions where transgression of duties occur, and prevent the possibility of illicit enrichment.

The attorney general's office of the nation, from the highest institutional level, will guarantee compliance with the law and the correct performance of public duties, through its own initiative or at the request of the interested parties.

b. Broadening of rights and duties

The rights and guarantees accorded by the constitution must be expanded and others must be introduced that will acknowledge freedom, personal property and favorable conditions for one's integral personal development. There must be more strict protection for the dignity, reputation and honor of people, and also the safeguarding of privacy, personal life and the home.

A totally new area for our legal system must be confronted: that of duties. We must establish a social obligation to work in accordance to one's capacity. Nobody can claim the benefits of social life if they don't perform their work within their capabilities, providing a material, scientific or cultural contribution to the community. Active participation in social development must be an obligation for everyone. The safeguarding and protection of social and state property must also be implemented.

Our legal norms cannot continue to be bastions promoting individualism and the egotistical exaltation of those things that an alienated man would seek, but instead, must encourage citizens towards solidarity with others and to work towards the collective interests.

c. Democratization of territorial administration

The direct participation of the people in decision making should take place, predominantly, in their places of residence, where a person carries out most of their activities as a social member of a group. Democracy is so much more authentic when it is directly exercised in one's immediacy. This is why a profound reconsideration of local government is required.

Those organizations that can best contribute to people taking direct control of local affairs should be added to the traditional municipality institution. To this end, we propose the creation of a new organization, the Community Cells, to work together with the current trade union and community institutions.

Formed by representatives elected by the community and workers' organizations, they must be the exponents — before their local municipality — of their needs and problems, thus constituting the nucleus of the great pyramid of planning, inspired by the authentic and democratic presence of the people. In collaboration with public services, the Community Cells must be capable of facilitating popular control over administrative institutions, thus contributing to the combat against the bureaucratic burden.

The same organizational principles of popular participation must be put into practice at a provincial and regional level, so that they associate and coordinate the actions of state services, municipalities and popular and workers' organizations. The initiatives adopted by the government toward this aim, are the beginning of a long road.

The administrative and territorial divisions, whose roots date back to the last century, demand a profound modernization. The region must be the economic unit that facilitates the formulation and application of development plans and programs. We have to provide it with adequate mechanisms and provide the most efficient link with state administrative bodies.

d. Democratization of Social Security
Cultural and Technological Development

On other matters, the social security system needs to be truly democratic. It will provide the same service and it will establish equal rights for all people, regardless of their employment or income.

Our country has entered the historical cycle of radical changes in values, conscience and the perception of itself as a people. New guidelines for life, attitude and behaviour begin to take shape. In this way, for example, voluntary work has mobilised more than two million compatriots, youth and adults of all ideologies and beliefs, authorities, parliamentarians, military personnel, ecclesiastics, etc. with the aim of spontaneously contributing to the great task of national construction.

On the other hand, the progress of the revolution and the change in the economic structure demands that we acknowledge the heightened role that science and technology have, particularly in the construction of a socialist economy, no less significant than the conquest of power by the workers.

We conceive this scientific and technological development as being directly linked to the people and not in isolation from it. That is why educational reform is urgent, to ensure the improvement of the cultural and scientific capacity of our compatriots.

The education authorities proposed a harmonious educational system that was presented as the National Unified School. It is not a jump in the complex process of educational development, but rather a decisive step forward in its evolution.

During its formulation historical factors were considered, in order to relate the changes as closely as possible to educational development in Chile. We hope to achieve an integrationist national education — not to be interpreted as cultural insulation — but to strengthen the personality itself of the country.

There is a third aim: the desire to provide permanent education to citizens, given that the accelerated development of science and technology demand that education be uninterrupted.

The aims of the National Unified School were distorted by some and questioned by others with respectable arguments. Faced with the latter, the government adopted the decision of postponing its implementation with the purpose of ensuring a dialogue, which is always open.

It's also necessary to give a lot of attention to the working conditions of our technicians and professionals, in order to stimulate them to contribute their knowledge towards the progress of the country. Chile needs the contribution of the whole creative capacity of its men and women. We must work hard to counteract the negative effects that the so-called "brain drain" has on us and the rest of the Third World, this being one of the worst burdens imposed by the hegemonic nations.

These are, succinctly put forward, some of the more urgent changes in the institutional system. As we have already said, they must find their way into a new constitution, without the legal order experimenting with solutions of continuity. The foundations of the new institutional norms will emanate from the collective experience and they will have to be directly discussed by all the people. The efficiency of the state apparatus, the democratization of political and economic power, the accelerated development of our country, depends to a great extent on its timely introduction.

This is how the government defines its position in the face of those who look to break down the democratic system by means of blocking Executive powers or through the annihilation of the state apparatus.

The role of the armed forces and order

In a modern society, like the one we envisage, the armed forces must be fully integrated. I wish to express the country's satisfaction with their performance, as well as the performance of police and investigations, in carrying out their patriotic tasks.

The armed forces, as well as fulfilling their usual role, have joined with representatives of popular parties and the workers confederation (CUT) to form part of the cabinet that I set up in order to put an end to the subversive October strike.

A soldier of the republic — the commander-in-chief of the army, General Carlos Prats González, in his role as minister of the interior, took on the vice-presidency of the nation while I was absent from the country. The citizens have appreciated his correct and efficient performance.

It has been a constant concern of the government to promote and bring to fruition the development plans for the three branches of the armed forces in order to consolidate, even further, the strict fulfillment of the specific tasks assigned to them by national defense. In accordance with this, during 1972, laws were enacted to increase the size of the army and the air force and a similar law for the navy is awaiting approval by Congress. To this we must add the financial support granted for improvements and expansion in infrastructure, as well as the renewal of logistic and military material.

All this is being achieved despite the various difficulties affecting the country during the past year, because the government is clearly aware that the military institutions, specially their professional and technical ranks, must have at their disposal the adequate means to fulfill their responsibilities of national defense.

This policy will be continued because security and development must be combined harmoniously since an imbalance can only bring negative consequences for the country. This is the reason why the government has placed special emphasis on the participation of the armed forces in the socio-economic programs.

Those who describe this participation as a political act not only ignore the institutional position of the armed forces but also deny them the right to a thorough knowledge of the country and its problems, essential for planning National defense. The government will continue to promote this participation, which will allow Chile to count on a source of human potential of high moral and intellectual background.

The Supreme National Security Council (CONSUSENA), will be revamped with a more agile and expedited structure, allowing easier and permanent coordination of its activities in the service of National Security.

The political project of the government
Citizen Parliamentarians: In these moments, more than in others, it is imperative that we clearly show to the country the direction in which the transforming actions of the Popular Government are heading. The mandate we gained in 1970, later ratified, was to establish a social order, which will open routes to socialism. In the current stage of the revolutionary process, we are obliged to specify, where possible, some of the manifestations of the social, political and economic aspects of the transitional period we are currently going through.

Our objective is to organize the elements of the present reality which will be the base for the subsequent stages in the construction of a new society, one in which the workers will assume full economic and political power. This requires an ordering of economical activity so that the great potential generated by structural changes can be exploited. The elimination of large-scale land ownership, financial monopolies and a large part of the industrial monopolies have cleared the way to a greater rationalization of the national economy. It is now a matter of having the necessary energy and clarity to establish the planning which, channeling the initiative and responsibility of the workers, will prevail over the capitalist forces.

The reactionary forces are vividly aware of their political failure. They are intent on provoking economic disorder. They know that an economic crisis would generate a political crisis, creating the conditions that would allow fascism to become a mass movement. As president, I will impose economic and political order. As a revolutionary, I will combat the development of fascism in any of its forms: economic, political, ideological or terrorist.

Our success in overcoming the supporters of chaos will be Chile's success. Their defeat consolidates the development of an active and pluralist democracy. I am emphatic in stressing that the political liberties of the political opposition must be effective. This is how I have always conceived the evolution towards socialism in our country.

Chileans must be very conscious that pluralist liberties depend on our capacity to prevent economic and political chaos.

As president, I call on all democratic and patriotic citizens to participate in this enterprise.

The more vigorous and authentic our democracy is, the more effective and real will be the mass participation of the population in the new society. Participation is not a handout. It is a right. It has been achieved thanks to the efforts and sacrifices of many generations. In the process of transition to socialism, participation is a material necessity. We vigorously condemn the enormous damage that sectarianism and intolerance is causing in our revolutionary process. Against imperialism and reactionary forces, there can be no place for party-driven misunderstandings or divisions.

The ideological debate in the hearts of the workers precedes this government and will remain afterwards. It cannot be allowed to weaken the unity built around the uppermost class interests. The struggle among the democrats who support the government and the opposition cannot reach such a point as to facilitate the work of those who want to impose fascism.

To establish the basis for the new economic structure and the Popular State, the government relies on the drive provided by the social force of the workers. Whether it is from within or outside the Popular Unity, they strive and make sacrifices to put an end to the capitalist system. This deep current bypasses ideological discrepancies and today unites the majority of our compatriots.

Faced with this revolutionary reality, Congress can organize a majority that will put itself at the service of the reordering of the economic-political system. It must not preserve the old structures. The government and Congress will be able to coincide in the critical dialogue about our most pressing needs. Otherwise, the present contradictions of the institutional regime will become more acute.

The Popular Government appeals to the conscience and class awareness of all the workers. Their social gains, their political liberties, their organizations, their power to challenge the forces of national and imperialist capitalism, their capacity to build a new society, these are great instruments. The national and international reactionary forces can destroy them. They aim to sweep away all the gains of the workers. Faced with a threat so real and present, the workers will not allow themselves to be used. Their economic demands cannot be utilized by the bourgeoisie against the government and the revolutionary process. Social discipline and conscious effort must be present at every workplace. Chile demands more production, more productivity.

The dreams, the creative capacity, artistic talent, revolutionary will, the experience of the process itself, all converge in the crucible of our homeland.

This great crucible fuses the commitment and dreams of the young, women and men. Chile and its future are held in their arms, the arms of the people.

We shall win!

19

Report to the Nation on the Military Uprising of June 29, 1973

Allende reports from La Moneda palace on that morning's heroic response by several individuals and the armed forces and Carabineros (national police) to an attempted military coup d'état by a dissident tank regiment. Some observers believed the coup attempt might be a "dress rehearsal" for a more thorough-going coup later, one that in fact did take place in less than 10 weeks. On June 29, however, General Pinochet sided with the constitutional government even though he later headed the September 11 coup d'état that ended democracy in Chile and took Allende's life. The high degree of tension surrounding this speech of Allende's is suggested by the president's brief reference to an earlier "incident that occurred on Costanera [Avenue] with General Prats." An upper-class reactionary woman was sitting in a car that had pulled alongside Prats' car at a stop light. She recognized Prats and apparently insulted him verbally and gestured in a threatening manner. This caused a nervous Prats to pull a pistol form his holster (perhaps Prats recalled too well the murder of General Schneider. In fact, 15 months later Prats and his wife were assassinated in Buenos Aires on orders from General Pinochet). Allende provides details of the day's events that are both entrancing and chilling to read today.

One moment, one moment. [Interrupted by chanting] One moment, comrades. Please, one moment. People of Chile, dear comrades of Santiago, I have assumed the responsibility of calling the people to inform them. Therefore I ask you to listen to me, because it is fundamental for each one here and each one who is listening on the radio to be fully aware of what has happened and also to understand the task he has to fulfill from now on.

That is why I ask not to be interrupted, either by applause or by shouts of slogans. The moment is too difficult, and my responsibility requires me to ask, more than ever, that the people understand how much I expect their serenity and firmness.

I want to render homage to those who have fallen. I especially want to pay homage to the loyal forces of the Chilean Army, the national navy and the air force. Sgt Rafael [Villena] was murdered at the door of the Defense Ministry. He was attached to the Second Army Division at general headquarters under the command of General Sepúlveda. I render homage to five civilians who lost their lives as a result of the underhanded, antipatriotic action, contrary to the doctrine of the armed forces, by that rebel group: to Leonita Reyes, to Victoria Sánchez Carranzo, a reporter, to Leonardo [Erlinse], a foreign newsman, to Luciano [Caro] and to Carlos [Fuentes]. I wish to emphasize that there are five persons seriously wounded at the central hospital, one at the workers hospital, and another at the [word indistinct] hospital — a total of seven seriously wounded. There are 11 persons seriously wounded at the military hospital from the army ranks. Twelve civilians have been shot who are less seriously wounded.

In addition to informing you, I have called you so that with the revolutionary zeal and firmness characteristic of the people, you may render homage to the armed forces of Chile, the *Carabineros*, and the Investigations Corps, which through their stand crushed the seditious attempt.

Now I will give you details about the past events: At 08:55 this morning I was called by the under-secretary of the interior, Comrade Daniel Vergara. He uttered a single sentence which revealed all: "Comrade President, we have tanks in front of La Moneda on Constitution Square. They are firing. I am informed that there are tanks surrounding La Moneda. I want you to know, Mr. President, that we are all here. We will do our duty." Minutes later, a *carabineros* second sergeant who belongs to the Moneda guard raised, with the aid of another *carabinero*, the flag of the homeland in the midst of the bullets. Their names: Second Sgt. Mario Humberto Mequis and Luis Venegas Alba, a *carabinero*.

What had happened? A group from Armored Regiment Number Two, led by ex-commander Souper, who was to be removed today from his post and who is now under arrest and definitively removed. The military courts will determine the sanctions to be applied to him and his accomplices. [Shouts and applause]

I repeat: Silence comrades!

That regiment surrounded La Moneda. Yesterday morning General Sepúlveda, chief of the Second Zone, announced proven facts. He charged that a very small number of officers had attempted on Wednesday morning to mobilize this same regiment. His charges, made at a press conference, were scoffed at by the reactionary press and gave rise to statements to the contrary.

The government adversaries presumed and maintained that those statements were a maneuver by us to prevent continuation of the investigation concerning the incident on Costanera [Avenue], which involved General Prats, who was so unjustly and stupidly attacked by the opposition radios and newspapers for the action he took.

Now the events prove that the government does not deceive or lie. Yesterday afternoon the defense minister went to the Senate and delivered the background information we had available, and in that session he was told that no credit was given to what the ministers had to say when what the senior military officers stated could not be believed. In the face of such an attitude, the defense minister left the Senate, making it clear once more that this government tells and will always tell the truth. [Applause, extensive chanting from the crowd]

Continuing with the information, I must point out that the seditious group fired repeatedly at the presidential palace. Moreover, they also fired at the Defense Ministry. The defense minister's offices were partially destroyed, as were several offices occupied by generals of the republic. They knew that Air Force Commander-in-Chief General Ruiz was inside that ministry, as well as Navy Commander-in-Chief Admiral Raúl Montero and the navy chiefs and officers. General Prats had left his home and gone first to the military school, then to the Tacna Regiment.

I want to stress the extraordinary damage to the Defense Ministry. A tank crushed the door and fired its gun inside the ministry. Shots were fired at the building. In the same manner, there were more than 500 shots fired at La Moneda. Sixteen offices in the Foreign Ministry have been almost destroyed, and more than 100 windows broken. When all this was happening I had already contacted the Defense Minister, Commanders-in-Chief Montero and Ruiz, and the interim *Carabineros* director general, General Viveros.

At that time Daniel Vergara called me again and told me: "Mr. President, we have received an order to surrender from the mutineers. Our decision — and here is the *Carabineros* officer in charge of the palace guard — is not to do it."

I told him: "There is a historic phrase that Lieutenant Pérez is going to repeat as a reply to the insolence of the rebels. Tell them what history said: 'The guard may die, but it will not surrender'." [Applause, shouts]

I pay tribute to the palace guard composed of *Carabineros* [applause] and to the young guard lieutenant, Mr. Pérez. I pay tribute to the investigations detectives who were here at La Moneda and who rapidly took their places to fight. I pay tribute to the personnel serving in La Moneda. Not one of them tried to leave. On the contrary, they said they would stay. And the majority of them are noncommissioned officers in the Chilean Navy. [Applause]

I pay tribute to the few government officials, men and women, who were at the presidential palace as well as at offices of the Interior Ministry, the Presidency and the Foreign Relations Ministry.

I pay tribute to the young newspaperwoman Verónica Ahumada, to whom I spoke four times and whom I urged to leave. She said: "I am here to keep the president informed." [Applause]

While the events were taking place at the Defense Ministry and the *Carabineros* directorate general, which was also fired upon while the interim director and the general of the *Carabineros* were there — I repeat, while these events were taking place, the army commander-in-chief together with Generals Pinochet, Pickering, Urbina and Sepúlveda prepared the plan to suppress the subversives. He ordered mobilization of the Buin and Tacna Regiments, the Noncommissioned Officers School, the Infantry School, the Telecommunications School and the Parachutists School. [Applause]

And General Prats took charge of the Noncommissioned Officers School. In the same manner, the *Carabineros* director general had mobilized the special group and the tanks. He had seen to it that two battalions and six tanks were deployed around the presidential house where I was in continuous control. And from there I spoke to the people twice by radio, first to tell them to trust the armed forces, *Carabineros* and Investigations Police; and second to tell them to occupy the enterprises and industries that were in their work centers, the pro-government leaders and political militants in their centers. I also told the people to regroup in four or five sectors, to be ready in case we needed them to fight along with the Chilean soldiers. [Applause]

Soldiers were in downtown Santiago, from the Noncommissioned Officers School, Infantry School, Telecommunications School and Parachutists School. They were in the Alameda sector. They were advancing on Mapucho station to make a geographic indication to the Buin Regiment headed by its commander and led by General Pinochet. At that time General Pickering, chief of military institutes, was advancing with another column near the Defense Ministry.

An event that history will record occurred when General Prats arrived at the Alameda. Alone, with two officers whose weapons were pointing downward, he spoke with four of those who were occupying the rebel tanks. They surrendered their arms to him and deferred to his high military rank. When he arrived at the fifth tank, the officer there said: "I will not surrender, General," and he tried to use his weapon.

General Prats' aide, Major Zabala, saved his life by pointing his gun at the rebel officer and taking away his gun. [Applause]

What a grand lesson for those who hours earlier had insulted and wronged the army commander-in-chief, and through him, the institution he heads, for the attitude he assumed yesterday on Costanera.

General Prats himself obtained the surrender of most of the tanks. The tank crews panicked and were surrounded by troops led by General Sepúlveda, who had been joined by *Carabineros* forces. The crews surrendered to the regiment from which they had rebelled under General Bonilla and the new commander Mr. Ramírez, who headed the regiment. [Applause]

I arrived there with three aides and a group of *Carabineros* and of course with tanks, just in case. I arrived when there were still snipers, or should I say, hypocrites firing from the Finance Ministry. I was met at the entrance to the presidential palace by General Prats, the *Carabinero* commander-in-chief, and General Pinochet. I want to stress that when General Prats had already obtained the surrender of five tanks, the commander-in-chief of the air force, General César Ruiz, and navy commander-in-chief Raúl Montero, bravely and in solidarity, came from the Defense Ministry to join General Prats. [Applause]

While I was greeting general Prats several shots rang out, and about 20 hit the palace. Moments later Santiago was an apparently peaceful city. However, fascists bombed the Radio Portales radio station.

Now there are cowardly civilian instigators, accomplices knocking on the doors of the embassies to seek asylum and flee Chile. Let the people judge the attitude of these bullies, who have been trying to undermine the armed forces, and only after obtaining minimal support from them when the moment came, fled and are now trying to elude justice. I hope they will not be able to succeed. [Shouts of "No! No!"] As was to be expected, the immense majority belong to the ill-named "Fatherland and Liberty." [Shouts]

As of today, we will call them "Anti-Fatherland and Cowardice." The people should recall the great rally we held on Thursday the 21st — where I explained how this country was almost in rebellion and on the verge of civil war; how the bourgeoisie and fascist sectors who are now united and linked to foreign interests were trying to prevent the government's progress, and especially to halt the economic advances of the People's Government.

I pointed out how they wanted to paralyze the nation, to deprive it of the essential laws while we were facing those dark moments which we would have to experience in the future.

Our main concern was to obtain laws that would allow us to fight inflation and prevent us from falling into a holocaust. I condemned the passing of laws without proper financial backing and the refusal to pass the law on economic rights.

I recounted the terrorist activities unleashed to create panic, the destruction of party headquarters, attacks against leftists and Popular Unity members. I pointed out that we were experiencing the same dark days as those of September 4, 1970, and November 3, which were climaxed by the murder of General René Schneider. They tried to do the same now.

I well know and I have said that not all our opponents have the same dastardly attitude as the coupists. Some have refused to join the coup, and we must point this out. Others speak of democracy and constitution. They use the word democracy to shield and protect themselves, but they violate the constitution and are antidemocratic and pro-fascists.

The three commanders in chief, whom I invited, should be arriving now. But first, I want general Prats to know that I want the people to hail him. [Applause]

At this moment I have here beside me Army Commander-in-Chief General Carlos Prats. [Applause] I have here beside me Admiral Raúl Montero. [Applause] I have here beside me Air Force Commander-in-Chief General César Ruiz. [Applause] One moment, please, one moment.

I also want you to salute Comrade Alfredo Joignant, director of investigations, whose corps observed an attitude of great loyalty and firmness.

Comrades [Allende interrupted by shouts], comrades, comrades, comrades: The people know what I have repeatedly told them. The Chilean revolutionary process has to follow its own path in accordance with our history, our institutions, our characteristics. Therefore, the people must understand that I have to be faithful to what I say. We will make the revolutionary changes within democratic pluralism, democracy and freedom. This does not mean — hear me well — this does not mean that we will tolerate the antidemocrats, the subversives, and least of all the fascists, comrades. [Applause and shouts]

Comrades, I speak to you today in the same way that I have spoken to you before. Some of you may not like it, but you have to understand what this government's real position is. Hear me well and with respect. I am not going to close Congress, because it would be absurd to do so. I am not going to do it. If it is necessary, I will send a bill to convoke a plebiscite, so that the people may make a pronouncement. Now, I want the people to keep the commitment that they contracted on Thursday the 21st. Tomorrow back to the routine again, to greet the free homeland. Back to work again, to recover the lost hours caused by the stoppage on Thursday. Tomorrow every one of you — to work more, to produce more, to make more sacrifices for Chile and for the people. [Applause]

And immediately to learn from the experience of the October strike and of the seditious attempt of today.

But before this, I want to point out that from afar fraternal voices came to say that they were with Chile. I spoke with the president of Argentina. He called me to say that his people, his government and General Perón were with Chile at this moment. The president of Mexico, Luis Echeverría, also called to tell me: "Mr. President, the people of Mexico and I are with your people and with you." And the cable and telephone brought the words of Cuba: [Applause] My friend Major Fidel Castro was there to tell me: "I know you are going to win. The people and the armed forces together will always win. We have full confidence in the Chilean people and in you, Comrade Allende." From afar, very far, voicing the feelings of millions of men, came the fraternal words, words which have the value of heroism. From North Vietnam, from way over there, came the fraternal spirit.

Comrade workers, we have to organize. We have to create people's power that is not antagonistic to or independent from the government, that is the fundamental force and the lever that the workers possess to advance in the revolutionary process.

20

Last Words Transmitted by Radio Magallanes

September 11, 1973

It is Chile's darkest hour, one that Allende prophetically says will bring down "infamy" on the heads of "those who have violated their commitments." Inside La Moneda, the presidential palace, Allende and a handful of followers defend themselves with bazookas and machine-guns, repeatedly refusing to surrender. The 65-year-old Chilean President uses a palace hookup with a radio station to address the Chilean people one last time before bombers force the station off the air. In what he calls "this gray and bitter moment," Allende persists in his "faith in Chile and its destiny." The "calm metal" of his voice intones to Chile's workers: "much sooner than later the great avenues through which free men walk to build a better society will open." Allende's press secretary Frida Modak later recalls: "I shall never forget the last time I saw Allende, his head covered by a helmet, his hand holding the machine-gun."

I will pay with my life defending the principles so dear to this homeland. Infamy will descend upon those who have violated their commitments, have failed to live up to their word, have broken the doctrine of the armed forces.

The people must be alert and vigilant. You must not let yourselves be provoked, not let yourselves be massacred, but you must also defend your conquests. You must defend the right to construct through your own effort a dignified and better life.

A word for those who, calling themselves democrats, have been instigating this uprising; for those who, saying they are representatives of the people, have been confused and acting stupidly to make possible this step that flings Chile down a precipice.

In the name of the most sacred interests of the people, in the name of the homeland, I call to you to tell you to keep the faith. Neither criminality nor repression can hold back history. This stage will be surpassed; it is a hard and difficult moment.

It is possible they will smash us, but tomorrow will be the people's, the workers'. Humanity advances toward the conquest of a better life.

Compatriots: It is possible that they will silence the radios, and I will take my leave of you. In these moments the planes are flying overhead. They may riddle us with bullets. But know that we are here, at least with this example, to show that in this country there are men who know how to meet their obligations. I will do it as commanded by the people and by my own conscientious will of a president who bears the dignity of his charge... [interruption]

...Perhaps this is my last opportunity to address myself to you. The air force has bombed the towers of Radio Portales and Radio Corporación. My words are not tainted by bitterness, but rather by deception. I hope they may be a moral punishment for those who have betrayed the oath they took as soldiers of Chile... Admiral Merino, who has designated himself commander of the navy, Mr. Mendoza, the callous general who only yesterday declared his loyalty to the government, and has been named director general of the *Carabineros* police.

In the face of these facts, the only thing left for me to say to the workers is: I will not resign! I say to you that I am sure that the seed that we now plant in the dignified conscience of thousands and thousands of Chileans cannot be definitively buried.

They have the power, they can smash us, but social processes are not detained, not through crimes nor power. History is ours, and peoples make it.

Workers of my country. I want to thank you for the loyalty which you have always shown, the trust which you placed in a man who was only the interpreter of the great desires for justice, who gave his word that he would respect the constitution and the law, and I did just so.

In this moment of definition, the last thing I can say to you is that I hope you will learn this lesson: foreign capital and imperialism united with reactionary elements, created the climate for the armed forces to break with their tradition, that belonging to General Schneider, and which Commander Araya reaffirmed, a victim of the same social sectors which right now are in their homes, waiting to take power with another's hand to continue defending their huge estates and privileges.

I address myself above all to the modest women of our country, to the peasant woman who believed in us, to the working woman who worked more, to the mother who knew of our concern for her children. I address myself to the professionals of our land, to the patriotic professionals, to those who were working against the sedition carried out by the professional schools, class ridden schools which defend the advantages which capitalist society gives them.

I address myself to the youth, to those who sang, who gave their joy and spirit to the struggle. I address myself to the Chilean man: to the worker, the peasant, the intellectual, to those who will be persecuted because fascism has already been present in our country for many hours: those terrorists who have been blowing up bridges, cutting railway lines, destroying oil and gas pipelines, in the face of the silence of those who have had the obligation of raising their voices. History will judge them.

Radio Magallanes will surely soon be silenced, and the calm metal of my voice will no longer reach you. It does not matter. You shall continue to hear it. I shall always be at your side, and you will remember me at least as a dignified man who was loyal to his country.

The people must defend themselves, but not sacrifice themselves. The people must not let themselves be leveled or mowed down, but neither can they let themselves be humiliated.

Workers of my homeland! I have faith in Chile and its destiny. Other men will overcome this gray and bitter moment where treason tries to impose itself. May you continue to know that much sooner than later the great avenues through which free men walk to build a better society will open.

Long live Chile! Long live the people! Long live the workers! These are my last words. I am sure that my sacrifice will not be in vain; I am sure that it will at least be a moral lesson which will punish felony, cowardice and treason.

Chronology: Chile 1962-1975

Sources: Appendix to Church Committee Report reproduced on the Internet by Róbinson Rojas Research Unit Consultancy <http:// www. soft.net.uk/rrojasdatabank/index.htm> [the "Church Committee," named after its chairman Senator Frank Church, was the U.S. Senate Select Committee to Study Governmental Operations in Respect to Intelligence Activities]; James D. Cockcroft, *Latin America: History, Politics, and U.S. Policy*, 2nd ed. (Belmont, CA: Wadsworth Publishing/Thomson Learning, 1997), 531-565; Congressional Research Service, Library of Congress, "Chile: A Chronology," Appendix A of *United States and Chile During the Allende Years, 1970-1973: Hearings before the Subcommittee on Inter-American Affairs of the Committee on Foreign Affairs, U.S. House of Representatives* (Washington, D.C.: U.S. Government Printing Office, 1975); Hedda Garza, *Salvador Allende* (New York and Philadelphia: Chelsea House Publishers, 1989); "ITT and Chile," *Report of the Senate Foreign Relations Subcommittee on Multinational Corporations*, June 21, 1973; *NACLA Report on the Americas*, May-June 1999.

1962

Special Group [select U.S. government officials including the CIA] approves $50,000 to strengthen Christian Democratic Party (PDC); subsequently approves an additional $180,000 to strengthen PDC and its leader, Eduardo Frei. Throughout early 1960s, the U.S. Department of the Army and a team of U.S. university professors develop "Project Camelot," which calls for the coordinated buildup of civilian and military forces inside Chile, with U.S. support, into a force capable of overthrowing any elected left-coalition government.

1963

Special Group approves $20,000 for a leader of the Radical Party (PR); later approves an additional $30,000 to support PR candidates in April municipal elections.

April 8 — Municipal elections results show PDC has replaced PR as Chile's largest party.

1964

April — Special Group approves $3,000,000 to ensure election of PDC candidate Eduardo Frei.

May — Special Group approves $160,000 to support PDC slum dwellers and peasant organizations.

September 4 — Eduardo Frei elected president with 55.7 percent of the vote.

1965

303 Committee [a group of U.S. officials including CIA representatives] approves $175,000 to assist selected candidates in congressional elections.

March 7 — PDC wins absolute majority in Chamber of Deputies; becomes largest party in Senate.

November 15 — Salvador Allende, in an interview reported in the *New York Times*, suggests the United States was among certain "outside forces" that had caused his defeat in the 1964 presidential election.

1967

June 16 — Edward M. Korry replaces Ralph A. Dungan as U.S. Ambassador to Chile. 303 Committee approves $30,000 to strengthen a faction of the Radical Party.

1968

July 12 — 303 Committee approves $350,000 to assist selected candidates in March 1969 congressional elections.

1969

March 1 — Congressional elections reflect an increase in support for the National Party and a resulting loss in Christian Democratic strength.

April 15 — At a meeting of the 303 Committee the question is raised as to whether anything should be done with regard to the September 1970 presidential election in Chile. The CIA representative pointed out that an election operation would not be effective unless an early enough start was made.

October 21 — Army units stationed at Tacna, Chile, revolt, ostensibly for the purposes of dramatizing the military's demand for higher pay. The revolt, engineered by General Roberto Viaux, is widely interpreted as an abortive coup.

1970

March 25 — The White House "Committee of 40," headed by National Security Council director Henry Kissinger and in charge of U.S. plans to prevent Allende's ascendancy to the presidency or, failing that, to destabilize his regime until a military coup can overthrow him, meets and approves $125,000 for a "spoiling operation" against Allende's Popular Unity coalition (UP).

June — Kissinger tells the "Committee of 40" that should Allende win Chile's elections "I don't see why we need to stand by and watch a country go communist due to the irresponsibility of its own people." The possibility of an Allende victory in Chile is raised at an ITT Board of Directors meeting. John McCone, former CIA Director, and, at the time, a consultant to the Agency and a Director of ITT, subsequently holds a number of conversations regarding Chile with CIA Director Richard Helms. Helms' 1970 notes prophesy that an economic squeeze on Chile will cause its economy to "scream."

June 27 — "Committee of 40" approves $300,000 for additional anti-Allende propaganda operations.

July 16 — John McCone arranges for William Broe (CIA) to talk with Harold Geneen (ITT). Broe tells Geneen that CIA cannot disburse ITT funds but promises to advise ITT on how to channel its own funds. ITT later passes $350,000 to the Alessandri campaign through an intermediary.

August 18 — National Security Study Memorandum (NSSM) 97 is reviewed by the Interdepartmental Group; the Group considers options ranging from efforts to forge amicable relations with Allende to opposition to him.

September 4 — Popular Unity candidate Salvador Allende wins 36.3 percent of the vote in the presidential election, defeating National Party candidate Jorge Alessandri (34.9 percent) and Christian Democrat Radomiro Tomic (27.8 percent). Final outcome is dependent on October 24 vote in Congress between Allende and the runner-up, Alessandri. Traditionally, the candidate with a plurality of popular votes wins the congressional runoff.

September 8 and 14 — "Committee of 40" approves $250,000 for the use of Ambassador Korry to influence the October 24 congressional vote.

September 9 — Harold Geneen, ITT's Chief Executive Officer, tells John McCone at an ITT Board of Directors meeting in New York that he is prepared to put up as much as $1 million for the purpose of assisting any government plan designed to form a coalition in the Chilean Congress to stop Allende. McCone agrees to communicate this proposal to high Washington officials and meets several days later with Henry Kissinger and Richard Helms.

September 15 — President Nixon instructs CIA Director Helms to prevent Allende's accession to office. The CIA is to play a direct role in organizing a military coup d'état. This involvement comes to be known as Track II. Years later, Helms was convicted of perjury for lying to the U.S. Senate about the CIA's foreign and domestic covert activities.

September 16 — At an off-the-record White House press briefing, Henry Kissinger warns that the election of Allende would be irreversible and that an Allende-led Chile could become a "contagious example" that "would infect" NATO allies in southern Europe. He also expresses doubt that Chile would experience another free election. [An ex-aide to Kissinger later noted that "Henry thought Allende might lead an anti-U.S. movement in Latin America more effectively than Castro, just because it was the democratic path to power."]

September 29 — A CIA official, at the instruction of Richard Helms, meets with a representative of ITT. The CIA officer proposes a plan to accelerate economic disorder in Chile. ITT rejects the proposal.

October — CIA contacts Chilean military conspirators; following a White House meeting, CIA attempts to defuse plot by retired General Viaux, but still to generate maximum pressure to overthrow Allende by a coup; CIA provides tear gas grenades and three submachine guns to conspirators. ITT submits to White House an 18-point plan designed to assure that Allende "does not get through the crucial next six months."

October 9 — Constitutional amendments are introduced into Chile's Congress and later passed as, in effect, a condition for ratifying Allende's election as president. The amendments limit government interference in political parties, education, the "free press," and the armed forces. Allende's power to appoint commanding officers is limited, although he is still allowed to promote officers in the armed forces and *Carabineros* (national police). Allende is obligated to preserve the jobs of the previous administration's state functionaries.

October 14 — "Committee of 40" approves $60,000 for Ambassador Korry's proposal to purchase a radio station. The money is never spent.

October 16 — A secret "eyes only" CIA headquarters cable to the CIA station chief in Santiago [made public years later] gives "operational guide" based on Kissinger's review of covert coup plotting. "It is firm and continuing policy that Allende be overthrown by a coup," the cable states.

October 22 — After two unsuccessful abduction attempts on October 19 and 20, a third attempt to kidnap Chilean Army Commander-in-Chief General René Schneider results in his being fatally shot, reportedly by right-wing elements angry at his failure to take military action against Allende.

October 24 — The Chilean Congress votes 153 to 35 in favor of Allende over Alessandri.

November 3 — Allende is formally inaugurated President of Chile.

November 12 — Allende announces he is renewing diplomatic, commercial and cultural relations with Cuba.

November 13 — "Committee of 40" approves $25,000 for support of Christian Democratic candidates.

November 19 — "Committee of 40" approves $725,000 for a covert action program in Chile. Approval is later superseded by January 28, 1971, authorization for nearly twice the amount.

December 21 — President Allende proposes a constitutional amendment establishing state control of the large mines and authorizing expropriation of all foreign firms working them. Both he and the Christian Democratic presidential candidate Tomic had campaigned on a platform calling for nationalization of the copper mines.

December 30 — President Allende announces he will be submitting a bill to Congress nationalizing private domestic banks "in order to provide more credit for small and medium businessmen."

1971

January 5 — Chile establishes diplomatic relations with the People's Republic of China.

January 28 — "Committee of 40" approves $1,240,000 for the purchase of radio stations and newspapers and to support municipal candidates and other political activities of anti-Allende parties.

February 12 — Chile and Cuba sign a $20 million trade agreement.

February 27 — The U.S. Department of Defense announces it is canceling the planned visit to Chile of the nuclear carrier Enterprise, earlier welcomed by Allende. All Chile's political parties denounce the decision as a slight to Chileans.

March 22 — "Committee of 40" approves $185,000 additional support for the Christian Democratic Party (PDC).

April 4 — Allende's Popular Unity (UP) coalition garners 49.7 percent of the vote in a four-way field in 280 municipal elections. For the first time in Chilean history, people 18-21 years old could vote. Their support contributed to the UP's huge margin of victory. A CIA-funded fascist group, *Patria y Libertad* (Fatherland and Liberty), begins stepping up a campaign of sabotaging factory equipment to hobble the economy.

May 10 — "Committee of 40" approves $77,000 for purchase of a press for the Christian Democratic Party newspaper. The press is not obtained and the funds are used to support the paper.

May 20 — "Committee of 40" approves $100,000 for emergency aid to the Christian Democratic Party to meet short-term debts.

May 26 — "Committee of 40" approves $150,000 for additional aid to Christian Democratic Party to meet debts.

June 30 — State Department announces a $5 million loan for Chile's purchase of military equipment.

July 6 — "Committee of 40" approves $150,000 for support of opposition candidates in a Chilean by-election.

July 11 — In a joint session of the Chilean Congress, a constitutional amendment is unanimously approved permitting the nationalization of the copper industry, source of three-fourths of Chile's foreign exchange. The amendment provides for compensation to copper companies within 30 years at not less than 3 percent interest. Also nationalized are iron ore, steel and nitrates.

August 11 — The Export-Import Bank denies a Chilean request for $21 million in loans and loan guarantees needed to purchase three jets for the national LAN-Chile airline.

September — The chiefs of Chile's main foreign corporations – Anaconda Copper, Ford Motor Company, First National City Bank, Bank of America, Ralston Purina and ITT – meet with Secretary of State William Rogers and agree to an economic blockade of Chile. The CIA sets up a "coup team" at the U.S. embassy in Santiago and pays out millions of dollars to Chilean right-wing groups, newspapers, radio stations, and political figures to accelerate the destabilization campaign.

September 9 — "Committee of 40" approves $700,000 for support to the major Santiago newspaper, *El Mercurio*, which goes on to encourage acts of sedition against the Chilean government, including a military coup.

September 10 — President Allende approves Chile's participation in a joint naval exercise with the United States and several Latin American nations.

September 28 — President Allende announces that "excess profits" of $774 million in the prior 15 years will be deducted from compensation to be paid to nationalized copper companies. Earlier, separate Soviet and French teams of technocrats and economists had revealed several abuses by the foreign copper concerns. The opposition Christian Democratic and National parties announce their support of Allende's compensation policies in mid-October.

September 29 — The Chilean government assumes operation of the Chilean telephone company (CHITELCO). ITT had owned 70 percent interest in the company since 1930.

September 29 — Nathaniel Davis replaces Edward Korry as U.S. Ambassador to Chile.

November 5 — "Committee of 40" approves $815,000 support to opposition parties and to induce a split in the Popular Unity coalition.

November 10 — December 4 — Premier Fidel Castro conducts extensive goodwill tour throughout Chile.

November 30 — After a visit to Latin America, White House Director of Communications Herbert G. Klein tells reporters that he and presidential counselor Robert H. Finch had received the "feeling" that the Allende government "won't last long."

December 1 — The Christian Democratic and National Parties organize the "March of the Empty Pots" by women to protest food shortages and the visit of Premier Castro to Chile.

December 15 — "Committee of 40" approves $160,000 to support two opposition candidates in January 1972 by-elections.

1972

January 19 — President Nixon issues a statement warning that, in cases of expropriated U.S. company properties, should compensation not be reasonable then new bilateral economic aid to the expropriating country might be terminated and the United States would withhold its support from loans under consideration in multilateral development banks.

February 29 — New York Supreme Court blocks New York bank accounts of Chilean government agencies.

March 21-22 — Syndicated columnist Jack Anderson charges that secret ITT documents (later made public) reveal that ITT had dealt regularly with the CIA in efforts to prevent Allende's assuming the presidency in 1970 or, failing that, to bring him down afterwards. In October 1970, ITT had submitted to the White House an 18-point plan of economic warfare, subversion and sabotage against Chile, to be directed by a special White House task force and assisted by the CIA, aimed at precipitating economic chaos whereby the Chilean armed forces "will have to step in and restore order." One ITT option sent to Kissinger was the halting of all loans by international and U.S. private banks. [Actually, neither the Inter-American Development Bank nor the World Bank had granted new credits to Chile since Allende assumed the presidency, even denying emergency relief to victims of the 1971 earthquake.] Anderson also revealed that in exchange for the Nixon administration's assistance in toppling Allende, ITT had offered to contribute several hundred thousand dollars to the Nixon campaign for the 1972 U.S. presidential election.

April 11 — "Committee of 40" approves an additional $965,000 for support to *El Mercurio.*

April 24 — "Committee of 40" approves $50,000 for an effort to splinter the Popular Unity coalition.

May 12 — President Allende submits a constitutional amendment to the Chilean Congress calling for the expropriation of ITT's holdings in the Chilean telephone company.

June 16 — "Committee of 40" approves $46,500 to support a candidate in a Chilean by-election.

July 24 — Allende attacks the United States for "deliberately restricting" Chile's credits in 1970-72 and for imposing "a virtual economic blockade" on Chile. [In 1972 Kennecott Copper Company had begun orchestrating an embargo against all Chilean copper exports to the rest of the world. Then, in early 1973, copper prices began plummeting in reaction to President Nixon's persuading the U.S. Congress to legislate the release of U.S. copper stockpiles, thereby creating a glut on the world market.]

August 21 — Allende declares a state of emergency in Santiago province after violence grows out of a one-day strike by most of the capital's shopkeepers.

September 21 — "Committee of 40" approves $24,000 to support an anti-Allende businessmen's organization.

October 10 — The Confederation of Truck Owners launches a nationwide strike backed by the opposition parties. This leads to the government's declaration of a state of emergency, not lifted until November 5 when the new military Interior Minister General Carlos Prats negotiates a strike settlement.

October 26 — "Committee of 40" approves $1,427,666 to support opposition political parties and private sector organizations in anticipation of March 1973 congressional elections.

November 4 — In a speech honoring the 2nd anniversary of the Popular Unity government, Allende defiantly proclaims the start of "the definitive defeat of the fascist threat."

December 4 — Speaking before the General Assembly of the United Nations, President Allende charges that Chile has been the "victim of serious aggression" and adds, "we have felt the effects of a large-scale external pressure against us."

December 8 — U.S. announces that in May 1972 it had agreed to extend $10 million in credit to Chile for purchase of a C-130 air force transport and other equipment, possibly tanks, armored personnel carriers and trucks.

1973

January — Inflation reaches 200 percent.

February 12 — "Committee of 40" approves $200,000 to support opposition political parties in the congressional elections.

March 4 — In the congressional elections, Allende's Popular Unity coalition wins 43.4 percent of the vote, a 7 percent increase over its vote in the 1970 presidential race.

March 22 — Talks between the U.S. and Chile on political and financial problems end in an impasse.

May 10 — A three-week copper strike continues at El Teniente mine and a state of emergency is declared in that region. The most determined strikers are the executive and management staff.

June 5 — Chile suspends its foreign shipments of copper as miners' strikes continue.

June 15 — Allende meets with copper strikers, and the majority of unskilled workers vote to accept his offer and return to work.

June 20 — Thousands of physicians, teachers, and students go on strike to protest Allende's handling of the 63-day copper strike. The workers confederation (CUT) calls a general strike next day in support of the government.

June 21 — Gunfire, bombings, and fighting erupt as government opponents and supporters clash during the huge CUT pro-government strike. The opposition newspaper, *El Mercurio*, is closed by court order for six days following a government charge that it had incited subversion. The following day an appeals court invalidates the closure order.

June 28 — The army announces the crushing of a "barracks revolt" against the commanding officers and the government.

June 29 — Rebel tank and armored personnel carriers seize control of the downtown area of Santiago and attack the Defense Ministry and the presidential palace before troops loyal to the government surround them and force them to surrender. This is the first military attempt to overthrow an elected Chilean government in 42 years. The abortive coup was led by Colonel Roberto Souper, who reportedly was about to be arrested as the head of the "barracks revolt" uncovered by army officials the day before.

July 2 — Copper miners agree to return to work, ending a 76-day strike that cost the government an estimated $60 million and crippled the country's economy.

July 26 — Truck owners throughout Chile go on strike, once more crippling the economy.

August — Christian Democrats hint broadly that they favor a coup and the party's newspaper runs an article claiming the government has been taken over by a "Jewish-communist cell." To assuage big business, Allende approves the eviction of workers from the more than 1,000 workplaces they have occupied. In some factories troops are required to do the job, and some workers are killed.

August 2 — The owners of more than 110,000 buses and taxis go on strike.

August 3 — At a press conference, Allende charges that 180 acts of terrorism against railroads, highways, bridges, pipelines, schools and hospitals had been committed since the assassination of his naval aide-de-camp a week earlier.

August 7 — The navy announces quashing of a servicemen's revolt in Valparaíso.

August 8 — Allende announces formation of a new cabinet including the three chiefs of the armed forces and the chief of the national police (*Carabineros*).

August 20 — "Committee of 40" approves $1 million to support opposition political parties and private sector organizations.

August 23 — General Carlos Prats resigns as Allende's defense minister and army commander, explaining in his letter of resignation that his participation in the cabinet had caused a left-right split in the army and stating that he was forced to resign by a "sector of army officers." General Augusto Pinochet Ugarte is named army commander on August 24. Prats' resignation is interpreted as a severe blow to Allende.

August 27 — Chile's shop owners call another anti-government strike.

September 4 — An estimated 750,000 supporters of Allende's government march in the streets of Santiago to celebrate the third anniversary of his election, chanting "Allende, Allende, the people will defend you!" In a radio and television address, Allende tells them to "be alert, very alert, without losing your serenity." The Confederation of Professional Employees begins an indefinite strike.

September 5 — The governing Popular Unity Coalition charges the navy with imprisoning and torturing leftist marines. Allende next day disassociates himself from the statement.

September 8 — Commenting on a 2-hour gun battle between air force troops and leftist factory workers, former under-secretary of transport Jaime Faivovich declares, "The armed forces are provoking the workers... the military coup is already underway."

September 11 — The Chilean military overthrows the government. Surrounding the presidential palace with tanks, armored cars, riflemen, and jet fighter-bombers by air, they issue an ultimatum to Allende to either resign or surrender. Allende refuses to do either and dies during the battle. In the days immediately following the coup, thousands of Chileans are killed or simply "disappear," as the military establishes complete control over the country.

September 13 — The new military government names Army Commander Pinochet President, dissolves Congress, and goes on to end all democratic institutions. Pinochet dismantles Allende's programs and installs a wholly free-market economy. He abolishes elections, makes strikes and unions illegal, and imposes strict censorship of books, the press, and school curriculums. Entire university departments (such as sociology) are shut down.

September-October — The Junta declares all Marxist political parties illegal and places all other parties in indefinite recess. Press censorship is established, as are detention facilities for opponents of the new regime. Thousands of casualties are reported, including summary executions and "disappearances." Many years later, mass graves of some of the victims are discovered.

October 15 — "Committee of 40" approves $34,000 for an anti-Allende radio station and the travel costs of pro-Junta spokesmen.

1974

June 24 — "Committee of 40" approves $50,000 for political commitments made to the Christian Democratic Party before the coup.

September 16 — President Ford acknowledges the earlier U.S. covert operations in Chile.

October 25 — The Inter-American Commission on Human Rights of the Organization of American States (OAS) reports "grievous violations of human rights" in Chile.

December 30 — Responding to reports of widespread human rights violations in Pinochet's Chile, the U.S. Government cuts off military aid.

1975

June 20 — Pinochet declares there "will be no elections in Chile during my lifetime nor in the lifetime of my successor."

July 4 — Chile refuses to allow the UN Commission on Human Rights to enter the country.

October 7 — The UN Commission on Human Rights reports "with profound disgust" the use of torture as a matter of policy and other serious violations of human rights in Chile.

Chronology

SALVADOR ALLENDE'S LIFE

Sources: Hedda Garza, *Salvador Allende* (New York and Philadelphia: Chelsea House Publishers, 1989; "Salvador Allende G." <http://members. xoom.com/_XOOM/chilerebelde/compa2.htm>

June 16, 1908 — Born Salvador Allende Gossens in Valparaíso, Chile

1922-25 — After family travels to northern Chile, Allende returns to Valparaíso where he hangs out at shoe repair shop of Juan Demarchi, an old Italian anarchist who introduces him to chess and Marx

1926-33 — After obligatory stint in military service, Allende studies medicine at University of Chile, Santiago

1931 — Arrested during demonstrations against Ibáñez regime

July 1931 — Ibáñez flees Chile

1932 — Marmaduke Grove declares "Socialist Republic of Chile"; his government overthrown 12 days later; Allende arrested

1933 — Allende receives medical degree; helps found Socialist Party; co-authors a book on structure of national health

1935 — Exiled for six months to fishing village of Caldera

1936 — Helps found Popular Front and becomes leader of its Valparaíso branch

1937 — Elected to Congress

1938 — Pedro Aguirre Cerda elected president

1939 — Allende marries Hortensia Bussy Soto; becomes Minister of Health

1941 — Ríos elected president after death of Aguirre Cerda

1942 — Allende resigns cabinet post

1943 — Elected secretary general of Socialist Party

1945 — Elected to Senate

1947 — Socialist Party divides over anticommunist "Law of Permanent Defense of Democracy" (known as "*Ley Maldita*" or "Cursed Law"); Allende joins Popular Socialist Party

1952 — Rejoins Socialist Party; runs for president; loses to Ibáñez

1953 — Elected to Senate; becomes its vice-president following year

1958 — Runs for president; barely loses to Alessandri

1964 — Runs for president; loses to Frei

1966-69 — Serves as president of the Senate

1968 — After the murder in Bolivia of his friend Che Guevara, an Argentine-born internationalist revolutionary leading a guerrilla insurrection there, Allende personally accompanies four of Guevara's Cuban guerrilla comrades to Tahiti

1969 — Helps organize the multiparty Unidad Popular (UP – Popular Unity)

1970 — Runs for president, wins; starts six-year term as president

1971 — Nationalizes copper and other mining industries; accelerates land reform program

1972 — Addresses UN General Assembly, condemning U.S. "destabilization campaign" and economic embargo

1973 — Truck owners' strike; Carlos Prats resigns as commander-in-chief of army and is replaced by General Pinochet

September 11, 1973 — Allende dies in presidential palace during military coup; Pinochet assumes power

Appendix

POPULAR UNITY PROGRAM

Allende conducted his 1970 electoral campaign on the Popular Unity Program, drafted by a coalition of political parties led by the Socialist Party and the Communist Party. This program was presented directly to the people largely through Allende's speeches and the "Popular Unity Committees" set up in almost every workplace or neighborhood during the election campaign. The Popular Unity Program represented an alternative way to develop Chile's economy and political democracy. Recognizing people's frustrations with the failures of "reformist" and "developmentalist" solutions, which the Alliance for Progress promoted," the program promised to "bring to an end the rule of the imperialists, the monopolists and the landed oligarchy and to initiate the construction of socialism." In other words, the Popular Unity Program called for economic growth based on equal access to economic resources and for social development based on equal access to political resources for every Chilean. Today, nearly 30 years since the end of Chile's expanded democracy under Allende, the Popular Unity Program still offers a useful and consistent alternative to the capitalist model which excludes a large portion of society from the fruits of economic growth. This alternative program spells out in some detail the different reforms needed to initiate the "transition toward socialism," including the steps to be taken to achieve a grass-roots democracy and a strong representative, pluralist state that will assure the economic success of the necessary reforms.

Program presented to the Chilean people for the presidential election campaign in 1970

INTRODUCTION

The parties and movements of which the Popular Unity's Coordinating Committee is composed, without prejudice to our individual philosophy and political delineations, fully agree on the following description of the national situation and on the program proposals which are to constitute the basis of our common effort and which we now present for consideration by the whole nation.

Chile is going through a grave crisis, manifested by social and economic stagnation, widespread poverty and deprivation of all sorts suffered by workers, peasants,[1] and other exploited classes as well as in the growing difficulties which confront white collar workers, professional people, small and medium businessmen, and in the very limited opportunities open to women and young people.

These problems can be resolved in Chile. Our country possesses great wealth such as copper and other minerals, a large hydro-electric potential, vast forests, a long coast rich in marine life, and more than sufficient land, etc. Chile also has a population with a will to work and progress and people with technical and professional skills.

WHY HAVE WE FAILED?

What has failed in Chile is the system — a system which does not correspond to present day requirements. Chile is a capitalist country, dependent on the imperialist nations and dominated by bourgeois groups who are structurally related to foreign capital and who cannot resolve the country's fundamental problems — problems which are clearly the result of class privilege which will never be given up voluntarily.

Moreover, as a direct consequence of the development of world capitalism, the submission of the national monopolistic bourgeoisie to imperialism daily furthers its role as junior partner to foreign capital, increasingly accentuating its dependent nature.

For a few people it is good business to sell off a piece of Chile each day. And every day this select few make decisions on behalf of all the rest of us. On the other hand, for the great majority of Chileans there is little to be gained from selling their labor and brain power and, in general, they are still deprived of the right to determine their own future.

The "reformist" and "developmentalist" solutions, which the Alliance for Progress promoted and which the Frei Government adopted, have not changed anything of importance in Chile. Basically, the Christian Democrat Government was nothing but a new government of the bourgeoisie, in the service of national and foreign capitalism, whose weak efforts to promote social change came to a sad end in economic stagnation, a rising cost of living, and violent repression of the

---

[1] The word peasants and peasantry should be taken to include small proprietors, agricultural wage laborers, sharecroppers, migrant and temporary rural laborers, smallholders who rent their land and other types of agricultural workers. (The translator)

people. This experience demonstrated once more that reformism cannot resolve the people's problems.

The development of monopoly capitalism prevents the extension of democracy and exacerbates violence against the people. As "reformism" fails and the people's capacity to struggle increases, the most reactionary sectors of the dominant classes who, in the last analysis, have no recourse but to use force, become firmer in their position. The brutal forms of violence perpetrated by the Frei Government, such as the activities of the Riot Police Unit, the beating up of peasants and students, and the killing of shantytown dwellers and miners, are inseparable from other and no less brutal forms of violence which affect all Chileans. People living in luxurious houses while a large part of the population lives in unhealthy dwellings or has no shelter at all also constitutes violence; people who throw away food while others lack the means to feed themselves also commit violence.

Imperialist exploitation of backward economies takes place in a variety of ways: through investments in mining (copper, iron, etc), industrial, banking and commercial activities; through the control of technology which obliges us to pay exaggerated sums for equipment, licenses and patents; through American loans with crippling conditions which require us to purchase from the U.S.A. and with the additional obligation to transport these purchases in North American ships. Just one example of imperialist exploitation is the fact that from 1952 to date, the United States invested US$7.473 billion in Latin America and received back US$16 billion.

Imperialism has taken resources from Chile equivalent to double the value of the capital accumulated in our country throughout its history. American monopolies, with the complicity of bourgeois governments, have succeeded in taking over nearly all of our copper, iron and nitrate resources. They control foreign trade and dictate economic policy through the International Monetary Fund and other organizations. They dominate important branches of industry and services, they enjoy statutory privileges while imposing monetary devaluation, the reduction of salaries and wages and the distortion of agricultural activities through their agricultural surpluses policy.

They also intervene in education, culture and in the communications media and they try to penetrate the armed forces, making use of military and political agreements.

The dominant classes, acting as accomplices in the process and unable to defend their own interests, have increased Chile's foreign indebtedness over the last ten years. It was argued that the loans and arrangements with international bankers would increase economic development. But the only result is that today Chile holds the record of being one of the world's most indebted countries in proportion to its population.

In Chile government and legislation is for the benefit of the few — that is they only serve the large capitalists and their hangers-on, the companies which dominate our economy, and the large landholders whose power still remains almost intact.

The owners of capital are only interested in making more money and not in satisfying the needs of the Chilean people. For example, if it appears to be a good business proposition to produce and import expensive cars they use our economy's scarce resources for this purpose, ignoring the fact that only a minute percentage of Chileans have the means to purchase them and that there are far more urgent needs to be satisfied. The improvement of public transport and provision of machinery for agriculture are obvious examples of such urgent needs.

The groups of businessmen who control the economy, the press and other communications media, the existing political system, and the threats to the state, when it hints at intervention or refuses to favor all these interests, are an expensive burden on the Chilean people. For these groups to deign to continue "working" — since only they can afford the luxury of working or not — the following conditions are necessary. They have to be provided with all kinds of assistance. Important businessmen pressure the state under the threat that, unless the help and guarantees they request are authorized, there will be no private investment. They have to be allowed to produce the products they want with money belonging to the whole Chilean people, instead of producing the goods needed by the great majority; and to transfer the profits obtained to their foreign bank accounts. They wish to be allowed to dismiss workers if they ask for better wages; and to be permitted to manipulate food distribution and stockpile food products in order to create artificial shortages and thereby raise prices in order to continue enriching themselves at the expense of the Chilean people.

Meanwhile, a large proportion of those people who actually produce face a difficult situation. Half a million families lack housing and as many or more live in appalling conditions lacking sewage, drinking water, light and healthy conditions. The population's education and health requirements are insufficiently provided for. More than half of Chile's workers receive wages which are insufficient to cover their minimum vital needs. Every family suffers from unemployment and unstable employment. The chances of employment are impossible or uncertain for countless young people.

Imperialist capital and a privileged group not exceeding 10 percent of the population receive half of the National Income. This means that out of every 100 escudos produced by Chileans, 50 end up in the pockets of 10 of the oligarchy and the other 50 have to be shared among 90

Chileans from the poor and middle classes.

The rising cost of living creates havoc in people's homes, especially for the housewife. According to official statistics, the cost of living has risen almost 1,000 percent in the last 10 years.

This means that every day Chileans who live from the proceeds of their work are robbed of part of their salaries or wages. The same happens to retired people, craftsmen, independent workers and small scale producers, whose meager incomes are daily eroded by inflation. Presidents Alessandri and Frei gave assurances that they would put an end to inflation. The results are there for all to see. The facts prove that inflation in Chile is the outcome of deeper causes which are related to the capitalist structure of our society and not to increases in incomes, as successive governments have tried to make us believe in order to justify the system and restrain workers' incomes.

On the other hand, the large capitalist can defend himself from inflation and what is more he profits from it. His property and his capital become more valuable, his construction contracts with the state are revalued, and the prices of his products always rise ahead of wage increases.

A large number of Chileans are underfed. According to official statistics, 50 percent of children under 15 years of age are under-nourished. This affects their growth and limits their learning capacity. This shows that the economy in general and the agricultural system in particular are incapable of feeding Chile's population in spite of the fact that Chile could support a population of 30 million people right now — that is, three times the present population.

Yet, on the contrary, each year we must import hundreds of thousands of dollars worth of food products.

Most of the blame for the food supply and nutritional problems of the Chilean people can be attributed to the existence of *latifundia* [large estates] which are responsible for the backwardness and misery which characterize the Chilean countryside. Indices of infant and adult mortality, illiteracy, lack of housing and ill health in the rural areas are markedly higher than for the cities. The Christian Democrat Government's restricted Agrarian Reform Program has not resolved these problems. Only the peasants' struggle, backed by the whole nation, will resolve them. The present struggle for land and the abolition of the *latifundia* is opening up new perspectives for the advance of the Chilean people.

The growth rate of our economy is minimal. In recent five year periods the average rate of growth has been scarcely two percent p.a. per capita; and since 1967 there has been no growth at all. On the contrary, we have moved backwards according to the Government Planning Office's figures. This means that in 1966 each Chilean had more goods than he has today, which explains why the majority are discontented and are looking for an alternative for our country.

The only alternative, which is a truly popular one, and one which therefore constitutes the People's Government's main task, is to bring to an end the rule of the imperialists, the monopolists, and the landed oligarchy and to initiate the construction of socialism in Chile.

THE ORGANIZED PEOPLE IN UNITY AND ACTION

The growth in size and organization of the labor force and the growing struggle and consciousness of its own power reinforce and propagate criticism of the established order, the desire for profound change and conflicts with the established power structure. There are more than three million workers in our country whose productive efforts and enormous constructive capacity cannot be put to good use within the present system, which only exploits and subjects them.

These organized forces, in a common effort with the people to mobilize those who are not sold out to national and foreign reactionary interests, could destroy the present system and, by means of this united struggle on the part of the large majority of Chileans, progress could be made in the task of liberating themselves. The Popular Unity alliance has been formed precisely for this purpose.

The imperialists and the country's dominant classes will struggle against a united people and will try to deceive them once again. They will say that freedom is in danger, that violence is taking hold of the country, etc. But each day the popular masses are less and less taken by these lies. Social mobilization is growing daily, and is now reinforced and encouraged by the unity of the left-wing groups.

In order to encourage and guide the mobilization of the Chilean people toward the conquest of power, we will set up Popular Unity Committees in every factory, farm, poor neighborhood,[2] office or school, to be run by the militants of the left-wing movements and parties and to be composed of the thousands of Chileans who are in favor of fundamental change. These Popular Unity Committees will not only constitute electoral organizations. They will interpret and fight for the immediate claims of the masses and above all they will learn to exercise power.

---

[2] The word used in the original Spanish text is "población" and refers to various types of low-income housing areas in towns and villages. These include slums, illegally occupied squatter settlements, temporary shantytowns and permanent but poor housing developments promoted by the government and housing associations or constructed by means of self-help programs in which technical and material assistance is provided by the government. In the rest of this document references to low-income housing districts or low-income neighborhoods should be taken as referring to all these different low income housing areas. [The translator]

This new form of power structure which Chile needs must begin to develop itself right now, wherever people need to be organized to fight over specific problems and wherever the need to exercise this power becomes apparent. This system involving a common effort will be a permanent dynamic method for developing our program, constituting a practical school for the masses and a concrete way of deepening the political content of the Popular Unity at all levels. At a given point in the campaign the essential contents of this program, enriched by discussion with and the support of the people, and together with a series of immediate government measures will be set out in a People's Act (*Acta del Pueblo*) which the new People's Government and the Front which sustains it will regard as a mandate that cannot be renounced.

Support for the Popular Unity's candidate does not, therefore, only involve voting for a man, but also involves declaring oneself in favor of the urgent replacement of our present society, the basis of which is the power and control exercised by large national and foreign capitalists.

THE PROGRAM
Popular Power
The revolutionary changes required by Chile can only be carried out if the people of Chile take power into their own hands and exercise it in a true and effective manner.

In the process of a long struggle, the Chilean people have achieved certain democratic liberties and guarantees which will require vigilance and constant battle if they are not to be lost.

The revolutionary and popular forces have not united to simply fight for the substitution of one president of the republic by another, nor to replace one party by others in government but, rather, to carry out the profound changes which are required by national circumstances, based on the transfer of power from the old dominant groups to the urban workers, rural population and progressive sectors of the urban and rural middle classes. This popular triumph will therefore open up the way for the most democratic political government in the country's history.

As regards the political structure, the People's Government has the double task of preserving and making more effective and real the democratic rights and achievements of the working classes, and transforming present institutions in order to install a new system of power in which the working classes and the people are the ones who really exercise power.

The strengthening of democracy and working class progress
The People's Government will guarantee the exercise of democratic rights and will respect the social and individual liberties of all sectors of the population. The freedom of worship, speech, press and of assembly,

the inviolability of the home, and the right to unionize will be made effective, removing the present obstacles put up by the dominant classes to limit them.

In order to put this into practice, the unions and social organizations formed by manual workers, white collar-workers, peasants and rural workers, shantytown dwellers and inhabitants of low-income neighborhoods,[3] housewives, students, professional people, intellectuals, craftsmen, small and medium businessmen, and other groups of workers, will be called upon to participate in government decision making at the relevant level. For example, in the social security institutions we will establish a system of management by the contributors themselves, ensuring that the government bodies are elected democratically and by secret ballot. As for firms in the public sector, their governing committees and production committees must include direct representation of manual and white-collar workers.

The Neighborhood Committees (*Juntas de Vecinos*) and other organized groups of inhabitants of poor neighborhoods will have ways and means of controlling the activities of the pertinent national housing organizations and of participating in many aspects of their activities. It is not just a question of these particular examples, but of a new philosophy in which ordinary people achieve real and effective participation in the different organisms of the state.

Likewise, the People's Government guarantees the right of workers to employment and to strike, and the right for all people to obtain a proper education and culture, fully respecting all ideas and religious beliefs and guaranteeing the freedom to practice them.

All democratic rights and guarantees will be extended, by granting to social organizations real means of exercising their rights and creating the mechanisms which will allow them to participate in the different levels of the state's administrative apparatus. The power and authority of the People's Government will essentially be based on the support extended to it by the organized population. This is our notion of strong government — the very opposite of that held by the oligarchy and imperialists who identify authority with the use of coercion against the people.

The People's Government will be a multiparty one, composed of all the revolutionary parties, movements and groups. The executive will

---

3 The original Spanish text refers to "pobladores" which generally means "settlers." But in this context reference is being made to both inhabitants of shantytowns and squatter settlements and to the inhabitants of new low income housing estates constructed for or with the aid of working class people who are often immigrants from the countryside. In the rest of the text the word "pobladores" will usually be translated simply as inhabitants of poor neighborhoods and should be read as including the various categories just listed. (The translator).

therefore be truly democratic, representative and cohesive. The People's Government will respect the rights of the opposition as long as they are exercised within the legal framework.

The People's Government will immediately proceed to effectively decentralize the administration which, in conjunction with democratic and efficient planning, will eliminate the centralization of the bureaucracy, replacing it with real coordination between all parts of the administration.

The structure of the municipalities will be modernized according to the plans for coordinating the whole state administration, while granting them the authority due to them. They will become local organs of the new political organization, possessing sufficient finance and powers to enable them to deal with the problems of the local districts and their inhabitants, in conjunction and coordination with the Neighborhood Committees. The Provincial Assemblies must begin to operate with the same purpose in mind.

The police must be reorganized so that they can never again be used as a repressive force against ordinary people but, instead, ensure that the population is protected from anti-social behavior. Police procedures will be made more humane, effectively guaranteeing full respect for human dignity and physical integrity. The prison system and prison conditions at present constitute one of the worst aspects of the present judicial system and must be radically transformed with a view to reforming the lawbreaker.

A NEW INSTITUTIONAL ORGANIZATION: THE PEOPLE'S STATE

Political Organization

The new power structure will be built up from grass roots by extending democracy at all levels and by organizing the mobilization of the masses.

A new political constitution will validate the massive incorporation of the people into governmental power. We shall create a unicameral form of government with national, regional and local levels, and in which the Popular Assembly will constitute the supreme power. This people's assembly will be the only parliament, expressing the sovereignty of the people at the national level and in which all the various currents of opinion will be expressed.

This system will enable us to root out the evils suffered in Chile under dictatorial presidencies and corrupt parliamentary rule. The powers and responsibilities of the president of the republic, the ministers, Popular Assembly, regional and local government organizations and political parties will be precisely redefined and coordinated in order to ensure the functioning of the legislature, efficiency in government and above all respect for the will of the majority.

All elections will take place simultaneously in an orderly process so as to establish the necessary harmony between the different expressions of the popular will and to ensure that these are expressed coherently.

Organizations representing the people may only be created by means of secret and direct universal suffrage of men and women of over 18 years of age, including civilians and military personnel, and literate and illiterate people. The members of the Popular Assembly and other organizations representing the people will be subject to control by the electors through consultation procedures, which would also allow for their mandate to be withdrawn. A rigorous code of conduct will be established requiring deputies or high-level civil servants to lose their mandate or post if guilty of acting on behalf of private interests.

The economic policy instruments to be used by the government will constitute a national system of planning, and they will be executive instruments to be used to direct, coordinate and rationalize government activities. The operational plan must be approved in the Popular Assembly, and workers' organizations will play a fundamental role in the planning system.

The regional and local organs of government in the new People's State will exercise authority in the relevant geographical areas and they will have economic, political and social powers. In addition they will be able to make proposals to and criticize the higher levels. However, in exercising their powers these regional and local bodies must work within the limits set by national laws and by the overall social and economic development plans. Social organizations with specific attributes will be integrated into each of the different levels of the People's State. It will be their duty to share responsibilities and develop initiatives in their respective spheres of influence as well as analyze and solve the problems within their competence. These attributes will not in any way limit the complete independence and autonomy of these organizations.

From the very day the People's Government assumes power it will provide ways of ensuring that the influence of the workers and people is brought to bear on the administrative decisions adopted and on the control over the operation of the state administrative machinery. These constitute decisive steps in the elimination of an over-centralized bureaucracy which characterizes the present administrative system.

The Organization of Justice
The organization and administration of justice must be based on the guaranteed principle of autonomy and on real economic independence.

We visualize the existence of a Supreme Court whose members are appointed by the People's Assembly, the only limitation being the natural suitability of the members. This court will be free to determine the internal, personal or corporate powers of the judicial system.

It is our intention that the new administration and organization of justice will come to the aid of the popular classes; it will operate more rapidly and in a less burdensome fashion.

Under the People's Government a whole new concept of the judicial process will replace the existing individualistic and bourgeois one.

National Defense
The People's State will pay special attention to the preservation of national sovereignty, which it also views as being the duty of every citizen.

The People's State will remain alert before those threats to our territorial integrity and the country's independence, which are encouraged by the imperialists and by those groups of the oligarchy in power in neighboring countries who encourage expansionist and retaliatory pretensions as well as repressing their own people. The People's State will establish a modern, popular and patriotic concept of the nation's sovereignty based on the following principles:

(a) The guarantee of the national integrity of all branches of the armed forces. In this sense we reject the use of these forces to repress the people or their participation in activities of interest to foreign powers;

(b) The provision of technical training with contributions from any modern military science, as deemed convenient to Chile and in the interests of national independence and of peace and friendship among peoples;

(c) The integration of the armed forces into different aspects of national life and the increase of their contribution to social life.

The People's State will find ways of making possible for the armed forces to contribute to the country's economic development without prejudice to its primary task of national defense.

Following these lines, it will be necessary to provide the armed forces with the necessary material and technical means and to establish a just and democratic system of remuneration, promotion and retirement, which guarantees economic security to personnel in all ranks while serving in the forces and on retirement, and which provides real possibilities for promotion through the ranks on the basis of individual merit.

THE CONSTRUCTION OF THE NEW ECONOMY

The central policy objective of the united popular forces will be the search for a replacement for the present economic structure, doing away with the power of foreign and national monopoly capital and of the *latifundia* in order to initiate the construction of socialism.

Planning will play a very important role in the new economy. The main planning organs will be at the highest administrative level, and the decisions, which will be democratically determined, will be executive in character.

The Socially Owned Sector

The process of transformation in our economy will begin with the application of a policy intended to create a dominant state sector, comprising those firms already owned by the state and the businesses which are to be expropriated. As a first step, we shall nationalize those basic resources like large-scale copper, iron and nitrate mines, and others which are controlled by foreign capital and national monopolies. These nationalized sectors will thus be comprised of the following:

1. Large scale copper, nitrate, iodine, iron and coal mines.
2. The country's financial system, especially private banks and insurance companies.
3. Foreign trade.
4. Large distribution firms and monopolies.
5. Strategic industrial monopolies.
6. As a rule, all those activities which have a strong influence on the nation's social and economic development, such as the production and distribution of electric power, rail, air and sea transport, communications, the production, refining and distribution of petroleum and its by-products, including liquid gas, the iron and steel industry, cement, petrochemicals and heavy chemicals, cellulose and paper.

In carrying out these expropriations, the interests of small shareholders will be fully safeguarded.

The Privately Owned Sector

This area includes those sections of industry, mining, agriculture and services where private ownership of the means of production will remain in force.

In terms of numbers these enterprises will constitute the majority. Thus, for example, in 1967 out of 30,500 firms (including artisan establishments) just 150 firms monopolistically controlled the entire market, received most of the assistance from the state, and most of the bank credit, and exploited the rest of the country's businessmen by selling them raw materials at high prices while buying their output at low prices.

The firms which compose this sector will benefit from the overall planning of the national economy. The state will provide the necessary technical and financial assistance for the firms in this sector, enabling them to fulfill the important role which they play in the national economy, when the number of people they employ and the volume of output they generate is taken into account. In addition, the patenting system, the customs tariffs, and the social security and taxation systems will be simplified for these firms and they will be assured of adequate and just marketing of their products.

These firms must guarantee the rights of workers and employees to fair wages and working conditions. Both the state and the workers in the respective firms will make sure that these rights are respected.

The Mixed Sector

This sector will be termed mixed because it will be composed of enterprises combining both state and private capital.

The loans or credits granted to the firms in this sector by development agencies may take the form of contributions, thereby making the state a partner rather than a creditor. The same holds in those cases in which the firm obtains credits with the backing or guarantee of the state or one of its agencies.

Intensification and Extension of the Agrarian Reform

In our view the agrarian reform process should be complementary to, and simultaneous with, the overall transformation which we wish to promote in the country's social, political and economic structure, such that its implementation is inseparable from the rest of our overall policy. Existing experience in this matter has shown up gaps and inconsistencies which suggest a reformulation of the policy for the distribution and organization of land ownership on the basis of the following guidelines:

1. Acceleration of the agrarian reform process, expropriating the holdings which exceed the established maximum size according to the characteristics of the different regions, including orchards, vineyards and forests, without giving the landowner the priority right to select the area to be retained by him. The expropriation may include the whole or part of the expropriated farm's assets (machinery, tools, animals, etc.).
2. The immediate cultivation of abandoned and badly exploited state lands.

3. Expropriated land will be organized preferably on the basis of cooperative forms of ownership. The peasants will be given titles which confirm individual ownership of the house and garden allocated to them, and the corresponding rights over the indivisible land of the cooperative as long as they continue to be members. When the circumstances warrant it, land may be allocated to individual peasants, with the organization of work and marketing being promoted on the basis of mutual cooperation. In addition, lands will be allocated to create state agricultural enterprises using modern technology.

4. In certain qualified cases land will be allocated to small farmers, tenants, sharecroppers and trained agricultural workers.

5. *Minifundia* properties [tiny land parcels] will be reorganized by means of progressively cooperative forms of agricultural work.

6. Small and medium peasants will be given access to the advantages and services provided by the cooperatives operating in their geographical area.

7. The defense of the indigenous Indian communities which are threatened with usurpation of their land will be ensured, as will be the democratic conduct of these communities, the provision of sufficient land and appropriate technical assistance and credit to the Mapuche people and other indigenous groups.

Policy For Economic Development

The government's economic policy will be carried out by means of a national system of economic planning and through control mechanisms, guidelines, production credit, technical assistance, tax and foreign trade policies, as well as through the management of the state sector of the economy.

The policy objectives will be:

1. To resolve the immediate problems of the working classes. In order to achieve this we shall divert that part of the nation's productive capacity at present used to produce expensive and unnecessary products for high income groups to the production of cheap, high quality mass consumption goods.

2. To guarantee work and adequate wages to all Chileans of working age. This will involve devising a policy which generates a lot of employment while making adequate use of national resources and adapting technology to national development requirements.

3. To free Chile from subordination to foreign capital. On the one hand, this means expropriating imperialist capital and implementing a policy for increasing our capacity to self-finance our activities and, on the other, it means that we must determine the

conditions under which non-expropriated foreign capital may operate, and achieve a greater degree of technological independence and greater independence in international transport, etc.

4. To secure rapid and decentralized economic growth, which will develop the country's productive forces to a maximum, achieving the optimum use of the available human, natural, financial and technical resources in order to increase labor productivity and satisfy the need for greater independence in the development of the economy, as well as those needs and aspirations of the working population which are compatible with a dignified human life.

5. To implement a foreign trade policy which will tend to develop and diversify our exports, open up new markets, achieve growing financial and technological independence and put an end to the successive scandalous devaluations of our currency.

6. To take all necessary measures to achieve monetary stability. The fight against inflation is already implicit in the announced structural changes. But it must also include measures which adjust the money in circulation to the real needs of the market and include the control and redistribution of credit and efforts to keep interest rates low. Measures must also be taken to rationalize marketing and commerce, to stabilize prices and to prevent price increases which emanate from the demand structure and reflect expenditure patterns of the high income groups.

The achievement of these objectives is guaranteed by the fact that it will be the organized masses who will exercise economic and political power, a situation which is represented by the existence of the public sector and of the overall planning of the economy. Government by the people will ensure the fulfillment of the indicated targets.

SOCIAL TASKS

The Chilean people's social aspirations are both legitimate and possible to satisfy. For example, Chilean citizens want decent housing without crippling rent increases, schools and universities for their children, adequate wages, a once and for all end to increases in the cost of living, stable employment, appropriate medical attention, street lighting, sewers, drinking water, surfaced roads and pavements, a just and efficient social security system, which is not based on privilege and which does not provide starvation level pensions, telephones, police, nursery schools, sport fields, holidays, tourism and popular beach resorts.

The satisfaction of these rightful aspirations, which in fact constitute rights which society must recognize, will be the principle concern of the People's Government.
The basic aspects of government action will be:

(a) The definition of an income policy, with the immediate creation of committees, which, with the participation of workers, will determine what constitutes a subsistence wage and minimum wages in different regions of the country. As long as inflation continues, wage readjustments related to the cost of living will be decreed by law. These adjustments will be made every six months or whenever the cost of living rises by more than five percent.
High-level salaries in all government departments, and above all the salaries of those appointed directly by the President, will be limited to levels which are compatible with national circumstances. Within a certain technically determined period, we shall begin to set up a system of equal minimum wages and salaries for equal work, wherever the work is done. This policy will first be introduced in the public sector, gradually being extended to the rest of the economy respecting, however, the differences made possible by varying levels of productivity in different firms. In the same way we intend to eliminate wage and salary discrimination between men and women or for reasons of age.

(b) To unify, improve and extend the social security system, maintaining all the legitimate advances made so far, eliminating the abuse of privilege, inefficiency and bureaucracy, improving and speeding up treatment and attention, extending social security to groups of workers not yet included, and making the contributors responsible for the administration of their Social Security Schemes, which should function within the overall planning framework.

(c) To provide all Chileans with preventive and curative dental and medical care financed by the state, by employers and by social security institutions. The whole population will join in the task of protecting public health. Medicines, etc. will be provided in sufficient quantities and at low cost, on the basis of a strict control of laboratory costs and the rationalization of production.

(d) Sufficient funds will be provided for a large housing program. The industrialization of construction will be developed, controlling prices and limiting the amount of profits made by the private or mixed enterprises operating in this field. In emergency situations, plots of land will be allocated to those families requiring them, also providing them with technical and material assistance to build their own houses.

One aim of the People's Government's housing policy is for every family to become a house owner. The system of readjustable rents will be eliminated. The monthly mortgage or loan repayment and rents, to be paid by house purchasers and tenants respectively, will not exceed 10 percent of family income as a general rule. We shall undertake the remodeling of cities and suburbs to prevent poor people being forced to the outskirts, respecting the interests of such inhabitants of redeveloped areas as small businessmen, by assuring them of a future in the same area.

(e) Full civil status of married women will be established, as will equal legal status for all children whether born in or out of wedlock, as well as adequate divorce legislation which dissolves legal ties and safeguards the woman's and children's rights.

(f) The legal distinction between workers and white collar employees will be ended, both being classed as workers in future and the right to unionize will be extended to all those who do not have this right at present.

CULTURE AND EDUCATION
A New Culture For Society
The social process, which will begin when the working class wins power, will develop a new culture which considers human labor with the highest regard, which emphasizes the desire for national assertion and independence and which develops a critical understanding of present reality.

The profound changes which have to be undertaken require a socially conscious and united people, educated to exercise and defend their political power, and scientifically and technically prepared to develop the transitional economy towards socialism, and a people wide open to creativity and the enjoyment of a wide variety of artistic and intellectual activities.

If, today, the majority of intellectuals and artists fight against the cultural distortions of capitalist society and attempt to convey their creative efforts to the workers and link themselves to the same historical destiny then, in the new society, they will continue this effort but from a vanguard position. A new culture cannot be decreed. It will spring from the struggle for fraternity as opposed to individualism, for the appreciation rather than disdain of human labor, for national values rather than cultural colonization, and from the struggle of the popular masses for access to art, literature and the communications media and the end of their commercialization.

This new state will involve the whole population in intellectual and artistic activities not only by means of a radically transformed educational system but also through the development of a national system to promote popular culture. A large network of Local Centers for Popular Culture will encourage ordinary people to organize themselves and exercise their rights to participate in and promote culture. This system of popular culture will stimulate literary and artistic creativity and it will multiply the links between writers and artists and a very much larger public than their existing one.

A Democratic, Integrated and Planned Educational System

Action by the new government in this field will concentrate on providing the best and most extensive educational facilities possible.

Both the general improvement in the working classes' living conditions and the recognition of the responsibilities borne by teachers at different levels will influence the extent to which these proposals are fulfilled. Also, a National Scholarship Program will be established which will be sufficiently broad as to ensure the inclusion and continued education of all Chilean children, especially the children from working class and peasant backgrounds.

Furthermore, the new government will implement an emergency plan for the construction of schools, relying on contributions of national and local resources mobilized by grass-roots organizations. Luxury buildings which are needed as premises for new schools and boarding schools will be expropriated. In this way, it is hoped to create at least one integrated school (both basic and middle levels[4]) in each rural district, and in each urban residential district and low-income neighborhood.

In order to provide the special requirements needed for the proper development of pre-school age children, and to facilitate the incorporation of women into productive work, we shall rapidly expand our nurseries and nursery school systems, granting priority to the most needy groups in our society. As a result of this policy, the children of urban and rural workers and peasants will be better prepared to start school and continue to benefit right through the normal school system.

To make the new teaching system a reality, new methods are required which put emphasis on the active and critical participation of students in their teaching, instead of perpetuating the passive attitudes they are expected to adopt at present.

In order to rapidly repair the widespread lack of culture and education resulting from the present system, we shall set in motion an

---

[4] The basic level of education lasts eight years commencing at six years of age, and the middle level lasts four years, following completion of the basic level. (The translator)

extensive popular mobilization campaign aimed at the rapid elimination of illiteracy and the raising of the educational level of the adult population. Adult education will be mainly organized around work centers, until it is possible to have a permanent system of general, technical and social education for workers.

The transformation of the educational system will not only be the task of technically qualified people. It is also a task requiring study, discussion, decision and implementation by teachers', workers', students' and parents' organizations within the general framework of national planning. Internally, the planning of the schools system will pay particular attention to the need for integration, continuity and diversification in teaching.

In the executive management of the educational system there must be real representation of the aforementioned social organizations, which will be integrated into the Local, Regional and National Education Committees.

In order to achieve effective educational planning and turn the idea of a unified national and democratic school system into a practical reality, the new government will take over responsibility for private educational establishments, starting with those educational institutions which select their pupils according to criteria of social class, national origin, or religion. This will be done by integrating the staff and other resources of the private education sector into the state system.

Physical Education

The People's Government will be constantly concerned to ensure that physical education and participation in all kinds of sports is possible right from the earliest years at school and in all youth and adult social organizations.

University Democracy and Autonomy and the Role of Universities

The Popular Unity Government will give strong backing to the University Reform process and it will resolutely push forward this reform. The democratic outcome of this reform process will constitute an important contribution by universities to the revolutionary development of Chile. On the other hand, the reorientation of academic teaching, research, and extension functions towards national problems will be encouraged by the People's Government's own initiatives.

The state will allocate sufficient resources to the universities to ensure the fulfillment of their functions and to ensure that they become fully democratic public institutions. In line with this, the members and employees of the universities will be responsible for running their respective institutions.

As class privilege is eliminated from the whole of the educational system, it will be possible for children of working class background to enter university and for adults to gain access to higher education either by means of special scholarships or through a system which simultaneously combines study and work.

The Mass Media
The mass media (radio, publishing, television, the press and cinema) are fundamental in helping to develop a new culture and a new type of man. For this reason it is necessary to redefine their purpose, putting emphasis on their educative role and ending their commercialization, and to adopt measures which allow social organizations the use of these communications media, eliminating the harmful effects of the monopolies. The national system of popular culture will be particularly concerned with the development of the film industry and the preparation of social programs for the mass media.

THE PEOPLE'S GOVERNMENT'S FOREIGN POLICY
Aims
The main lines of emphasis of the People's Government's Foreign Policy are:

The assertion of full political and economic autonomy for Chile
The establishment of diplomatic relations with all countries, irrespective of their ideological and political position, on the basis of respect for self-determination and in the interests of the Chilean people.

Ties of friendship and solidarity will unite Chile with dependent or colonized countries, especially those who are fighting for their liberation and independence.

The promotion of strong inter-American and anti-imperialist sentiments based on foreign policies which are the expression of entire nations rather than on policies formulated solely by foreign ministries.

Efforts by nations to achieve or maintain self-determination will be given decided support by the new government as a basic condition for the existence of international peace and understanding. As a consequence, our policy will be one of alertness and action in defense of the principle of nonintervention and we shall resist any attempt by the imperialist nations to discriminate, pressure, invade or blockade. We shall reinforce our relationships, trade and cultural exchanges and friendship with socialist countries.

Greater national independence
The active defense of Chilean independence means that we must denounce the present Organization of American States as an agent and

tool of American imperialism, and fight against all forms of Pan-Americanism which are implicit in this organization. The People's Government will attempt to create an organization which is really representative of Latin American countries.

It is considered absolutely necessary to review, denounce or renounce, as befits each case, those treaties or agreements which involve commitments limiting our sovereignty, and, in particular, treaties of reciprocal assistance, pacts of mutual aid or other pacts which Chile signed with the United States.

The government will reject and denounce foreign aid and loans which are extended for political reasons, or involve conditions requiring the investments derived from those loans to be made in ways which prejudice our sovereignty and are against the people's interests. Likewise, we shall repudiate all types of foreign charges imposed on Latin American raw materials such as copper and the obstacles put in the way of free trade which, over time, have made it impossible to establish collective trade relations with all countries of the world.

International solidarity

The People's Government will demonstrate effective and militant solidarity with those struggles in which people are fighting for freedom and for the construction of a socialist society.

All forms of colonialism and neocolonialism will be condemned and we will recognize the right of those peoples subjected to these systems to rebel. Likewise, we shall condemn all forms of economic, political and military aggression provoked by imperialist powers. Chile's foreign policy must be one of condemnation of North American aggression in Vietnam, and one of recognition of an active solidarity with the heroic struggle of the Vietnamese people.

In the same way, the Chilean people will demonstrate meaningful solidarity with the Cuban Revolution, which is the vanguard of revolution and construction of socialism in Latin America.

The Middle Eastern nations who are struggling against imperialism can count on the solidarity of the People's Government, which supports the search for a peaceful solution based on the interests of both the Arab and Jewish peoples. We shall condemn all reactionary governments which promote or practice racial segregation and anti-Semitism.

Policy for Latin America

With regard to Latin America, the People's Government will advocate an international policy which asserts the identity of Latin America in the world.

It is our view that Latin American integration must be built on the basis of economies which have liberated themselves from imperialist forms of dependency and exploitation. Nevertheless, we shall maintain an active policy of bilateral agreements in those matters of interest for the development of Chile.

The People's Government will take action to resolve border problems which are still outstanding on the basis of negotiations which exclude imperialist and reactionary intrigues, and which take into account both the interests of Chile and the interests of the peoples in neighboring countries.

Chilean foreign policy and its diplomatic expression must break away from its bureaucratic habits and lack of initiative. Moreover, our foreign policy must derive from the peoples of many nations with the double purpose of, on the one hand, taking up the lessons learned from their struggles for application in the construction of our socialist society and, on the other, of offering them our experience, in such a manner that it is in the very practice of the idea that we shall build up the international solidarity for which we are fighting.

FIRST 40 MEASURES OF THE PEOPLE'S GOVERNMENT

1. An End To Enormous Salaries! We shall put a limit on the high salaries earned by those appointed directly by the president. We shall not allow people to hold simultaneously various paid posts such as advisory posts, directorships, representatives.

   We shall do away with administrative promoters and political mongers who use their official positions to promote their own ends and the interests of their friends and business and political acquaintances.

2. More Advisers? No! All civil servants will belong to the normal staff grades and none will be exempted from the Administrative Statute's conditions. We will not have any more advisers in Chile.

3. Honest Administration. We shall put an end to favoritism and grade jumping in the public administration. It will not be possible to remove civil servants from their posts without due cause. Nobody will be persecuted for their political or religious beliefs. We shall ensure the efficiency and honesty of government officials and the civil treatment of the public.

4. No More Unnecessary Foreign Trips. Foreign journeys by government officials will not be allowed except for those which are really necessary in Chile's interests.

5. No More Use Of Government Cars For Pleasure. Under no circumstances will the government's cars be used for private purposes. Those vehicles which are available will be used in the service of the public: for transporting school children, for transporting people requiring medical attention from low-income housing districts, or for police duties.

6. The Civil Service Will Not Enrich Its Employees. We shall establish strict control over the incomes and property of high level public officials. The government will no longer allow public officials to use their position to enrich themselves.

7. Fair Pensions. We must put a stop to millionaire level pensions whether they be for parliamentarians or any other public or private group, using the resources to improve pensions at the lower end of the scale.

8. Fair And Timely Retirement. We will give retirement rights to all people over 60 years of age who have been unable to retire because their contributions have not been paid.

9. Social Security For Everyone. We shall incorporate into the Social Security system all people in small and medium scale commerce, industry and farming, and independent workers, artisans, fishermen, small scale miners and housewives.

10. Immediate And Full Payment Of Pensions And Benefits. We shall finally pay the increases in pensions due to retired members of the armed forces and we shall arrange for the proper and due payment of retirement pensions and widow's pensions under the Social Security System.

11. Protection Of The Family. We shall set up a ministry for the protection of the family.

12. Equal Family Allowances. All family allowances will in future be fixed at the same level.

13. Children Are Born To Be Happy! We shall provide free education, books, materials, exercise books, etc. for all children throughout the basic level.

14. Better Meals For Children. We will provide breakfast for all children in the basic level and lunch for those children whose parents cannot provide it.

15. Milk For All Chilean Children. We guarantee a daily ration of half a liter of milk to all Chilean children.

16. Family Welfare Clinics In All Poor Areas. We shall set up family welfare clinics in all working class neighborhoods, slums and squatter settlements.

17. Real Holidays For All Chilean Students. The best pupils selected from the basic educational level throughout the country will be invited to the Presidential Palace at Viña del Mar.

18. Control Of Alcoholism. We shall overcome alcoholism, by providing possibilities for a better life and not by repressive means. We shall stop abuse of the drinking laws and licensing regulations.

19. Housing, Lighting And Drinking Water For All Chileans. We shall undertake an emergency plan for the rapid building of

houses. Also, we shall ensure the provision of drinking water and electric lighting in every block.

20. No More Readjustable "CORVI" Payments. CORVI, the Housing Corporation's dividends and the loan repayments it receives will no longer be readjusted in line with rising prices.

21. Fixed Price Rents. We shall fix rents at an amount corresponding to 10 percent of family income as a maximum. Key rights will be abolished immediately.

22. Vacant Sites, No! Housing, Yes! We shall build on all disused public, semi-public and municipal sites.

23. Property Taxes On Mansions Only. We shall free from the payment of property taxes the owners of dwellings with a surface below 80 square meters as long as the owner lives there permanently and the house is neither a luxury house nor a beach villa.

24. A Real Agrarian Reform. We shall intensify agrarian reform, which will also benefit medium and small scale farmers, *minifundia* holders, sharecroppers, employees and temporary rural laborers.

25. Medical Attention Without Bureaucracy. We shall eliminate all the bureaucratic and administrative obstacles which hinder or make difficult the provision of medical attention to contributors and unemployed people.

26. Free Medical Attention In Hospitals. We shall abolish payment for medicines and examinations in hospitals.

27. No More Artificially High Prices For Medicines. We shall drastically reduce the price of medicines by lowering the import duties and taxes on the raw materials.

28. Scholarships For Students. We shall establish the right of all good students to obtain a scholarship for the basic and middle school levels and university education, taking into account performance and the family's economic resources.

29. Physical Education And Popular Tourism And Holidays. We shall promote physical education and we shall establish sports fields in schools and all neighborhoods. Every school and low-income urban or rural housing district will have a sports field. We shall organize and promote low-income tourism and holidays.

30. A New Economy To Put An End To Inflation. We shall increase the production of items of popular consumption. We shall control prices and prevent inflation by immediately setting up the new economic structure.

31. No More Links With The International Monetary Fund. We shall renege the commitments with the International Monetary Fund.

We shall put an end to the continual shameful devaluation of the escudo.

32. No More Taxes On Food. We shall stop increases in taxes which affect basic food necessities.
33. Abolition Of The Sales Tax. We shall abolish the sales tax and replace it by another more just and efficient tax system.
34. No More Speculation. We shall severely penalize economic crimes.
35. No More Unemployment. We shall ensure the right of all Chileans to work and we shall prevent unjustified dismissals.
36. Work For All Chileans. We shall immediately create new sources of employment by implementing plans for public works and house building, by setting up new industries, and by carrying out development projects.
37. The Riot Police Unit Will Be Disbanded. We shall ensure law and order in lower and middle class residential areas and the protection of the individual. The police and detectives will be restricted to crime prevention duties. We shall disband the Riot Police Unit incorporating its members into the normal duties of police vigilance against delinquency.
38. An End To Class Justice. We shall set up a rapid and free legal procedure, in which the Neighborhood Committees will cooperate, to examine and resolve special cases such as quarrels, ruffianism, abandonment of the home and acts which disturb the community.
39. Legal advice bodies in all neighborhoods. We shall set up Legal Advice Bodies in all low-income neighborhoods and districts.
40. The Creation Of A National Institute Of Art And Culture. We shall create a National Institute of Art and Culture and schools for training in the arts in all districts.

THE 20 BASIC POINTS OF THE POPULAR UNITY GOVERNMENT'S AGRARIAN REFORM

ONE. Agrarian reform and agricultural development will not be isolated factors, but will form an integral part of the overall plan for transforming the economy into one which serves the whole people. This implies that agrarian reform will not only involve the expropriation of all *latifundia*, the distribution of land to peasant producers and rural laborers and the provision of the technical assistance and credits which are necessary to enable them to produce what Chile requires, but also includes the transformation of commercial and industrial relationships for the sale and purchase of products required by peasants for consumption and for production. The marketing and processing of agricultural output must be in the hands of the state or peasant or consumer cooperatives.

TWO. The benefits of agrarian reform will be extended to the groups of medium and small farmers, smallholders, employees, sharecroppers and temporary laborers who have so far been excluded from these benefits.

THREE. The peasantry, represented by unions, cooperatives and small scale farmers' organizations will replace the representatives of the large estates in all government departments and agencies. The Popular Unity Government will only deal with these representatives of the rural population because it is they who are the true representatives of the 98 percent of the population which lives from agricultural activities or depends on an income from agriculture.

At the level of the Ministry of Agriculture and Agrarian Reform, as it will then be called, under whose direct responsibility will be placed all branches of the state which deal with the agricultural sector, a National Peasant Council will be set up to advise the minister and top civil servants and officials of the various government agencies. This council will be democratically elected by the grass-roots peasant organizations.

At the same time Regional Peasant Councils will be formed in each of the country's agricultural zones in which the officials responsible for the zone and the elected peasant representatives will participate on an equal footing. All the measures necessary for implementing agrarian reform and agricultural development will be adopted in these National and Regional Peasant Councils — i.e. expropriations, land distribution, credits, marketing of products and inputs, etc.

FOUR. Agrarian reform will no longer be implemented on a farm by farm basis but by areas and, in each of these areas, productive work will be guaranteed for all peasants and rural laborers in the area either in direct work on the land, or in the processing and distribution of the products, or in the provision of the general services required in production.

FIVE. We shall employ new legal concepts to help us to achieve integration and cooperation by the united action of the various rural organizations of wage earners, employees, sharecroppers, temporary laborers and small and medium scale farmers. This will involve an increase in the number of tasks to be carried out by the unions, agrarian reform settlements (*asentamientos*),[5] rural cooperatives, indigenous

---

[5] *Asentamiento*. This was a transitional system adopted during the Christian Democrat Government and during the first year of the Popular Unity Government to manage the expropriated estates for a three to five year period. The *asentamiento* coincides with the boundaries of the old estate and is run as a unit on a cooperative basis by the agrarian reform corporation and *asentamiento* members. During the transitional period the peasants are trained to take over full management responsibilities and government

Indian communities, and other types and forms of small farmers' organizations, such as the small farmers' committees.

Furthermore, the People's Government will end the present mockery of the law whereby agricultural employers refrain from paying the two percent employer's contribution required by the law governing peasant unions inducing the bankruptcy of the rural workers' trade unions.

SIX. Areas under forest will also be included in the agrarian reform.

SEVEN. Only small- and medium-scale farmers will be excluded from expropriation, and only those larger-scale farmers whose social and economic contributions to agricultural production and rural community development are recognized by the peasants will have the right to retain some land. And in any case, the right to retain some land will not be accompanied by the preferential right to select this piece of land, since it may be necessary to offer other land so as facilitate the restructuring of peasant holdings.

EIGHT. Working capital will be included in expropriations so that, right from the very beginning, expropriated holdings have the capital necessary for farming operations.

NINE. Technical assistance to peasants will be provided without charge and special credit, technical assistance and training programs will be drawn up for the most disregarded groups, especially the indigenous Indian communities.

TEN. Each peasant will have family rights to his house and garden. Production will be organized preferably under the cooperative system, though in special cases individual cultivation and ownership of land may be considered.

ELEVEN. By means of credit, technical assistance, regional and national planning, we shall orient production towards high priced products both for export and for the home market. Credits for certain types of labor intensive products, such as pigs and poultry, will be reserved for small farmers and other peasants to help increase their income and improve their social and economic situation.

---

agencies provide technical assistance and credit. According to the law the peasants may decide whether the land will be divided into individual holdings or be organized and operated on a cooperative basis on the expiration of the *asentamiento* period, though the government may impose cooperative ownership operation if there are overriding technical reasons for doing so. (The Translator)

TWELVE. At an early stage of the People's Government the Agrarian Reform Law will be fully enforced, making use of all powers that the present government does not wish to use or has not been able to use, such as allocating land to cooperatives, defending the interests of sharecroppers and tenants, reorganizing irrigation areas and systems, etc. The necessary amendments to the present Agrarian Reform Law will be discussed and approved by the National and Regional Peasant Councils before being sent to Parliament.

THIRTEEN. The state will guarantee the purchase of that part of the peasants' output which is not marketed at official prices through the normal channels, and gradually the state will make anticipatory contracts for all livestock and agricultural output which is planned according to the country's needs.

Advance credits for production will be granted to small peasants in cash only, and not in the form of credit notes as happens in most cases at present and which involves the further exploitation of those peasants who can only get their credit notes discounted at burdensome rates and on unfavorable terms.

FOURTEEN. Agriculture-based industries will preferably be located in the agricultural regions which at present suffer most severely from agricultural unemployment or underemployment.

FIFTEEN. The state will nationalize all monopolies controlling the marketing, preparation and processing of livestock and agricultural products or the necessary inputs for agricultural production. These enterprises will be either directly managed by the state, with advice from the Peasant Councils, or they will be handed over to rural cooperatives.

SIXTEEN. A national social security system for all rural workers will be set up, especially including those small farmers who are at present excluded from social security. In the same way, we shall ensure that social security arrangements for farmers and agrarian reform settlements will be continued.

SEVENTEEN. Special programs will be undertaken to improve and to construct rural housing because, until now, peasants and rural workers have been excluded from all previous housing improvement programs.

EIGHTEEN. We shall set up rural hostels in the principal towns in agricultural areas, so that passing migrants and temporary laborers or peasants on business in town have somewhere to lodge which also provides them with support and guidance in carrying out their tasks, especially in relation to public services, education, health, etc.

NINETEEN. A general policy for education will be developed through adult literacy programs, publications of books, newspapers and radio programs for the rural population, and through courses on agricultural technology in line with the region's production plans. At the same time, theatre, art and other cultural activities will be promoted, which will help develop the character of rural communities.

TWENTY. A special effort will be made to push ahead with plans for the protection of natural resources, forestation plans, etc., and with plans for making better use of irrigated areas.

Select Bibliography

I. Speeches and interviews by Allende

Allende Gossens, Salvador. *Archivo Salvador Allende*. 20 v.s, edited by Alejandro Vitker. Chapingo, Mexico: Universidad Autónoma Chapingo, 1990.

_____ *Chile: historia de una ilusión. Discursos-conferencias-entrevistas-programa Unidad Popular*. Buenos Aires: Edita La Señal, 1973.

_____ *Chile's Road to Socialism: Salvador Allende*. Edited by Joan E. Garces, with an introduction by Richard Gott. Baltimore: Penguin Books, 1973.

_____ "First Annual Message to the National Congress, May 21, 1971," and "Postscript," in Régis Debray, *The Chilean Revolution: Conversations with Allende*. New York: Pantheon, 1971.

_____ "Inaugural Address in the National Stadium, Santiago, November 5, 1970," and other selected speeches or speech excerpts, in Dale L. Johnson (ed.), *The Chilean Road to Socialism*. New York: Anchor, 1973.

_____ *La revolución chilena*. Buenos Aires: Editorial Universitaria de Buenos Aires, 1973.

_____ *Obras escogidas 1933-1948*. Edited with an introduction by Patricio Quiroga Zamora. Santiago: Instituto de Estudios Contemporáneos, 1988.

_____ *Salvador Allende: Su pensamiento político*. Santiago: Empresa Editora Nacional Quimantu Limitada, 1972.

_____ *Selección de discursos de Salvador Allende*. La Habana: Ed. de Ciencias Sociales, Instituto Cubano del Libro, 1975.

II. Web sites with more words of Allende

A la memoria del Presidente Salvador Allende < http://www.home.ch/~spaw1140/allende/>

Allende: la biografía de un político ejemplar <http://members.xoom.com/chilerebelde/compa2.htm>

DerechosChile <http://www.derechoschile.com/english/resour. htm>

In Memory of Salvador Allende <http://www.neravt.com/left/allende.htm>

La página de Salvador Allende <http://members.tripod.com/~Mictlantecuhtli/Allende/Allepiv.html>

Photographs of Allende <Index of /~hvelarde/Chile/Salvador .allende> Róbinson Rojas Research Unit Consultancy <http://www.soft.net. uk/rrojasdatabank/index.htm>

III. Biographies of Allende

Garza, Hedda. *Salvador Allende*. New York and Philadelphia: Chelsea House Publishers, 1989.

Levretski, J. *Salvador Allende*. Moscow: Editorial Progreso, 1978 [Spanish and Russian editions only].

See also novels by Isabel Allende and Fernando Alegría for fictionalized accounts of parts of Allende's life and times that are remarkably close to the truth.

IV. Films and Videos

The Battle of Chile, widely acclaimed three-part documentary film by Patricio Guzmán, 1975-1978

Chile: Hasta Cuando? Sixty minute color film documentary by award-winning Australian director David Bradbury, 1987

Chile, I Don't Take Your Name in Vain. Fifty-five minute color video on 1983 mass protests from Icarus Films, 1984

Chile, Obstinate Memory (Chile, la memoria obstinada), by Patricio Guzmán, notable for its interviews with Chilean youth who know nothing about Allende, 1997

Interview with President Salvador Allende. Thirty-one minute color film directed by Saul Landau and Haskell Wexler, 1971

Missing. Feature length film by prize-winning director Costa Gravas on kidnap and murder of U.S. journalist Charles Horman after 1973 coup, 1982

Salvador Allende. Fifty-two minute color video by Patricio Enríquez, co-production of INA-PIXART-RADIO QUEBEC-TV 5, 1980

Salvador Allende Gossens: A Testimony (Salvador Allende Gossens: un témoignage). Eighteen-minute film of Canadian miners meeting with Allende in 1972, available from National Film Board of Canada <http://www.onf.ca/FMT/E/MSN/14/14022.html>

Also from Ocean Press

AFROCUBA
An Anthology of Cuban Writing on Race, Politics and Culture
Edited by Pedro Pérez Sarduy and Jean Stubbs
What is it like to be Black in Cuba? Does racism exist in a revolutionary
society that claims to have abolished it? How does the legacy of slavery
and segregation live on in today's Cuba? *AfroCuba* looks at the Black
experience in Cuba through the eyes of the island's writers, scholars and
artists.
ISBN 1-875284-41-9

BAY OF PIGS AND THE CIA
Cuban Secret Files Reveal the Story Behind the Invasion
By Juan Carlos Rodríguez
No CIA document or other account of the mercenary invasion of Cuba in
1961 can be read in the same way after the publication of Cuba's story of
the Bay of Pigs and its aftermath.
ISBN 1-875284-98-2

CIA TARGETS FIDEL
The Secret Assassination Report
This book presents the internal report prepared by the CIA in 1967 on its
own plots to assassinate Cuban President Fidel Castro. Introduced by
former head of Cuban counterintelligence Fabián Escalante.
ISBN 1-875284-90-7

CUBA: TALKING ABOUT REVOLUTION
Conversations with Juan Antonio Blanco by Medea Benjamin
A frank discussion on the current situation in Cuba, this book presents
an all-too-rare opportunity to hear the voice of one of the island's
leading intellectuals. This new edition features a new essay by Blanco,
"Cuba: 'socialist museum' or social laboratory?"
ISBN 1-875284-97-7

DEADLY DECEITS
My 25 Years in the CIA
By Ralph W. McGehee
A new, updated edition of this classic account of the CIA's deeds and
deceptions by one of its formerly most prized recruits.
ISBN 1-876175-19-2

REBEL LIVES
A new series from Ocean Press

I WAS NEVER ALONE
A Prison Diary from El Salvador
By Nidia Díaz
Nidia Díaz (born María Marta Valladares) gives a dramatic and inspiring personal account of her experience as a guerrilla commander during El Salvador's civil war. Seriously wounded, she was captured in combat by Cuban-exile CIA agent Félix Rodríguez. Nidia Díaz was the FMLN's Vice-Presidential candidate in 1999.
ISBN 1-876175-17-6

PRIEST AND PARTISAN
A South African Journey of Father Michael Lapsley
By Michael Worsnip
The story of Father Michael Lapsley, an anti-apartheid priest, and how he survived a South African letter bomb attack in 1990 in which he lost both hands and an eye.
Foreword by Nelson Mandela
ISBN 1-875284-96-6

SLOVO
The Unfinished Autobiography of ANC Leader Joe Slovo
A revealing and highly entertaining autobiography of one of the key figures of South Africa's African National Congress. As an immigrant, a Jew, a communist, a guerrilla fighter and political strategist — and white — few public figures in South Africa were as demonized by the apartheid government as Joe Slovo.
Introduction by Nelson Mandela.
ISBN 1-875284-95-8

MY EARLY YEARS
By Fidel Castro
In the twilight of his life, Fidel Castro reflects on his childhood, youth and student days. In an unprecedented and remarkably candid manner, one of the century's most controversial figures, describes his family background and the religious and moral influences that led to his early involvement in politics.
Introductory essay by Gabriel García Márquez
ISBN 1-876175-07-9

Also from Ocean Press

JOSE MARTI READER
Writings on the Americas
An outstanding new anthology of the writings, letters and poetry of
José Martí—one of the most brilliant and impassioned Latin
American leaders of the 19th century.
ISBN 1-875284-12-5

FIDEL CASTRO READER
The voice of one of the 20th century's most controversial political
figures — as well as one of the world's greatest orators — is
captured in this new selection of Castro's key speeches over 40 years.
ISBN 1-876175-11-7

CUBAN REVOLUTION READER
A Documentary History
Edited by Julio García Luis
An outstanding anthology presenting a comprehensive overview of
Cuban history and documenting the past four decades, highlighting
40 key moments in the Cuban Revolution up to the present day.
ISBN 1-876175-10-9

CUBA AND THE UNITED STATES
A Chronological History
By Jane Franklin
Based on exceptionally wide research, this updated and expanded
chronology relates in detail the developments involving the two
neighboring countries from the 1959 revolution through 1995.
ISBN 1-875284-92-3

PSYWAR ON CUBA
The Declassified History of U.S. Anti-Castro Propaganda
Edited by Jon Elliston
Newly declassified CIA and U.S. Government documents are
reproduced here, with extensive commentary providing the history
of Washington's 40-year campaign to destabilize Cuba and under-
mine its revolution.
ISBN 1-876175-09-5